HOME-GOING

The Journey from Racism and Death
to Community and Hope

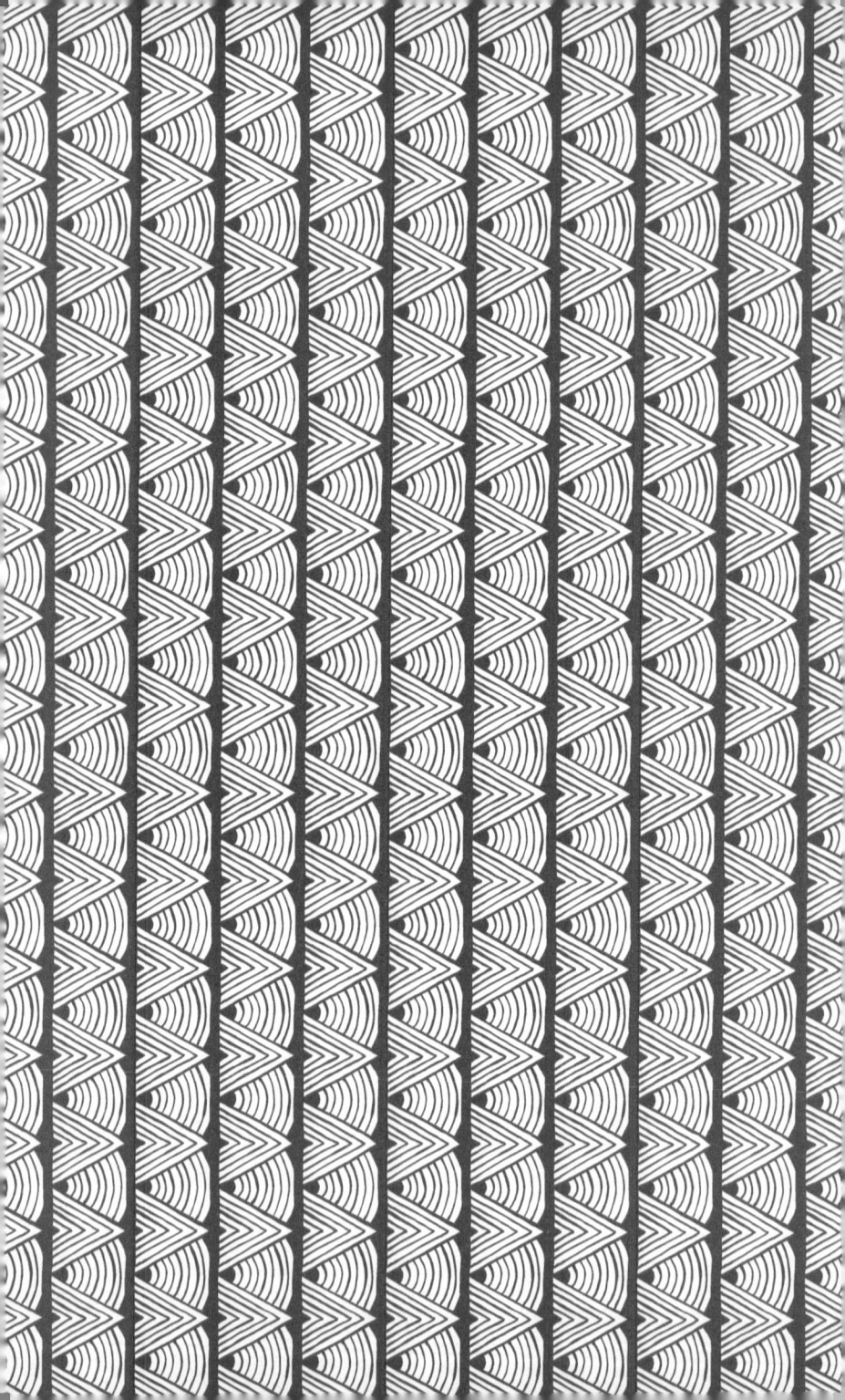

HOME-GOING

The Journey from Racism and Death to Community and Hope

PATRICK SAINT-JEAN, SJ

ANAMCHARA
BOOKS

IngramSpark paperback edition ISBN: 978-1-62524-866-4
eBook ISBN: 978-1-62524-865-7

Cover design by Ellyn Sanna.
Interior design by Micaela Grace.

This book is written for YOU.

Deep listening is an act of surrender.
We risk being changed by what we hear.

—VALARIE KAUR

Please listen.

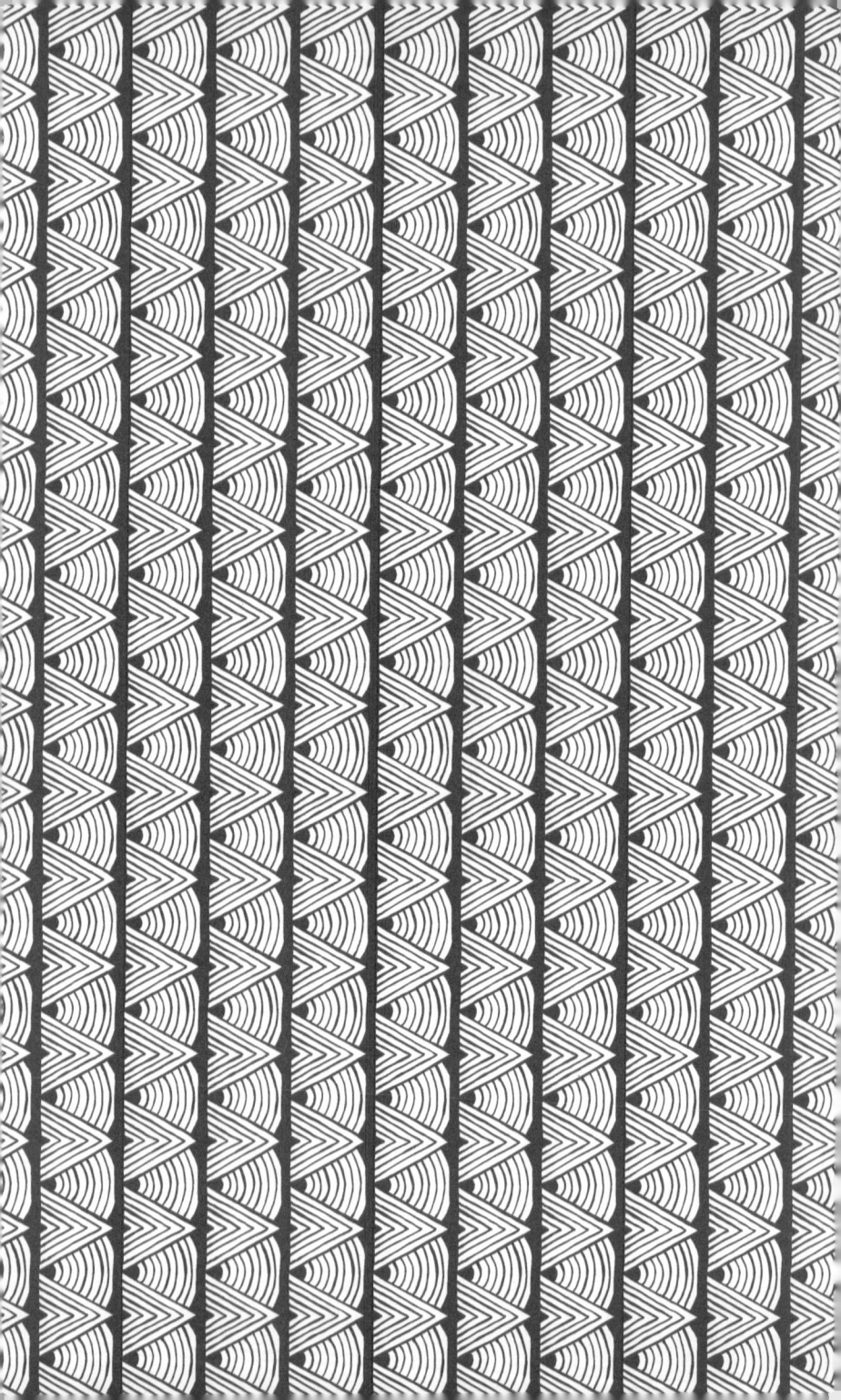

I would also like to express
a deep and sincere gratitude to all children.
Without ever knowing,
they gave me the courage,
hope, and commitment
I needed to engage with this difficult topic.
And so, I dedicate this book to the children,
especially my godsons and goddaughters,
including little Robin Alexander.
May this book help build a better world
for you all to inherit.
Thank you for carrying on the
work of love and justice.

CONTENTS

I'm going home, yes, I'm going home.
One of these days, going home.
Won't be long, going home.
You'll look for me, going home.
I'll be gone, yes, I'm going home.

—AFRICAN AMERICAN SPIRITUAL

INTRODUCTION

WATER JOURNEYS

Wade in the water, wade in the water!
Wade in the water, children,
God is gonna trouble these waters!
See that band all dressed in white?
God is gonna trouble these waters!
It look like a band of the Israelites.
God is gonna trouble these waters!

—AFRICAN AMERICAN SPIRITUAL

"A HUMAN BEING IS A STORY," IS AN
African saying. As a psychotherapist, I know we
understand each other best when we hear each
other's stories. And so, let me begin with a story.

Not so long ago, relatively speaking, the Igbo people of West Africa were going about their ordinary lives, just like we do today.

Oh, I know: in many ways, their ordinary lives weren't at all like ours, but try to ignore the ways they are different.[1] Instead, use your imagination and see all the ways these people are just like you and me. Like you and me, they laugh and talk with their friends; they adore their children (even though their children can also drive them crazy); they fight with their spouses and then have make-up sex; they do their work, sometimes with joy, sometimes with grumbling; and they worship a God they love and trust. They have dreams and ambitions, hopes and fears. Like all human beings, they can be cruel, and their culture is far from perfect. They are you. They are me.

And then their entire life is gone. Slave traders, both African and European, capture thousands and thousands of them, men, women, and children; royalty, high priests, chiefs, ordinary folks. Their heads are shaved, and they are stripped naked, their individual identities and names stolen. More than one in every ten of them die in the crowded, stinking ships that carry them across the Atlantic. Imagine, if you can, that this is you, your family, your friends. Even if you survive the Middle Passage,[2] your individual identity is dead, your ordinary life is dead, your safety is dead, your role in society is dead, and your sense of how the world works is dead. The slave ships stink of death.

Now, let me tell you about seventy-five Igbo who survived their journey from West Africa. On a spring day in 1803, they stepped onto land for the first time in some eighty days. Remember, you're there too. You're breathing in your first breath of clean air; you're stretching your cramped muscles; you're staggering a little because for more than two months, you've been lying on a wooden deck, crammed tight between other human bodies. The rags you clutch around your naked body are stiff with urine and excrement, and your elbows and hips have rubbed against the floor where you were chained until the tips of the bones broke through the skin. You're weak, frightened, and numb with grief and homesickness. You don't know what will happen next—but you're thinking it can't be worse than the ship.

At the Savannah slave market, though, as you talk with fellow Africans who have been in this strange world longer, you begin to realize there is only death and more death for you here. You and the other seventy-four in your group are sold together to a rich white man, and then you're packed into another ship, a smaller one this time, which will take you some eighty miles south to the white man's plantation. There, you'll be expected to do hard labor from sunup to sundown (and even longer during harvest time).

In Frederick Douglass's autobiography, he described what happened to him when he first experienced the reality of slavery's endless labor:

> I was broken in body, soul, and spirit. My natural
> elasticity was crushed, my intellect languished, . . .
> the cheerful spark that lingered about my eye died;
> the dark night of slavery closed in upon me; and
> behold a man transformed into a brute![3]

This is what lies in store for you and the other Igbo.

As you travel aboard the small ship in the darkness below deck, you talk with your fellow captives, telling them all you have learned about slavery in this new land. Your high chief is in the group, and he demonstrates the authority he still possesses by leading you all in prayer. He reminds you that you are not alone; the Life-Giver is with you, as are the ancestors, and they will give you their strength.

Then, as you talk in whispers, a decision takes shape. I imagine the furtive conversations must have been much like those that took place on Flight 93 on September 11, 2001: a mixture of terror, courage, and finally, inevitability. Like the passengers on that plane, you and your fellow Igbo decide to risk your lives by snatching control from your captors. Alone, you would never attempt such a thing, but together, connected to one another and to your shared ancestors, you know you are strong. Like the separate strands that twist together to make a rope, you and your kinspeople are stalwart.

Your brave venture succeeds. The white men jump off the ship and swim toward shore, only to drown before they reach it. You and your companions shout with triumph.

Unfortunately, none of you know how to navigate the boat, and while you are still cheering, the ship runs aground off St. Simons Island. When you disembark, your heart sinks. You see no path, not even a narrow opening, through the thick undergrowth that edges the water.

"This is not the end," says your chief. "The Water Spirit brought us," he chants, "and the Water Spirit will bring us home."

As an African, you know water is not only the source of physical life, but it also allows you to step out of this world into the Other World. Where there is a threat of death, water restores life. It is essential for the spiritual journey.[4]

And so, trusting in the Water of Life and Death, each of you takes up the chant as you fall into line. *The Water Spirit brought us, the Water Spirit will bring us home.* Your voices twine together, rising louder and louder into the night until they become a single song that fills everything: *The Water Spirit brought us, the Water Spirit will bring us home.*

One by one and all together, each of you walks straight into the deep water. . . .

And here's where the story splits into two.

Death and Life

If you're white and you've happened to hear this story, you most likely believe the Igbo Landing on St. Simons Island is the site of a mass suicide. And now we come back down to earth, because you're really *not* one of those people, those poor Black people. What those people went through was a tragedy, you say, but now you're merely a spectator, watching seventy-five Black folk march to their deaths by drowning. How sad, how terrible. It's not the sort of story that's fun to think about, so quick, put it out of your mind and forget it!

But if you're Black? Well, you probably know there's a different ending to the story. In this alternate ending, those seventy-five people don't drown. Instead, they walk on the water, just like Jesus. Of course no one can walk all the way from the

Georgia Coast to Africa, so after a while, something even more wonderful happens: they "walk up on the air like climbin up on a gate. And they flew like blackbirds . . . black, shiny wings flappin against the blue up there."[5] Another account of the "flying Africans" says they rose up "into the air with a great shout; and in a moment were gone, flying, like a flock of crows, . . . miles on miles, until they passed beyond the last rim of the world and disappeared in the sky like a handful of leaves."[6]

So that wasn't a mass suicide. It was a home-going. It wasn't death. It was life. And that's what this book is actually about: not death but life.

And it's also about the power of community.

Community

I don't mean that we're going to talk about life, and then we'll *also* talk about community. No, I believe that life and community are pretty much one and the same. In the African tradition of *Ubuntu*, we cannot exist without one another; relationships are what make us human. Meanwhile, the growing field of environmental science tells us that the entire universe is a network, with each thing (each person, animal, plant, stone, planet, star) dependent on all the rest in this vast community.

But the Western world turned away from this understanding at some point during the so-called Enlightenment, and instead of community responsibility and connection, "rugged individualism" became de rigueur. Dog-eat-dog was the societal rule; in competition this fierce, you can only win by harming your opponent. This perspective looks like pure foolishness to the African. "They share one stomach, yet they fight over food," says an African proverb.

Today, Western society not only emphasizes the privileges and achievements of the individual; it also tries to break down the rest of the world into discreet categories, with "experts" in each field of study. A geologist and a neurobiologist have little in common, just as the expertise of a brain surgeon and a podiatrist overlap very little if at all. Quantum physicists, however, are pointing the way toward a new understanding (except that it's actually very old—the European world just needs to rediscover it). As physicist Fritjof Capra wrote: "Gradually, physicists began to realise that nature, at the atomic level, does not appear as a mechanical universe composed of fundamental building blocks, but rather as a network of relations, and that, ultimately, there are no parts at all in this interconnected web. Whatever we call a part is merely a pattern that has some stability and therefore captures our attention.... Quantum theory thus reveals a basic oneness of the universe. It shows that we cannot decompose the world into independently existing smallest units. As we penetrate into matter, nature does not show us any isolated "building blocks," but rather appears as a complicated web of relations between the various parts of the whole."[7]

Many scientists believe now that trees and fungi communicate with each other and depend on one another. The neurons in your brain only fire in response to an electric signal firing at them from another brain cell. Coral reefs communicate with fish. Dogs sense when their human companions are about to have a seizure. Everything interacts. Everything communicates. Nothing is excluded.

And, according to African spirituality, nothing dies, not really. The BaKongo people[8] had a visual representation of this reality; if you look at the cover of this book, you'll see it at the center of the light. This cross within a circle is known as the Kongo cosmogram; Africans call it the *dikenga* or the *Yowa cross.*

The Kongo Cosmogram

The outer circle of the dikenga represents the cycle of life. Everything is included within this circle, without any hierarchy and without any sense of linear time. The horizontal line that divides the circle is known as *Kalunga,* "the threshold between worlds," the deep waters that separate the world of the living and the world of the dead.[9] The vertical line, stretching from the circle's highest to lowest points, indicates the ongoing relationship between life and death, including the vital, active connection between the ancestors (what we call the "dead") and the living. Communication between these two worlds is constant; it is the ever-present conversation that underlies human life. [10] The invisible world constantly interacts with the visible one, wrote African religious historian Simon Bockie, "for both are part of the vast cosmological plan of life and death," a plan of "continuous, unbroken communal order."[11]

The vertical and horizontal lines create a cross at the middle of the circle, a "crossroads" where life and death intersect. This is the "vanishing point," the place where all dualistic conflicts are resolved: life and death, male and female, young and old are all united into a single powerful force. When you plunge into the deep waters here, you are transformed. You come into the presence of the Life-Giver.[12] God has no symbol within the Kongo cosmogram, however, because the entire dikenga exists within the Life-Giver. How can you indicate a specific point for Someone who is not limited to any location in either time or space? How can you represent Something that is everywhere?

The dikenga is more than a visual illustration, more than a symbol. It is, in fact, much more like the Catholic understanding of a sacrament: an instrument of Divine power; a visible, tangible expression of spiritual reality. Traditional African communities participate in this reality in countless ways: in the structure of the days of their week; in the architectural design of their homes; in teaching practices with their young; in the hours of the day; in funeral rituals; in song and dance: and even in women's hairstyles. Human life itself, from conception until death and then beyond, is a living dikenga.[13] To draw a dikenga and then stand upon its center, "singing the point," is a powerful meditation ritual that connects a person to both the ancestors and God.[14] Enslaved Africans carried the hope of the dikenga within them; they drew its circle-cross on pottery[15] and hid it within their burial grounds and beneath the foundations of plantation homes.[16]

Our story about the seventy-five Igbo is also an illustration of the Kongo cosmogram. Whether the Igbo flew on strong wings over the water or drowned in its cold depths doesn't really matter from the perspective of the dikenga. Either way, they entered Kalunga. They passed from this life into the life that is to come. Factual or not, this story is *true*, and its truth has inspired and encouraged Black people for centuries.

White people have their own myths of courage and hope, but there's a difference I've noticed. From *Beowulf* to Spiderman movies, the white stories focus on a single heroic individual who, because of his unique powers (and yes, white heroes are usually male), rises above other human beings to do something extraordinary. But remember, as this African proverb states: *Until the lion tells the story, the hunter is always the hero!* Unlike the Western hero story, made famous by Joseph Campbell, African stories are more ambivalent, leaving room to embrace multiple points of view. African heroes are not solitary; they are groups of people working together, just as the seventy-five Igbo did.

The Network of Life

At each point in the Igbos' story, their connections with each other were what generated their courage and strength. If you had been a single Igbo suffering alone below the ship's deck, you would not have had the courage to fight for your freedom—but because you belonged to a community, a community that even death could not destroy, you were strong.

Note that the kind of community we're talking about is a *network,* where each member retains its individual irreplaceable value. We're not speaking of a *melting pot,* where everything gets boiled down into a homogenous mush, with the taste of the Eurocentric ingredients overpowering all the others. A melting pot has nothing to do with the reality of true life, where each member of a living web contributes in essential ways to the well-being of all the rest of that inter-connected community. As Ralph Ellison reminded us, "The heel bone is, after all, connected, through its various linkages, to the head bone."[17]

Racism, however, damages the living network that con-nects us to one another. In doing so, it weakens us all—not just Blacks but whites too. Racism ruptures the web of life. Racism *is* death. We cannot speak of racism without talking about death—and we cannot talk about antiracism without affirming life.

To quote Capra again, "The more we study the major problems of our time, the more we come to realise that they cannot be understood in isolation. They are systemic problems, which means that they are interconnected and interdependent."[18] We make a mistake if we think racism will be solved merely by convincing individuals to see things dif-ferently; racism stretches far beyond any single person's prej-udice. It is a systemic problem, poisoning entire networks of our society, each interacting with all the others: education, the economy, physical and mental health, nutrition, the court system, law enforcement, medicine, and countless other systems. Left to grow unchallenged, racism brings physical and spiritual death. This is the understanding on which I wish to build our discussion of death, racism, and the Black experience.

The Nature of Death

According to a BaKongo creation myth, God created humanity in order to make another "self," someone not only *like* God but someone who actually participated in the Divine Selfhood. However, as time went by, human beings began to be lazy. They became self-absorbed, no longer curious about the world outside themselves and no longer able to perceive the pain of other lifeforms that did not share in the Selfhood of God in the same way they did. They had no urge to help or heal, no desire to sing or paint or dance. So God withdrew from human beings. At the same time, however, the Divine One created a new way to reenter God-self—death. Thus, the death that comes from natural causes, without hatred or violence, is salvation. It is the ultimate restoration, allowing human beings to once more become partners with the One who gives all life.[19]

As English-speaking Westerners, we have no words to differentiate between a violent death and a death that comes naturally at the end of a long life. For us, death is death. Death is the full stop at the end of our lives.

From an African perspective, however, not all deaths are the same. Violent death from racism and hatred is perceived far differently from the death that is a triumphant transition into another world. One is an enemy; the other is a friend. And yet at the same time—from a Christian perspective, at least—a violent death cannot rob the joyous reality of transition into another, fuller, deeper life.

"The last enemy to be deactivated," says the Bible, "is death."[20] The Greek word used here for "enemy" is *echthros,* a word that comes from the same root as "hatred." According to Madeleine L'Engle in her young-adult fantasy *A Wind in the Door*, the echthroi are our spiritual enemies, and their main strategy is "making someone not know who he is."[21] Racism is surely one of the echthroi's forms in our world, a terrible force that works to deny others their God-given identities, to make them doubt their worth and beauty. This theft of identity and meaning is, I believe, the Bible's understanding of death. The forces of hatred that seek to negate and destroy are the true enemy.

When we go off target, the Bible says, the consequences are death.[22] But what is the target—and what does death mean in this context? I believe Jesus described the target he had in mind: "Love the Eternal One your God with all your heart and all your soul and all your mind," going on to add, "Love your neighbor as yourself."[23] When we fail to follow this double command, we join forces with the echthroi. At the end of the day, if we place the ego's desire for power and control ahead of the well-being of others, the only "targets" we hit are oppression, discrimination, bigotry, and injustice.

And yet this is the mindset that has been normalized since at least the seventeenth century, when philosopher René Descartes described human beings as naturally "masters and owners." (By "human beings," he meant white European males, who by right could possess and use an inanimate world that included women, people with black skin, and Nature.) We have the option to take a far different route, however, as Kenyan philosopher James Ogude has explained, emphasizing a "different form of consciousness that does not privilege the self" but instead, understands that the self can only "realize itself is through others" (with "others" being not only human beings but also the natural world of plant and animal, water, air, and soil; and the spiritual world).[24] The interwoven lacework of life is a biological, social, and spiritual reality. The rugged individualism that says, "My own happiness is the thing I value most" breaks the mutual life-giving bonds within this web—and it is ultimately a dead end: a full stop to creativity and growth and possibility.

Throughout this book, we will speak of death from both perspectives: destruction versus fulfillment, the end versus transformation. Both perspectives are real; neither one can cancel out the other, and yet ultimately, I believe, life—Divine Life—triumphs.

The Goals of This Book

I have been contemplating writing this book for many years. I am a Black man, but few of us in the Western world are immune to the death dilemma: that urge to ignore death because death frightens us and to also look away from the systemic death that threatens our entire world. As a Christian, as a Jesuit, and as a Black man, my ego hesitates to unveil my insecurities. When it comes to death, I want to have an impeccably curated public persona, projecting only faith and confidence out into the world, rather than my hidden wounds of fear and sorrow.

But then I remember the courage of those Igbo people—ordinary people (like me, like you) who found, both in each other and in their spiritual beliefs, what they needed to become extraordinary. They did not play make-believe about death; they fully realized the danger they faced—but they faced it together, with the courage and vulnerability that gives absolutely everything to whatever lies ahead. That, in my mind, is the true definition of hope.

In this book, we will venture past death and racism into the region of hope and community. We too will take a "water journey,"[25] walking in the ancient footsteps of my people, borrowing from their courage and wisdom. Together, we will examine the ways racism and death intersect, and we will learn from the history and traditions of Black people. Many of the issues I bring up apply not only to Blacks but also to all people of color. Because I am a Black man with my ancestral roots in Africa, this is where I have focused my attention. I am writing what I know—but I also want to acknowledge that Blacks are not the only people of color who suffer the death that is racism. The Indigenous peoples of the Americas have faced ongoing death ever since the first white person stepped onto their lands; the Asian community also continues to endure the violence and discrimination that greeted it when it first came to America; and even the US Centers for Disease Control and Prevention (CDC) acknowledges the heavy costs of racism born by Latinos and Latinas.[26] In 2021 alone, 555 human beings died as they tried to enter the United States by crossing her southern border, while more than 1,500 immigrants drowned in the Mediterranean trying to reach Europe—and these groups also died because of racism.

Regardless of the color of our skin, however, we will all face the same challenges: To believe in a life that death cannot conquer. To walk in the hope of life rather than the fear of death. To find ways to rebuild the interactive life-giving system on which we all depend. To that end, I have included a simple prayer exercise or meditation practice at the end of each chapter. Use them if they're helpful to you; skip over them if they're not.

Sankofa is an African concept that means "return to your past in order to move forward." It is often associated with the African proverb, "It is not wrong to go back for that which you have forgotten." From the African perspective, the past is necessary to the present. As Miriam Makeba, the great African empress of song, said, "In the West the past is like a dead animal. It is a carcass picked at by the flies that call themselves historians and biographers. But in my culture the past lives."[27]

And so, let us work together, you and I, to reclaim the living past—with all its beauty and creativity, as well as its terror and ugliness—so that we can look toward a better future. Embedded in the history of Black experience is the rich wisdom of Africa. We have tried long enough to fix America's problems using Euro-American thinking. Let us now claim the African legacy that belongs to us all, for genetically, we share a common mother: we are all descended from a single African woman who lived about 200,000 years ago.[28]

So come, sisters and brothers, and follow me. We will plunge into the life-and-death waters of Kalunga, and then—together, like those long-ago Igbo—we will find our way to a safer, larger home, a home where no one is excluded.

Jordon's river is deep and cold,
Kills the body but not the soul.

—AFRICAN AMERICAN SPIRITUAL

MEDITATION PRACTICE

The Akan people of Africa believe that what makes a "living soul" is an inherent, ongoing destiny.[29] Their concept of destiny is, however, a bit different from ours. For them, destiny is the thing within us that pulls us toward the Creator, the way iron filings are pulled by a magnet. Death is a part of that destiny, but not in a pessimistic or hopeless way. Instead, death is the necessary opening that allows us to draw closer to God than we can in this life. Death is part of our very selfhood. Just as a little girl already carries within her ovaries the eggs that may one day be fertilized and become her children, we carry within our bodies the as-yet-undeveloped reality of our deaths. Dying is a developmental stage in our maturity as individuals.

Take some time now to think about your death. From the moment you were born, you carry your death with you. Does that frighten you or depress you? Allow yourself to feel whatever emotions arise from the fact of your own death.

Now imagine the Kongo cosmogram, the circle with the cross at the center. Picture yourself standing on the center point, the place where death and life intersect. All around you is water. If you dive into the water, you will enter death—and then the life that lies beyond death. How do you feel as you stand there? Does the thought of diving into the water frighten you? Is there anything exciting about it? Spend a few moments with your feelings, whatever they are. Notice them without trying to change them. Allow them to simply be.

Finally, picture yourself diving into those waters. What does it feel like? Is the water cold or warm? Can you see anything on the other side of the water? If so, what? (And if you can't, that's all right too.) What emotions do you experience as you swim through the water? Do you feel trapped—or free? Weak— or strong? Notice these feelings, but do not try to change them or shape them. Stay in this moment, swimming in the waters of life and death, for as long as feels comfortable to you.

Now, return to the present moment. You have shown great courage in going through this exercise, for it is not easy to face death. Spend a little time thinking about your relationship to life and death. Remind yourself that your identity comes from God. Claim its wholeness, allowing your death to be a part of that wholeness.

Repeat this meditation at least once a month. When you do, don't try to force feelings or images to arise—and don't avoid them either. Simply observe whatever comes. Notice if your feelings change as you repeat this exercise. You may want to journal your reactions, so you can compare how your attitudes may be developing and changing. Doing this exercise regularly will help you become more comfortable with death. It may also give you a sense of your larger, spiritual identity, one that transcends the circumstances of your life.

The sacred self's affirmation . . .
is its way of breaking through
those barriers and impediments
that seek to bind and enslave it.
The more I affirm my "God self,"
the less I confirm the capacity of others
to enslave and dehumanize. . . .
Affirming the truth of one's existence
creates freedom of self.

—CARLYLE FIELDING STEWART[30]

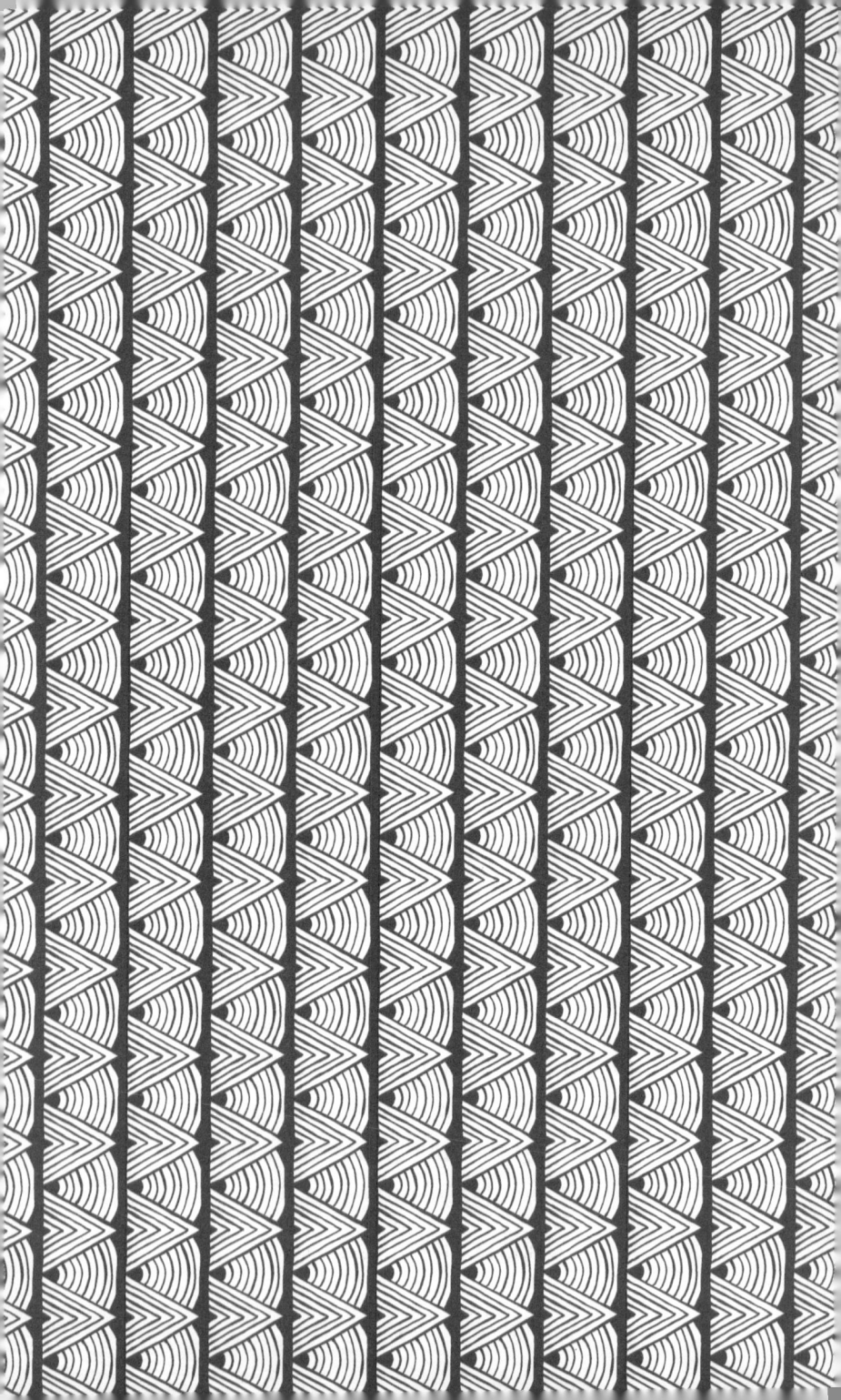

1

THE AGE
OF PANDEMIC

DEATH AND RACISM

*This virus has no eyes, and
yet it knows exactly
how we see each other and
how we treat each other.*

—KAMALA HARRIS[31]

*White Americans do not believe in death,
and that is why the darkness of
my skin so intimidates them.*

—JAMES BALDWIN[32]

DEATH IS A STRANGE THING. IT'S SOMETHING we will all experience, but it's also something none of us has experienced *yet*. It's a mystery, an uncertainty. It's dark.

Despite the common dualistic prejudice of Western thinking (good versus bad, light versus dark, white versus black), darkness does not equal evil. In the natural world, darkness is often fertile, filled with possibility. Because we cannot see what darkness holds, though, we feel out of control; death threatens our egos, those external shells we try so hard to protect—but a loss of control is always an opening, an opportunity for Divine possibility. "Life is the beginning of death" is an African proverb that speaks to the inevitability of death, but this reality need not overshadow our lives with pessimism and meaninglessness, because the opposite can be true as well: "Death is the beginning of life."

From a Western perspective, we imagine life as a straight line that starts with birth and ends with death. The African worldview sees things differently. Death does not end life; instead, it is merely a developmental milestone, the threshold into a deeper life. We cannot perceive the post-death phase of life with our current senses—for the African as for the Euro-American, death is dark—but within that darkness, lies promise and hope.

This does not diminish the pain death brings. Even Jesus, when confronted with the death of a friend, shed tears of sorrow.[33] I suspect Jesus could see farther into death's shadows than the rest of us can, and yet he still cried, just as we do when death takes those we love. I am grateful for the insights my African and Christian heritages give me—but at the same time, because of death, we who are a part of the African diaspora have shed far too many soul-fracturing tears.

The Inescapability of Death

My most intense personal experience of death happened more than a decade ago, when my grandmother died. Tatie, as I call her, was my best friend, my confidant, and my mentor. When I learned she was struggling with stage-four cancer, I faced a threat I could not see, and so I denied that it existed. I was accustomed to feeling in control of my life; I had always been able to use my intelligence or charm to get whatever I wanted, which had given me an illusion of self-sufficiency. I was the macho man, stronger than death. Nothing could touch me.

But Tatie died—and when she did, death was a reality I could no longer avoid. Now, it had become a constant companion, one that was always waiting for me. I was never truly alone, because death was always in the room with me. At night, it sat on the edge of my bed, leaning toward me as though it wanted to climb under the blankets and snuggle.

Still, I tried to pretend—not only to those around me but to myself as well—that none of this was happening. Outwardly, I appeared as I always had—cheerful, outgoing, successful— but inwardly, I was drenched with something mysterious and immense. I was sinking, I was drowning ... and unlike the Igbo in the story I told in the introduction, I did not recognize that my only hope lay in the very thing that threatened to destroy me: the waters of death.[34]

And then came 2020—and like the rest of the world, I could no longer avoid those fearful waters. I struggled to embrace this time as an opportunity for me to reshape my relationship with death, but I was nervous, uncomfortable, anxious. Death was everywhere I turned.

Not only did the COVID-19 virus kill at least three million people globally during 2020,[35] but gun homicides in the United States also increased by 35 percent, with almost five thousand more people losing their lives because of guns in 2020 than did in 2019.[36] American deaths in general increased by nearly 20 percent that year, the largest mortality spike in a hundred years.[37] After nearly a century of believing—or pretending, at least—that modern medicine had triumphed over death, we once again faced life's one unavoidable reality: *Death will come for us all. None of us can escape.*

COVID-19

And yet many of us still tried to deny it. We minimized the dangers of COVID-19; some of us even convinced ourselves that the whole thing was an elaborate hoax. If our own lives remained untouched, we allowed ourselves to believe we were immune to the illness that had stricken so many people around the world. We listened to the growing number of deaths—by the end of 2022, almost 7 million people, globally, had died because of COVID[38]—but the numbers were too big to grasp. Many of us remained numb to the very real grief that surrounded us.

In fact, in the United States, with its population of almost 330 million, most of the population *was* untouched. We didn't see corpses lying in the street or hear the wails of orphaned children. Many of the people who died from COVID were elderly, poor, or people of color. As Reverend William Barber pointed out:

> Before COVID-19, nearly 700 people died every day because of poverty and inequality in this country. The frontlines of this pandemic will be the poor and dispossessed—those who do not have access to health care, housing, water, decent wages, stable work or child care.[39]

If you were a healthy white adult with an adequate income, odds were good you could observe the pandemic from a distance (just as you had always observed those who lived and died in poverty).

Still, by the end of 2021, somewhere around 135 million people, globally, had lost people they loved and were in mourning due to COVID-related deaths.[40] Some medical experts referred to a "double public health crisis," one visible, one nearly invisible—coronavirus *and* "unmitigated grief."[41] "This pandemic of grief is one for which there is no vaccine," said grief therapist Robert Neimeyer.[42]

As a practicing psychotherapist, I've noticed that many Americans assume grief is not an expected aspect of human life. Instead, they seem to think of grief as a bothersome interruption of "normal life." When grief cannot be avoided, says the average American, people should do their best to "work through it" and put it behind them as quickly as possible. It's a linear process that begins and ends, according to this way of thinking, and it is also a private process that's not meant to be displayed or shared with the community as a whole.

But this understanding of death does not serve us well in our time of pandemic. It cuts us off from the very thing we need most—the life-giving support of the community—at a time when we are already struggling to hold on to our social connections. It puts many of us at risk for future problems, both medical and emotional. What's more, death is not only the cessation of biological life; the pandemic also put to death goals and dreams, economic stability, the very shape of our lives.

It may also have murdered many of our children's innocence and sense of security, as well as their health. A study found that as of December 2021, more than 200 thousand American children had been orphaned as a result of the pandemic. The study's authors concluded that this crisis situation may "result in a profound long-term impact on health and well-being for children." The authors go on to say that the death of parents "is associated with mental health problems, shorter schooling, lower self-esteem, sexual risk behaviors, and risks of suicide, violence, sexual abuse, and exploitation."[43] The study's authors remind us, however, that children can be resilient when they have ongoing connections to a community that supports them, sets boundaries for them, and commits to providing for their emotional and physical needs.

I have faith in the Black community's creativity and resilience (more on this in chapter 9), but I am also well aware that the pandemic has been harder on Blacks as a whole than on whites, weakening our cultural power. More than 65 percent of America's orphans are children of color. Many of the illnesses Blacks have at higher rates than whites—asthma, hypertension, heart and lung disease, and diabetes—are also the underlying conditions that put people at risk for more severe cases of COVID-19. When Black people get sick with COVID, they are ten times more likely to die than white people.[44]

To make things even worse, low-income people—who also tend to be people of color—have a greater risk of being exposed to the virus because they are often unable to practice social distancing. Lacking cars, many of them depend on public transportation to get to their jobs—if they still have jobs. Those who didn't lose their employment during the pandemic were often the ones who kept the "essential" functions of our economy operating. They were the nurses and health aides, the cleaners and farmworkers, the restaurant workers and cashiers. Their jobs did not allow them to stay home, and less than 10 percent of them had the option of working virtually from home (compared to more than 60 percent of workers with higher-income jobs).[45] Finally, when low-income Blacks caught the virus and were told to stay home and quarantine, it was often an impossibility for family members living in small apartments with a single bathroom.

So where I am going with all these numbers and percentages? I'm trying to help you understand that while the COVID-19 pandemic has shaken us all, it's been particularly devastating to the Black community and other communities of color. As Kamala Harris said, a virus is technically blind, and yet this one has pinpointed our weaknesses, attacking bodies that are already weakened by the centuries of racism embedded in our economy and health-care system. We cannot talk about the grief the pandemic caused without talking about racism. And we cannot face our chronic fear of death until we also face our racism.

Grief and Racism

As the Black community bears the burden of so much sorrow, it becomes even more vulnerable. According to grief expert Mary-Frances O'Connor, losing three or more loved ones puts stress on the human body that can lead to potentially lethal cardiovascular disease.[46] O'Connor and her colleagues also noted that grief can make the immune system teeter, leading to increased susceptibility to diseases.[47]

As O'Connor's studies of grief continued, she realized that the current (white) concept of grief is "too narrow in scope to encompass Black grief." She went on to say, "We must expand our definition of grief to account for the pain that occurs within the Black community after the loss of a loved one, the loss of land, the loss of a sense of safety, and the loss of members of the community due to direct and indirect acts of racist violence . . . including the unequal distribution of grief, vulnerability to premature death, and historic and ongoing violence."[48] As people of color, racism breaks our hearts, literally. It puts us at risk. It kills us.

In the introduction, I said that life and community are very nearly synonymous, because life only exists in interdependent networks—communities. Meanwhile, racism is tangled in the web of our society, like a malicious growth that severs the healthy, life-giving connections between us. In doing so, it negates the real meaning of life. If *community* is equivalent to *life,* then *racism* is equivalent to *death.*

Death comes for us all, of course—"Death is a robe we will all have to wear," says an African proverb—but racism is not natural death. It is murder. This was made starkly clear when police officer Derek Chauvin killed George Floyd by kneeling on his neck for more than nine minutes.

The "Other Epidemic"

For people like me (people with black skin), Floyd's murder in the early days of the pandemic was a bone-shaking, heart-shattering atrocity—but it was neither surprising nor new. Black people have always known, ever since the beginning of slavery, that racism is a lethal threat to our lives. For many white Americans, though, Floyd's murder was the first time they encountered racism at a visceral, emotional level. Because a young girl recorded the murder on her phone, we could all experience Floyd's death at a far more intense level than if we'd just read about it in the news. We heard his groans, his gasps for breath; we saw the indifference on the faces of the police officers. Black or white, we could *see* with our own eyes what racism looks like.

But George Floyd's murder was not unique. In 2020 alone, these people of color also lost their lives to racism-fueled police brutality:

- Andre Hill, age forty-seven, was shot and killed by officers in Columbus, Ohio, after he came out of his garage holding a cell phone in his hand.

- Manuel Ellis, age thirty-three, encountered police while walking home from a convenience store in Tacoma, Washington; he died after the officers punched him, Tasered him, and then knelt on him for at least six minutes. (The officers initially claimed Ellis had attacked them first, but eyewitnesses at the scene, as well as a video recording, told another story.)

- Rayshard Brooks, age twenty-seven, was shot and killed by officers after he fell asleep in his car outside a fast-food restaurant in Atlanta, Georgia.

- Daniel Prude, age forty-one, died from asphyxiation in Rochester, New York, when officers applied pressure to his throat while he was having a mental-health episode.

- Breonna Taylor, age twenty-six, died after being shot eight times in her apartment in Louisville, Kentucky, when police officers broke into the wrong house on a drug raid.

- Daunte Wright, age twenty, was shot and killed in Minneapolis after he was stopped for a traffic violation. (The officer said she had mistaken her gun for her Taser.)

- Johnny Bolton, age forty-nine, was shot and killed when police entered his Smyrna, Georgia, apartment on a no-knock drug bust; Bolton's name was not listed on the warrant.

- Angelo Quinto, age thirty, died from complications after a police officer in Antioch, California, knelt on his neck for five minutes; the police were initially responding to a call that Quinto was suffering from a mental-health crisis.

- Marcellis Stinnette, age nineteen, was shot and killed by the police while sitting in his car with his partner outside his house in Waukegan, Illinois. (His partner was also shot but survived.)

- Jonathan Price, age thirty-two, was trying to break up a fight outside a gas station in Wolfe City, Texas, when he was shot multiple times by police officers.

- Mickel Erich Lewis, age thirty-nine, was shot when he leaned into his car during a police stop for a minor traffic violation in Mojave, California.

- Walter Wallace, age twenty-seven, a man with mental-health issues, was shot fourteen times by police in Philadelphia when he walked toward them with a knife in his hand; his mother was at the scene and had been talking to her son, who was in the midst of a mental crisis.

- Kurt Andras Reinhold, a forty-two-year-old unarmed homeless man with mental illness, was shot and killed after police stopped him for jaywalking in San Clemente, California.

- Julian Edward Roosevelt Lewis, age sixty, was shot in his car after he initially fled from a traffic violation stop in Sylvania, Georgia.

- Robert D'Lon Harris, age thirty-four, was shot and killed by police in Vinita, Oklahoma, during a traffic violation stop.

- Dion Johnson, age twenty-eight, was shot and killed by a state trooper who found him sleeping in his car by the side of the road in Phoenix, Arizona.

- Maurice Gordon Jr., age twenty-eight, was shot in Bass River, New Jersey, after police stopped him for speeding (officers said they thought he was reaching for a gun).

- Shaun Fuhr, age twenty-four, was holding his child and running away from police in Seattle, Washington, when he was shot and killed. (Police were originally called because Fuhr was fighting with his partner, the mother of his child.)

- Donnie Sanders, age forty-seven, fled after being stopped for a traffic violation in Kansas City, Missouri, and was shot by officers who thought he was reaching for a gun. (He was later found to be unarmed.)

- Barry Gedeus, age twenty-seven, was shot and killed by officers as he was riding his bicycle home from a convenience store in Fort Lauderdale, Florida; the officers said he matched the description of someone who had committed a sexual assault.

- Jaquyn Oneill Light, age twenty, was shot in his home, in Graham, North Carolina, after he unintentionally collided with an officer who was entering his house.

- William Howard Green, age forty-three, was shot in Temple Hills, Maryland, while handcuffed inside a patrol car after being stopped for erratic driving.

If you skimmed over this list of names (thinking, *Yeah, yeah, I get the picture*), I ask you to please go back and read them over. These are the names of human beings who lived and loved and laughed. They have families, friends, and lovers who miss them and mourn them. As a Black man, I know they could easily have been my brothers or sister, my father or mother—or me.

If you are white, I ask you to try to share with me what that knowledge feels like. Imagine how you would feel if random, meaningless, violent death was always lurking in wait for you and your loved ones. Sit with that feeling until it sinks into your flesh and bones, until it begins to carve a rut in your neural pathways. And then remember the feeling. Come back to it often. I do not pretend this is easy. I am asking you to open yourself to a sorrow so vast, so deeply rooted, that none of us can fully grasp it. The number of people who have lost their lives to racism is too immense to fathom.

In 2020 alone, the actual list of people of color who died at the hands of police officers is far longer than what I just wrote. According to the website *Mapping Police Violence*, police killed a total of 484 people of color during 2020. The American Civil Liberties Union (ACLU) refers to these fatal police shootings in the time of COVID-19 as the "other epidemic."[49]

The ACLU report goes on to say: "The epidemic of police violence has been directly and disproportionately targeted at Black people. . . . Just as police are more likely to stop, frisk, arrest, and jail Black people than white people, they are more likely to shoot and kill Black people. One study found that young unarmed male victims of deadly force by police are 13 times more likely to be Black than white. . . . Stunningly, for young men of color, police use of force is now among the leading causes of death."[50]

This epidemic of violence did not end in 2020; in 2021, another 487 people of color lost their lives to police brutality,[51] and in 2022, another 366.[52] Reading the statistics, it's sometimes easy to forget that each number stands for an individual human being. It is also easy to find reasons to diminish these tragedies; after all, we say, the person who died had drugs in their system; they had a weapon; they were mentally unstable. They shouldn't have argued with the police; they shouldn't have tried to run away. These statements, even when they were true, cannot negate the incalculable value of the lives that have been lost. As Reverend Naomi Washington-Leapheart reminds us, each person who died at the hands of police "was not a problem for institutions to neglect, evaluate, control, pity, solve, or revile. He was a full human being who deserved the space to grow, stumble, and thrive."[53]

Living as we do in a system where the well-being of each individual depends on the well-being of every other individual, these deaths impact us all. Whether we realize it or not, each racist-driven death shakes the very core of all our lives. How can we make sense of so much death?

Unsettling Questions

"Death," said theologian John Shelby Spong, "must, therefore, raise the deepest and most unsettling questions with which human beings deal."[54] Indigenous cultures, as well as older versions of European culture, have always sought to answer these questions. In the modern Western world, however, we seldom devote our intelligence and energy to seeking the meaning of life and death. Our best minds are no longer theologians and philosophers; they are scientists whose goal is to extend life, not define it.

The scientific perspective doesn't seek to perceive or understand invisible, "spiritual" worlds. Instead, its goal is to determine visible, tangible causes and effects. From this perspective, we don't die because we are ready to enter a new world or a new phase of life, nor do we die because we live in a world where violence and racism hack holes in life's boundless interactions. No, science says we die because of technical problems within the machine that is the human body. "Science almost always assumes that problems have technical solutions," wrote ecologist Garrett Hardin. "A technical solution may be defined as one that requires a change only in the techniques of the natural sciences, demanding little or nothing in the way of change in human values or ideas of morality."[55]

Science, particularly medical science, has, however, worked from the assumption that white males are humanity's standard model. This means the "technical" perspective has been distorted and blinkered; any solutions it offers will also be fragmented and flawed.

Physician Harlan Krumholz calls for a transformation of scientific thought, particularly when it comes to racism. He pointed out that research into combatting major diseases (such as cancer, heart disease, diabetes, and so on) has been driven by public awareness. "Now imagine," Krumholz said, "if one of the leading causes of deaths was understood as simply being racism within society, and we galvanized that kind of interest and effort and accountability as we saw to make progress." Racism, Krumholz concluded, is the number-one cause of death among men, and the third leading cause of death for women. In other words, racism is a disease as lethal as cancer and heart disease—and it merits the same attention and commitment to problem-solving.

"We cannot simply be passive in saying, 'I'm not racist,'" Krumholz wrote. "We need to accept that our system has been racist since the beginning of time, and that we need to be actively anti-racist in seeking solutions, both with regard to our own behaviors and in regard to the systems that we work in. . . . [I]t cannot be accomplished by effective individuals alone. This allyship, the idea that we can all hold hands, work together, hold ourselves accountable, and make progress, is essential."[56] And there it is again: healthy, living communities work together, "holding hands." That is the only way we can fight death-dealing racism.

Perhaps Americans have handled the pandemic so poorly because we are unequipped to deal with grief. We look down at our phones. We mutter a few platitudes. (*Be strong. God knows what he's doing. You will come out of this a better person. I'll pray for you.*) And all the while, we pretend death is not in the same room with us.[57]

We do much the same thing with racism. It's no coincidence that the same segment of the population that gives no credence to critical race theory is also the segment that minimizes the true human cost of the COVID-19 virus, that also resists vaccination (because to be vaccinated would be to admit that the threat of death is real). But the problem isn't limited to conservatives or a single political party. This is a problem that belongs to us all.

Changed Perspectives

"Maybe," suggests journalist Eric Weiner, "we should let the pandemic change us."[58] The pandemic brought death and sorrow. It exposed and magnified the injustice and racism in our systems. But death is also always an opportunity. It is a place where hope is born. As Jesus said, "I tell you the truth: unless a grain of wheat is planted in the ground and dies, it remains a solitary seed. But when it is planted, it produces in death a great harvest" (John 12:24 TV).

Physics teaches us that energy cannot be created or destroyed; it can only change its form. The pandemic brought death—death by virus, death by racism, death by grief—but in all that death, there is also a release of energy, energy we can now use in new directions, for life instead of death, to support and build community rather than weaken and undermine it. In doing this, we must work together as equals. We must understand that just as the problem belongs to all of us, so does the solution. And finally, we must commit ourselves to the long, hard work of justice.

After the murder of George Floyd in May 2020, donations to social justice charities soared. "Woke" white folk, driven by guilt and pity, were eager to do whatever they could. They may at times have given more food than was needed or sent their money to organizations without any clear sense of how the funds would be used, but I believe the donations were well-intentioned. However, guilt and pity are seldom sustainable, and by December 2020, donations to antiracist causes had fallen back to their previous levels.[59]

Dear white reader, if you believe Black folk need your help, please let me gently break it to you: that's racist thinking. It's based on a model of hierarchy, where you reach down to those who are lower than you. The truth is—*you need Black people.* We need each other. As Martin Luther King Jr. put it, we all belong to the "inescapable network of mutuality," "the single garment of destiny." He went on to say, "I can never be what I ought to be until you are what you ought to be, and you can never be what you ought to be until I am what I ought to be. . . . This is the inter-related structure of reality."[60]

Within a network, there is no hierarchy; all are equal, and all are needed. My well-being is essential to yours, just as yours is to mine. But you are not my savior, and I cannot be yours. Together, however, we have a chance to learn, a chance to grow. Together, we can imagine a new vision of what it means to belong to the single vibrant organism that contains all life.

But we cannot do that without first facing death.

The Black Experience of Death

The Black experience of death is brutal and appalling. To look at it closely is uncomfortable, even agonizing. But it is necessary.

Elisabeth Kübler-Ross, the psychiatrist whose model shapes the modern world's understanding of death and dying, described the "stages of grief" as denial, anger, bargaining, depression, and acceptance.[61] When it comes to the death that is racism, many Americans are still in the denial stage.

America has suffered a terrible and ongoing death, one that began at the same time as its birth and continues still today—and yet many of us refuse to admit its reality. We want to believe our country is wonderful, a shining beacon of freedom; to admit that death lies at the very heart of who we are would disrupt that belief.

Denial is generally unconscious, though; it happens after a loved one's death because our minds simply can't grasp the reality that this person is no longer present (at least not physically); and it happens in a similar way when we confront our nation's racism. "Sometimes," wrote twentieth-century psychiatrist Frantz Fanon, "people hold a core belief that is very strong. When they are presented with evidence that works against that belief, the new evidence cannot be accepted. It would create a feeling that is extremely uncomfortable, called cognitive dissonance. And because it is so important to protect the core belief, they will rationalize, ignore and even deny anything that doesn't fit in with the core belief."[62] Racism and death do not fit in with our core beliefs as Euro-Americans.

Kübler-Ross's next stages are anger and bargaining. Over the centuries, we have hurled our anger at one another as one more way to avoid the pain. Anger can be the impetus for justice (see chapter 5 for more on this)—but if unexamined, it can also be destructive, keeping us mired in the ancient sources of our rage. As for bargaining, I believe donating to charities as a response to Black death and racism may demonstrate this aspect of grieving: *If I do this really good thing, then please, God, make the agony of racism go away.*

The time has come to face our pain.

Kübler-Ross describes what this involves: "After bargaining, . . . [e]mpty feelings present themselves, and grief enters our lives on a deeper level, deeper than we ever imagined. This depressive stage . . . is the appropriate response to a great loss . . . [but] is too often seen as unnatural: a state to be fixed, something to snap out of. . . . If grief is a process of healing, then depression is one of the many necessary steps along the way."[63]

I am not suggesting that as we examine the Black experience of death, we should eventually move on to acceptance, Kübler-Ross's final stage in the grieving process. This is not what healing looks like in this context—or rather, acceptance within this context does not mean complacency; it does not mean we continue to tolerate injustice. Instead, in Kübler-Ross's words, we "learn to reorganize roles, re-assign them to others or take them on ourselves. . . . We can never replace what has been lost, but we can make new connections, new meaningful relationships, new inter-dependencies . . . ; we move, we change, we grow, we evolve. . . . We start the process of reintegration, trying to put back the pieces that have been ripped away."[64] Racism has ripped away essential pieces of who we are as individuals, as well as who we are as a community. Antiracism is the ongoing work of restoring those pieces.

Too often, we focus on the white experience as the place that holds the solutions to racism. We try to find answers to our societal problems by working from the assumptions of the Euro-American worldview. But, as Audre Lorde reminds us, "The master's tools will never dismantle the master's house."[65] I believe it is the Black experience that will teach us something new, both as individuals struggling with our fear of death and as a broken community in need of healing. The African worldview is the therapeutic lens we need.

A worldview can be described as "a cognitive home that we all live in—an edifice of ideas that's arisen layer by layer over older constructions put together by generations past . . . the set of assumptions we hold about how things work: how society functions, its relationship with the natural world, what's valuable and what's possible. It often remains unquestioned and unstated but is deeply felt and underlies many of the choices we make in our lives. We form our worldview implicitly as we grow up, from family, friends, and culture, and once it's set, we're barely aware of it unless we're presented with a different worldview for comparison."[66]

The dominant Western worldview emphasizes the individual human as more important than the community as a whole, as well as more important than (and separate from) Nature. Furthermore, for many Euro-Americans, the use of resources and wealth is best determined in light of individual goals and desires; science is the source of truth; time is linear, oriented toward the future; and society is compartmentalized into segments that seldom or never interact.[67]

The worldview of the African diaspora is based on very different assumptions. Traditional Africans, as we mentioned in the introduction, understand all life and all truth as a web of connected systems that function both collectively and collaboratively within the ever-cycling circles of time. This understanding can be best expressed with the African concept we mentioned earlier: *Ubuntu*, "I am because we are." This way-of-being-in-the-world sees no separation between human beings, Nature, and the "spiritual world." The living dead (and I don't mean zombies but rather those who have crossed the threshold into another phase of existence) are still essential to the vast, vital fabric of life. We cannot understand the African concept of death without grasping the meaning of Ubuntu.[68]

During these pandemic years, in my psychotherapy practice, I've realized many Americans engage with death—their own, as well as the deaths of loved ones—with a sense of hopelessness. Regardless of their religious beliefs, the individuals with whom I worked saw death as the final goodbye. Instead of being the end of a chapter, death, from this perspective, is the end of the entire book. Death is where the story ends.

As a mental-health professional, I was trained to see grief as a disorder. I have certificates in grief and trauma, I belong to psychological associations that study grieving, and I have many hours of training in the treatment of grief. In reality, however, for much of my professional life, I was as much at a loss when faced with death as my patients were. I encouraged my patients to quickly "heal," "to recover," as though sorrow was a disease.

After my grandmother died, as I struggled to come to terms with the meaning of her death, I was forced to grope my way toward a healthier and more complete understanding of death in general. I too, like my patients, lacked a healthy relationship with it. I needed to integrate my spiritual beliefs (as both a Jesuit and a member of the African diaspora) with my professional training—because the Euro-American worldview is not enough. At first glance, it seems to elevate human identity higher than anything else, and yet all the while, it anticipates the final destruction of that very identity. It denies us hope in anything beyond this life.

In the Gospels, Jesus presents a very different perspective. "Don't get lost in despair," Jesus tells us. ". . . My Father's home is designed to accommodate all of you. If there were not room for everyone, I would have told you that. I am going to make arrangements for your arrival. I will be there to greet you personally and welcome you home, where we will be together. . . . I came to give life with joy and abundance" (John 14:1–3, 10:10 TV).

Although America calls itself a Christian nation, the teachings of Jesus are incompatible with the assumptions of the Western worldview. As a result, many of us store our religion in a little box we can set to one side where it has little or no relation to the rest of our lives. A religion like this fails to give us the hope we need as the foundation of a healthy community.

There is much we could learn from Africa. Our African roots belong to us all, both Black and white, and from them, we can learn (or relearn) what so many of us have failed to grasp from Jesus' message in the Gospels: the difference between the death that leads to still more life—and the death that negates and discards life. There, in those dark waters of both sorrow and resilience, we have opportunities to learn new truths.

My humanity is bound up in yours,
for we can only be human together.
We shall survive only together, black and white.
We can be human only together, black and white.

—DESMOND TUTU[69]

Jesus rejected hatred
because he saw that hatred meant death
to the mind, death to the spirit,
and death to communion with his Father.
He affirmed life; and hatred was the great denial.
To him it was clear:
Thou must make no division.

—HOWARD THURMAN[70]

SELF-ASSESSMENT EXERCISE

Researchers have found that during crises—such as the COVID-19 pandemic, political unrest, and individual traumas—many of us drop the self-care habits that were once normal parts of our lives.[71] Somehow, they no longer seem important—when actually, we need them more than ever in order to confront these crises with strength and resilience.

Take a moment to think about your life as it is today compared to what it was prior to 2020. What differences do you notice? Some of these were unavoidable, of course, but are there any practices you once engaged in that benefited your life, which you have since stopped doing? It might be a daily time for prayer or meditation, it could be an exercise program, it could be taking time to be alone—or making time to be with friends. It might be a creative practice, such as drawing, writing poetry, quilting, or playing a musical instrument. Whatever it is, how might you fit it into the "new normal" of your life today? Can you do that today—and then make a plan for continuing to remake a habit? Studies have found that just ten minutes of self-renewal every day can diminish depression and anxiety and build a new sense of joy in life.[72]

There must be always remaining in every life,
some place for the singing of angels,
some place for that which in itself
is breathless and beautiful.

—HOWARD THURMAN[73]

2

THE WORK
OF MOURNING

DEATH AS AN
OPPORTUNITY TO LEARN

*Learning might be the central task
of the grieving brain.*

—SUSAN H. SEELEY AND
MARY-FRANCES O'CONNOR[74]

*In order to see where we are going,
we not only must remember
where we have been,
but we must understand
where we have been.*

—ELLA BAKER[75]

IF MY GRANDMOTHER HAD NEVER DIED—IF Tatie were still alive and healthy, available for me to visit or call on the phone whenever I wished—would I still be the same person I am today?

No, I would not.

Tatie taught me more than I can describe during her lifetime; her life was a gift to me that shaped who I continue to be today. But in her dying, Tatie gave me other gifts, gifts she could not have given me if she had remained alive. Her death shapes who I am, just as her life does. I am a stronger, better person because Tatie lived—and I am also a stronger, better person because she died.

This is a strange paradox. I mourn Tatie every day. Her death continues to give me pain. And yet at the same time, her death has enlarged me, emotionally, intellectually, spiritually. I am not an emotional masochist, drawn to situations that cause me suffering, nor do I romanticize death—so how can something so hurtful be so essential to my sense of my own God-given selfhood?

Perhaps because Tatie, in her death, taught me the real meaning of hope.

Mourning versus Melancholia

My experience is not unique. Many psychologists have recognized this same therapeutic paradox.

The "work of mourning," a psychoanalytic term first used by Sigmund Freud,[76] implies that mourning is an active process; it is not static but rather leads somewhere. Freud contrasted mourning with melancholia, which he defined as being sunk in grief, unable to move forward. Mourning, said Freud, hears and responds to the call of reality, while melancholia chooses to mire itself in an unchanging fantasy world. Mourning expands our consciousness out into new insights; melancholia remains in the gloom of the unconscious. We *know* when we mourn, but melancholia shapes our lives without our awareness.

Freud defined melancholia as not only a reaction to the death of a loved one but also as "the loss of some abstraction . . . such as one's country, liberty, and ideal."[77] This ideological loss is similar to psychoanalyst Jacques Lacan's concept of the "second death," what he also called the "symbolic death"—a death that does not involve the cessation of physical life but rather the extinction of our symbolic universe and the devastation of our position within that universe.

America, I believe, has suffered this symbolic death, and as a result, she is stuck fast in melancholia. The ideals that are so important to her self-identity—freedom, equality, and opportunity—have been lost to racism ever since her birth; as a result, she is not who she thinks she is. She claims for herself labels such as "Land of Liberty," "land of opportunity," and "Leader of the Free World," but all the while, her idealism hides a malignant hemorrhage. Although racism is an undeniable aspect of her unconscious identity, she cannot locate the wound that is killing her slowly from within. She doesn't want to recognize what it is doing to the human beings who live within her society.

Freud's work on mourning and melancholia gave the Western world new psychological insights about itself, ones that are still being used today. At the same time, however, Freud's understanding of grief was cut short by his own system of beliefs. The work of mourning, he wrote, required a "testing of reality"[78]—but his understanding of *reality* was a limited and impoverished one. As a result, Freud's continued influence on our current culture contributes to our uneasy relationship with death.

An Open Space

First of all, let me say I'm uncomfortable with the word *loss* being used as the equivalent of *death*. This understanding implies we first "owned" something (or someone), and then it was taken from us. Then, in typical Euro-American fashion, we seek to "overcome the loss," filling up the "hole" with some new person, activity, or object, so we can proceed with our lives intact. Freud described this with monetary metaphors: we "buy" people and objects by attaching them to ourselves, and then we are forced to "sell" those attachments, creating in ourselves a sense that something is missing, which makes us "buy" still more new attachments.[79] The final goal of mourning, according to Freud, is "severance": when we are able to turn away from what we once loved and form new loves in its place.[80] This may be Freud's understanding of the "work of mourning," but it is not mine. As a member of the African diaspora, my struggles to understand death and mourning have led me in altogether different directions.

After my grandmother's death, one of my mentors encouraged me to join a grief group. The other members of the group were compassionate and kind, but I soon realized their objective was very much in line with Freud's understanding of mourning: they sought to remove the "sense of loss" we were each experiencing. "I just need to achieve *closure*," said one group member. This phrase brought to my mind the image of an open door—a door that, the group believed, needed to be firmly shut.

Shortly after this experience, a good friend said to me, "Patrick, you are causing yourself so much pain. It's time to move on from the loss of your grandmother. Tatie is gone. You need to fill the hole she left in your life with something new."

At this point, I was coming to realize how much Freud's ideas have shaped Euro-American thinking (even though Freudian thought is no longer taken seriously by most modern-day psychologists). I did not then (nor do I now) want to "move on" from my relationship with Tatie, nor do I want to replace her with anyone or anything. Her death causes me pain, but I claim that pain as my own, as part of me. It enriches me. It does not leave a hole in me, which would imply I am somehow less now than I was before she died (taking us back to the idea that death equals loss). Her death did, however, shake my certainties—the mental structure of my reality—leaving a *space,* an emptiness.

Tufwanga mu soba is an African proverb that means: "We die in order to undergo change."[81] Death, whether it is our own or a loved one's, clears an empty space where something new can come into being and grow. The African understanding perceives reality as countless intersecting vibrations, which send out waves—sometimes small, like the tiniest ripples on the surface of water, and sometimes huge, like a tsunami. When change happens, the literal translation of what an African would likely say, is, "My life has been waved (or shaken)."[82]

The larger the wave, the greater the destruction—and at the same time, the greater the potential for something radically new to come into being. A key concept within the Kongo cosmogram (described in the introduction) is that nothing ever survives in a fixed form. Nothing remains intact, and "change, mixture, and innovation are givens, not aberrations."[83] The world is continually changing because it is continually being created. Change means life—and this means that death, the biggest change we have yet to experience, is only *more life*. The Akan of Ghana have a proverb that says, "Death, for all his strength, cannot carry water from the river with a sieve." In other words, we cannot deny that death's cruel and irresistible grip on our lives—but at the same time, death does not have the power to rob us of the life that flows through us in an eternal stream of endless energy.

But that is not the way the Western world likes to see things. Instead, it teaches us to resist change—those alterations in ourselves, in others, and in the world around us that time brings—and perceive them as losses (as though the aspects of our lives were ours to own). Some of us envision heaven as a place where nothing changes, where we get to "keep" everything exactly as it always was. But what would we keep, in that case? If we could choose who to be in the afterlife, would we be our child selves with our fresh innocence intact? Would we be our young-adult selves, overflowing with ambition and physical energy? Or would we want to keep the wisdom that old age brought us? Clearly, the changes in our lives and circumstances—the so-called losses—bring with them new gifts. It's all a matter of perspective.

As I work with patients who are mourning, I've come to recognize that even the most painful death always engenders a state of possibility. Death vibrates through our lives and hearts, opening up new spaces. While the Western eye sees positive and negative space (or foreground and background), the African perceives no space as truly empty. In fact, the apparently empty spaces in the Kongo cosmogram contain "the knowledge between the lines," locations of rich potential and power.[84]

Seen from this perspective, the voids that death leaves do not diminish us. They are not *losses;* instead, they are places of possibility. They offer us opportunities to learn and grow, and in doing so, we expand rather than contract. We move into the territory of hope. Hope and learning are intertwined, says educator Herbert Kohl, for hope is "the refusal to accept limits."[85] Surprisingly, these two—hope and learning—can be the gifts of even the most agonizing death.

Grieving expert Mary-Frances O'Connor sheds light on what I will continue to refer to as the "work of mourning" (though this is not the vocabulary O'Connor uses). Sorrow, O'Connor has found, creates neurological changes in our brains.[86] These changes create the opportunity for new learning to take place. When that learning gets stalled, it's often because people are refusing to truly see the actual experience for what it is. Instead, they avoid thoughts, situations, or conversations that might make them have to face their pain. This avoidance gets in the way of growth. It keeps the sorrow as an unexamined, unacknowledged wound. It prevents the work of mourning from going forward.

Focusing on our sorrow rather than avoiding it, says O'Connor, means we will have to allow ourselves to feel the very real pain—but we will also have space to grow. She goes on to say, "From the perspective of the brain, if we're going to learn what life is like now, and we're going to learn what makes sense for us, what can be meaningful, we have to engage in new experiences. That's how the brain learns."[87]

We hate to acknowledge, however, the monstrous death that racism has dealt our nation. We are too afraid of it to allow ourselves to see any potential in its shadows. As author Fanny Brewster reminds us, "The sorrow of the African American slave has gone untold for centuries because . . . the greatness of the sorrow was too overwhelming to bear." Because we cannot face this sorrow, Brewster, goes on to say, "The racism of slavery moved underground and continues to survive in our institutions."[88]

Meanwhile, some Americans are saying it's unpatriotic to even mention the dirty secret hidden within the national psyche—and it's close to heresy to consider stepping into the space of racism's sorrow with the intention of learning something new there. The controversy over critical race theory is a good example of America's refusal to see the extent of her abysmal grief.

Critical Race Theory

Critical race theory boils down to simply this: racism's most deadly manifestation is not an interior emotion but a social construct that's embedded in our legal system. (It is also entrenched within our education, our health care, our law enforcement, our housing practices, and literally *all* aspects of our society.) Critical race theory has never been taught in public schools (it's an academic concept that's been in universities for more than forty years[89]), but its opponents can insist that it is being taught to America's children because they have expanded the definition of critical race theory to include pretty much anything that has to do with diversity and inclusion. They feel free to now define it as "Black-supremacist racism, false history, and the terrible apotheosis of wokeness."[90]

Here are just a few of the reactions critical race theory has elicited from Americans:

- In August 2021, a Pennsylvania school board unanimously voted to prohibit teaching critical race theory in classrooms by approving a "patriotism amendment" to the district's mission statement. The amendment forbids teaching concepts that cause people to "feel guilt or anguish . . . solely because of their race, sex, or religion." The board member who introduced the proposal stated, "Patriotism is not controversial. Period."[91]

- In March 2022, a former president told his followers, "Getting critical race theory out of our schools is not just a matter of values, it's also a matter of national survival. We have no choice. . . . If we allow the Marxists and Communists and Socialists to teach our children to hate America, there will be no one left to defend our flag or to protect our great country or its freedom."[92]

- In July 2022, the *National Review* reported: "If [teaching critical race theory is] not reversed, we could lose the next generation of Americans. The effort to indoctrinate students in progressive, anti-American ideologies that pervades our universities is also ravaging K–12 education."[93]

As a Black man, when I read news stories like these, I am enraged that my reality is being denied. To even acknowledge my experience is considered unpatriotic! I believe rage is fully justified (and we will discuss this further in chapter 5), but for the purposes of this book, I am doing my best to step back from my emotions and write from the perspective of a psychotherapist. I also want to step back from the binary vision that pits Black against white as two separate and opposing forces within our society. Instead, I am choosing to see through an African lens, where all things interact and are connected. As a Jesuit who practices Ignatian spirituality, I also believe life is meant to be a collaborative venture, with the words of Paul in his first letter to the Corinthians as our template:

> The human body has many parts, but the many parts make up one whole body. So it is with the body of

Christ. . . . If the foot says, "I am not a part of the body because I am not a hand," that does not make it any less a part of the body. And if the ear says, "I am not part of the body because I am not an eye," would that make it any less a part of the body? If the whole body were an eye, how would you hear? Or if your whole body were an ear, how would you smell anything? . . . The eye can never say to the hand, "I don't need you." The head can't say to the feet, "I don't need you." In fact, some parts of the body that seem weakest and least important are actually the most necessary. . . . If one part suffers, all the parts suffer with it, and if one part is honored, all the parts are glad. All of you together are Christ's body, and each of you is a part of it. (verses 12, 15–17, 21–22, 26–27 NLT)

If one part suffers, all the parts suffer with it. From this perspective, racism is neither a "Black problem" nor a "white problem"; it is a killing force within our single shared community. Racism weakens us all because it attacks the vital matrix in which we all live.

Believing that racism exists only in the hearts and minds of (a few bad) white people shifts attention away from societal issues and lays the blame on individuals, where it can be easily shrugged off. After all, we can't see inside each other's thoughts and emotions, and so we can all insist we don't have a racist bone in our bodies (as though racism, where it does exist, is a small and relatively unimportant bit of osseous tissue within a white person's skeleton). When racism is seen this way, it allows Americans to maintain their personal righteousness ("*I'm* not racist," insists even the most blatant racist), while avoiding the work of mourning and the opportunities to learn.

The concept that racism is systemic, however, turns our focus away from white emotions and attitudes to the Black experience within America's institutions and social systems. Critical race theory is based on the Black witness to truth, the truth many of us don't want to face: that death lies at the very foundation of our communal identity—and that this is not merely a historical fact, something that happened in the past, but also an ongoing reality. As Dr. King observed in his 1968 address to the American Psychological Association, the United States "is poisoned to its soul by racism and the understanding needs to be carefully documented," so that it becomes "more difficult to reject." Critical race theory is a step toward documenting America's poison.[94]

The Past Is Present

"How might we understand mourning, when the event has yet to end?" writes Sadiya Hartman. "When the injuries not only perdure, but are inflicted anew? Can one mourn what has yet ceased happening?"[95] Hartman points out an important problem when it comes to applying the "work of mourning" to racism.

Most adversities can be pinpointed in time: *this is the date when my grandmother died; that was the month I was laid off from my job; I'll always remember the year I was sick with long COVID*. Using the Western world's linear view of time, we think of mourning as beginning at the point where a tragedy divided our lives into *before* and *after*. But there is no "after" when it comes to racism. To believe that there is—that racism was something that happened only in the past—is just one more way for us to deny the reality of the ongoing grief. Here again, I find that the traditional African perspective is useful.

The Euro-American model of time is like a number line, in which we begin at a point of origin ("zero" on the number line) and move toward an end (a number that varies depending on what we're talking about). This linear view implies that the past is disconnected from the present and the future, which in turn means that we who live in the present do not have to accept responsibility for things that happened in the past, before our "zero points" (our birthdates).

The African model of time, however, sees the past as "invasive," "ever impinging on the present . . . not disjoined from the present."[96] At the same time, the African perspective also sees time and space as a single entity, which ultimately does not exist except through the perception of human consciousness. Consciousness is a force continually breathing throughout reality, independent of space-time, and so we are all connected; space-time cannot separate us since it is merely a construct of our neurology, necessary in a practical day-to-day way but irrelevant to the deep-set meaning of our lives. Within this wider perspective of space-time, we cannot escape our responsibility to do the work of mourning, opening ourselves not only to sorrow but also to new possibilities.

America's work of mourning requires, I believe, that we participate in Sankofa: returning to the past in order to heal the present. Then, as we confront the reality of racism and death, we will also find rich potential and hope, for in the Black experience lie answers to our current fears and failures. The Black experience is essential to our shared identity. When we realize that, we will finally be able to reclaim our kinship as blood sisters and brothers, members of the same ancient family.

A Lesson in Humility

The death of my grandmother was truly a learning opportunity for me. The challenge, I came to realize, was to let go of the reality I had created in my mind, so that I could be with Tatie in a new way, with a new understanding of reality.

This was not easy. I was an adult in graduate school, certain I already had a good grasp on life. For more than twenty years, I had been building my sense of self and my place in what I considered to be the "real world." I had been quite happy with the edifice I constructed, a bit smug even, complacent in my sense of my own power.

Tatie's death killed that old way of thinking. She was my closest friend, my confidant, my partner in crime. When she died, the depth of my sorrow swept me off my feet. I could not find a way around it. I yelled, I cursed, I broke things. I got in my car and roared down the highway, breaking the speed limit. I passed friends on the street and ignored them. I refused to answer my phone, and when friends kept calling and texting, I turned it off. And finally, when I was worn out from grieving,

I realized: Tatie's death was an opportunity to learn something that was as new as it was painful—humility.

To accept death means we accept we are not in control. We are not all-powerful. We are not the shining, competent people we thought we were.

Not long ago, as I was helping a good friend of mine process her grief after the death of a child, she said something I had never articulated before: "Death is the way we come to realize our new self. It's a chance for reinvention, rebirth. It offers regeneration that helps us survive when surviving is impossible." And maybe that's exactly it: death makes the survival of the old life impossible. If we want to continue to live, we must let the old way of being die—so that something new can be born. This, I believe, is also the challenge America faces.

Before the Civil War, many white Americans had a sentimental, sanitized image of death, seeing it as a sweet and flowery passage from this world's perils into a comfortable afterlife.[97] The war's bloody carnage (which for the first time was recorded with photographs) fractured this narrative. "The presence and fear of death," wrote historian Drew Gilpin Faust, "touched Civil War Americans' most fundamental sense of who they were, for in its threat of termination and transformation, death inevitably inspired self-scrutiny and self-definition."[98] Here, in the presence of death, America had an opportunity to learn: to see herself more clearly and begin the process of transformation into a better version of herself.

But she let the opportunity slip by, retreating into a renewed romanticization of death that allowed her to also turn her back on the reality of racism with her pride intact. America sought to bring "healing" to a divided nation by reuniting North and South, emphasizing the "heroism" of both—but as Bill Farrell observed, "this tearful, joyous, and spiritual family reunion could occur as it did only because the North abandoned black Americans in the South," leaving Blacks unsupported and vulnerable in the face of disenfranchisement, lynchings, segregation, poverty, malnutrition, and restricted access to education.[99]

The COVID pandemic has made America again confront the reality of death, offering us yet another opportunity to learn death's lessons in humility. We are not, after all, the proud and perfect nation that leads the entire planet into the bright world of freedom and democracy. Humbled by sorrow, we have the chance to let go of who we thought we were, in order to become something far better and more real.

And so, as you read this book, I ask you to join me in the work of mourning. In doing so, we will need to dig ourselves out of our centuries of melancholia, unstop our ears, and hear the call of reality. Only when we stop running away from death will be able to learn from the Black experience—and we can only do this by entering the full horror of America's five-hundred-year-old (and ongoing) sorrow.

> *Grief will always be prolonged,*
> *as long as injustice is prolonged.*
>
> —TASHEL BORDERE[100]

People wish to be settled;
only as far as they are unsettled
is there any hope for them.

—RALPH WALDO EMERSON

PRAYER RITUAL

Set aside some time to be alone. Turn off your phone; shut down your computer. Now, fill two bowls of similar size about half full of water and place them side by side on the floor or table (one on the right, one on the left), along with an empty cup. Sit cross-legged on the floor or in a chair at the table, and commit this space of time to God. Ask that the Divine Presence open this place and this moment into eternity, where all is alive, all is exactly as it should be.

Now place your hand in or over the bowl on the right. This water represents your experiences with racism and death. Call to mind a particular incident as you dip a cup of water from this bowl. Spend a few moments allowing yourself to feel the pain of the experience. Ask God to help you release anything in you that is clinging to this experience, anything that is getting in the way of new life and learning. When you feel you are ready to surrender this experience to God, pour the water in the cup into the left-hand bowl, saying, "I give this experience to you, the One who gives life to all, so that I may have more room in my heart to learn and grow."

Now dip the cup into the left-hand bowl. The water in this bowl represents the Water of Life, which is Jesus. As you pour it into the right-hand bowl, say to Jesus, "There is an empty space in my heart now. Fill it with your love and life. I am willing to change and grow—and as I do so, show me ways to bring change and growth into the world around me." Some of the water you are pouring from the left-hand bowl will be the same water you just put there from the right-hand bowl, but now it has been sanctified by love; it is both the same and not the same.

Repeat these steps, pouring from the right-hand bowl into the left-hand bowl and back again, as many times as you feel you need, each time calling to mind a different experience with racism or death. When you find your attention no longer as engaged with what you are doing, it is probably time to move on. Spend a few more moments in prayer, reflecting on any new realizations that have arisen. Then use the water in the bowls to water your plants, or pour it outside on the ground. You may also want to drink a little from each bowl.

I offer water that will become a wellspring within you that gives life throughout eternity.

—JESUS
(JOHN 4:14 TV)

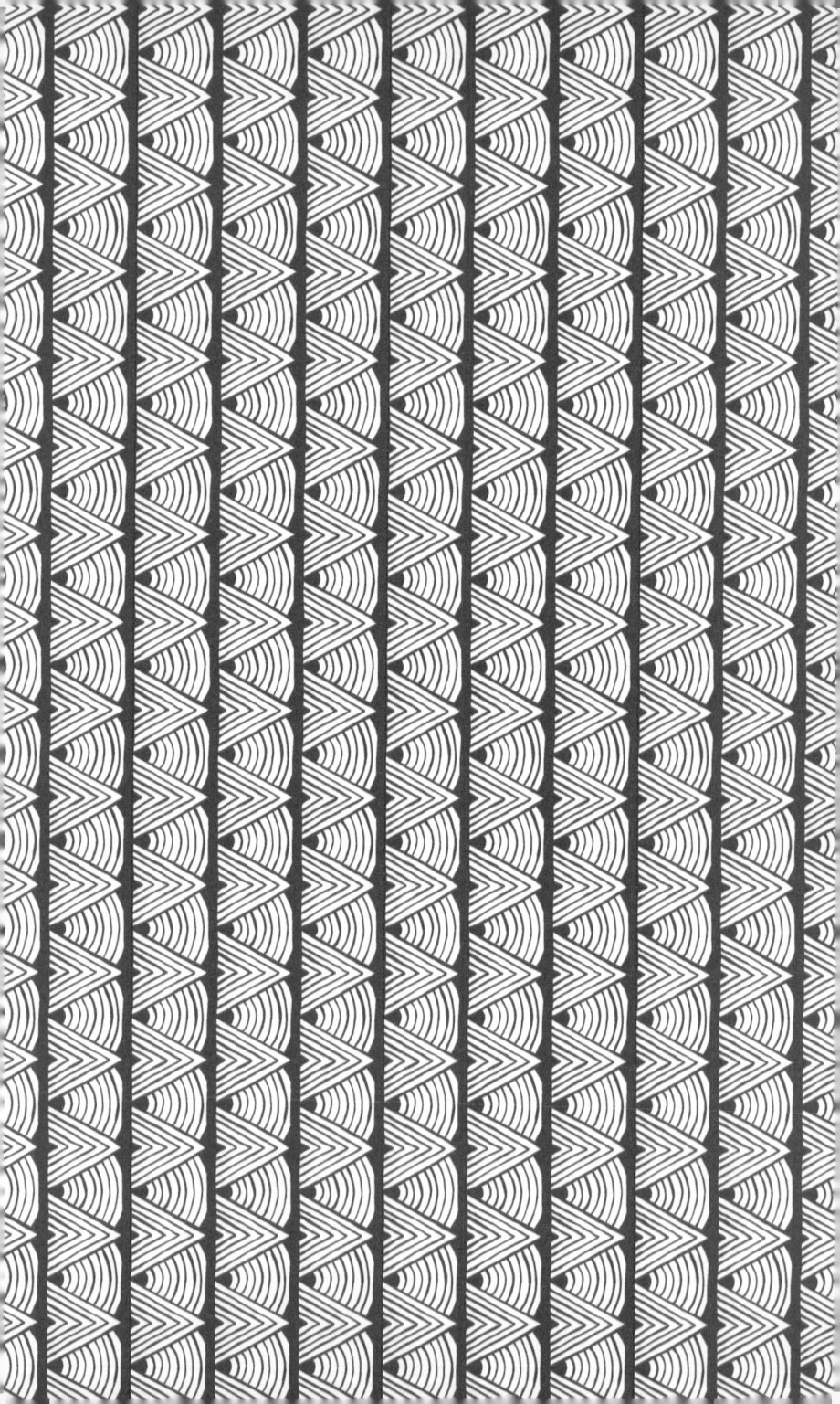

3

CLAD IN MOURNING

DEATH AS A NEVER-ENDING REALITY

*The trouble with us is that we
are always preparing to die.
You meet a white man early
Monday morning
and ask him what he is preparing to do . . .
he is preparing to start a business.
You ask a colored man . . .
he is preparing to die.*

—BOOKER T. WASHINGTON[101]

Black life has been, and continues to be, under siege.
With death and dying constituting Black life . . .
it permeates everything from our cultural productions
to the way we raise our children.

—KARLA HOLLOWAY[102]

ALL BLACKS KNOW IT'S NOT SAFE TO HAVE
black skin. If you are Black, it is not safe to walk to work[103]; it is
not safe to play with a toy gun[104]; it is not safe to have a broken
taillight or headlight on your car[105]; it is not safe to go for a ride
with your girlfriend[106]; it is not safe to be in your grandmother's
backyard[107]; it is not safe to fall asleep In your car[108]—or go
grocery shopping,[109] go to church,[110] water your neighbor's
garden,[111] sleep in your own bed,[112] play video games with your
nephew,[113] eat in the parking lot of a fast-food restaurant,[114] or
party at a bar.[115] It might not even be safe to go birdwatching,
not if you're Black.[116] As poet Claudia Rankine wrote, "The
condition of black life is one of mourning."

Rankine went on to speak of the "daily strain of knowing that as a black person you can be killed for simply being
black: no hands in your pockets, no playing music, no sudden
movements, no driving your car, no walking at night, no
walking in the day, no turning onto this street, no entering
this building, no standing your ground."[117] According to a
2022 Pew Research study, a third of all Black Americans worry
every day that they might be violently attacked because of

their race (compared to only 4 percent of white Americans).[118] "The unarmed slain black bodies," wrote Rankine, "turn grief into our everyday feeling that something is wrong everywhere and all the time."[119]

The modern-day Euro-American perspective says, "Hide your mourning away. It's private. Its time span is limited, so suffer through the best you can—perhaps with help from a therapist if you're emotionally weak—and then put it behind you." But in order to maintain this attitude, we have to altogether deny the Black experience; we have to hide the constant and tragic violence the Black community has sustained for centuries. And still sustains. This is the only way we can maintain our societal preference for a reality where death is a rare aberration, a minor sidebar to life's major themes.

It is getting harder and harder to do this. The Black Lives Matter movement, for example, insists that we look at death. It demands we participate in the never-ending mourning of the Black community. It puts death out in the open, where we have to see it, where we can no longer turn away and pretend it's not there. "Black Lives Matter aligns with the dead," wrote Claudia Rankine, "continues the mourning and refuses the forgetting."[120]

And yet some white Americans respond, "All lives matter," and with that generically true statement, they try to once more tuck death comfortably out of sight. And so, we do not confront or interrupt the violent progression of Black deaths; we simply look away. We use vague platitudes and generalities to shield our eyes:

Everyone dies sooner or later.
We all have our crosses to bear.
God knows what he's doing.
Time heals all wounds.
It's time to put this behind us and get back to normal.

(Those are the more gentle evasions. I've also heard: *Criminals deserve what they get* and *What do you expect from drug users?*)

These evasions do Blacks no good. We cannot refer to death as having happened somewhere to someone in the past, because, for the Black community, death is something that happens all the time, now, to us. In psychiatrist Frantz Fanon's words, we are constantly "clad in mourning."[121] Time will never heal our wounds, for those wounds are always fresh, always shedding new blood. We carry them both consciously and unconsciously; either way, we still wear the same heavy robes of sorrow our ancestors did some five hundred years ago.

The Maafa:
The Genocide of Enslavement

Maafa, a Swahili word that means "great disaster," refers to the millions of Black people who died in history's longest genocide. The number of humans who died because of the transatlantic slave trade is too immense to comprehend. The official UN estimate is 15 million,[122] but some scholars believe 150 million is a more accurate number[123]; others claim the number is far smaller—6 million or perhaps 11 million—but does a smaller number make the horror any less? Whether it's 6 million or 150 million,[124] I simply can't understand numbers that big; I struggle to find something to compare them to, so I can grasp the sheer enormity of human lives that were lost.

Okay, try this: Imagine that every single human being in New York City or London was brutally killed. That would be comparable to the smaller estimates of deaths-by-slavery. Or if we take the larger numbers, you could try imagining that every single person in Japan—or half of all the people in the United States—were murdered. Can you grasp that yet? I'm not sure I can. I think maybe the better approach would be this: remember the last time someone you love died; now imagine that happening over and over and over, one beloved individual after another, each one beautiful in their own way, each one infinitely precious. That's what slavery did. It murdered individual after individual. It shredded the intersecting strands of life that sustain us all.

Enslaved people died for a host of reasons. They died onboard the slave ships from illnesses that spread quickly below deck. Once they landed in America, they died from malnutrition[125]; they died from whooping cough and dysentery; at least half of all their babies died before they were a year old, probably from chronic undernourishment.[126] They died when a white man's punishment went too far.

Let yourself enter the experience of this former slave, Robert Fanner, and imagine his little brother Peter: "Every time that Peter would fall behind . . . [the master] would take him out and buckle him down to a log with a leather strap, and stand way back and then he would lay that long cowhide down up and down his back. [Peter] would split open with every stroke and the blood would run down. The last time he turned Peter loose, Peter went to my sister and asked her for a rag. She thought he just wanted to wipe the blood out of his face and eyes, but when she gave it to him, he fell down dead across the potato ridges."[127]

(Can you see that little boy? Does he make tears come to your eyes? Remember him. Do not let yourself forget Peter, for he deserves to be remembered.)

Finally, enslaved people died when they tried to escape. Some did manage to make it to freedom. Most, though, were captured, returned, and punished. In 1705, in Virginia, a law was passed that allowed whites to kill runaways without penalty. When one wealthy landowner, Robert "King" Carter, asked for permission to dismember his runaways, permission was granted.[128]

In 1712, in New York City, a group of enslaved Blacks lit fire to a building and then attacked the white men who rushed to put out the flames. The city's militia broke up the fight, and many Blacks fled into the forests of northern Manhattan (where they may have joined the indigenous tribe that lived there). Of the twenty-eight Blacks who were captured, "some were burnt [over a slow fire for many hours], others hanged, one broke on the wheel, one hung alive in chains," the governor reported to the King, "so that there has been the most exemplary punishment inflicted that could be possibly thought of." Twelve of the captured Africans cut their own throats rather than be returned to slavery.[129]

Enslaved Africans did not meekly accept slavery. They did not turn into the good-natured, simple-minded, loyal-to-the-master stereotypes that white novels and movies once portrayed. Instead, as often as they could, they rebelled.[130] They fought for their freedom—even if freedom meant death.

Suicide was common among enslaved Blacks, who many times considered it an act of power. On the slave ships that crossed the Atlantic, Africans refused to eat or leaped into the ocean. When they were held back from either of these options (ships' crews flogged and force-fed anyone trying to starve themselves, and many slave ships had netting around them to stop people from trying to jump), they found ways to strangle or hang themselves; some even tore open their own throats with their fingers. In America, enslaved Blacks jumped into rivers, leapt from windows and cliffs, ran into burning buildings, and cut their throats. Faced with the reality of enslavement, countless Africans chose death instead.

Olaudah Equiano was only ten years old when he was captured from his home in what is now Nigeria. "I was soon put down under the decks," he wrote, "and there I received such a salutation in my nostrils as I had never experienced in my life; so that, with the loathsomeness of the stench, and crying together, I became so sick and low that I was not able to eat, nor had I the least desire to taste anything. I now wished for the last friend, death, to relieve me; but soon, to my grief, two of the white men offered me eatables; and, on my refusing to eat, one of them held me fast by the hands, and laid me across I think the windlass, and tied my feet, while the other flogged me severely. I had never experienced any thing of this kind before; and although, not being used to the water, I naturally feared that element the first time I saw it, yet nevertheless, could I have got over the nettings, I would have jumped over the side, but I could not; and besides, the crew used to watch us very closely who were not chained down to the decks, lest we should leap into the water; and I have seen some of these poor African prisoners most severely cut for attempting to do so, and hourly whipped for not eating. This indeed was often the case with myself. . . . One day, two of my wearied countrymen who were chained together, preferring death to such a life of misery, somehow made through the nettings and jumped into the sea: immediately another quite dejected fellow, who, on account of his illness, was suffered to be out of irons, also followed their example; and I believe many more would have done the same if they had not been prevented by the ship's crew, who were instantly alarmed. . . . [T]wo of the wretches were drowned, but they got the other, and afterwards flogged him unmercifully for thus attempting to prefer death to slavery."[131]

Slaver J. P. Romaigne tells what this looked like from his side of the story: the Africans who jumped off the ship were "dancing among the waves, yelling with all their might what . . . seemed a song of triumph."[132]

Death was a way to wrench control from white hands; suicide allowed Blacks to assert their own personhood and reclaim their freedom (since dead bodies had no further use to white landowners). While Eurocentric Christianity condemned suicide as both a legal crime and a spiritual sin that would send you straight to hell, enslaved Blacks saw their freely chosen deaths as a way to rejoin their ancestors and return home to Africa. Each death by suicide was also a statement against slavery, one that played a role in the growing abolitionist movement. By choosing to die, enslaved Blacks revealed their humanity even as they declared their independence.[133] For them, death was a declaration of personhood, a way to reclaim life, and an affirmation of their homeland.

The Lynching Era

The abolition of slavery did not, however, bring an end to the premature deaths my people suffered. Between 1880 and 1998, across America, from the North to the South, whites lynched between four and five thousand Black women and men.

Is five thousand an easier number to imagine than six million? Or is it just one more number for your eyes to slide over and forget? According to the U.S. Census Bureau, a "small town" has a population of five thousand or fewer residents. Would you care if a small town was murdered, each one of its inhabitants strung up on a tree and hung? Would you take that sorrow as your own and carry it with you?

These violent public killings were a form of terrorism. Lynchings gave white people back the power that abolition had taken from them. Often victims were hung, but these were not business-like state executions; they also involved torture, mutilation, decapitation, and desecration. Some victims were burned alive. And the white community turned out to watch, as though a lynching was a parade. Photos were taken and souvenirs sold.

This happened. If you are white, sit with that. Imagine a mob murdering someone you love in the most hideous way possible. Imagine it happening to you. And now realize, this *did* happen to you, for we are all one body (as Christ said); we belong to a single tapestry of life that includes the past as much as the present. Your life bears the pain of each death on a lynching tree. And you can't squirm away from this knowledge; you can't tell yourself, *Lynching is wrong, of course, but those Black people probably did something wrong too.*

Do you want to know why Blacks were lynched? The reasons vary. One man was a waiter who told a white woman he needed a few moments before he could serve her; several men were killed for wearing their own World War II uniforms; many Black lynching victims had had consensual relationships with white women. Other reasons for lynchings were: voting, owning a prosperous farm, asking an employer for wages, teaching children to read, picking peaches from a neighbor's tree, starting an NAACP chapter, sending a Christmas card to a white girl, having too much money, being a civil rights worker, and driving or walking through a white neighborhood. Many times the lynchings were based on rumors that claimed a Black person had committed murder, arson, or theft. Vagrancy— being homeless—was also considered a crime worthy of lynching. And then there were the lynchings that were carried out simply because a group of white men "felt like killing" a Black person.[134]

Blacks fought back as best they could. Journalist Ida B. Wells reported the atrocity of lynching in her newspaper columns. W. E. B. DuBois published a photo essay that included the images from postcards showing the murder of a Black man. The Civil Rights Movement has its roots in Wells' and DuBois's efforts. Justice rose from lynching's darkness—but nothing can neutralize the atrocity.

I'm going to tell a story now that's painful to read. If you're Black, please feel free to skip over the next paragraph; you don't need to be triggered by one more account of a Black person's brutal death. But if you're a white person, I'm asking you to not look away. Every Black person you know carries the weight of stories like this one, in their minds, in their bodies, and even, I believe, in their DNA. The memories of death and anguish and injustice cling to all of us in the Black community, like heavy cloaks we can never take off.

In 1916, Jesse Washington, a seventeen-year-old Black boy with mental disabilities, was accused of raping and murdering the fifty-three-year-old wife of his employer. He was arrested and tried for the crime. Then, after a jury deliberated for four minutes, they declared him guilty—and a mob of white people dragged him to the city hall, where wood for a bonfire was already stacked. Along the way, the mob stripped off Jesse's clothes; they beat him and stabbed him, over and over, and then they doused him with gasoline. They cut off his fingers and toes and his penis for souvenirs. Finally, they kept him alive as long as possible, raising and lowering him into the fire with a chain. Jesse tried to climb the chain to escape the flames, but with no fingers, he could not grip the metal links. A crowd of more than ten thousand people (including Waco's mayor and chief of police) watched him die. Parents gave their children permission to leave school so they too could see the spectacle. Spectators, eager to get a good view, stood on cars and buggies, climbed into trees or onto the roofs of nearby buildings. Shouts arose from the crowd, said one newspaper report, like those heard during "a triumphal procession from a ball game that has been a big victory."[135] When at last, the boy was dead, they dragged his burned body through the streets.

That's an ugly, ugly story. So ugly I almost didn't tell you. But the thing is—it happened. On a warm spring day in Texas, a seventeen-year-old boy named Jesse Washington died a horrific death, surrounded by a mob of people who hated him for no reason other than the color of his skin. And his death wasn't unusual; it wasn't one of those awful but blessedly rare things that happen now and then. No, Jesse's story is just one among thousands of others like it.

So please, dear white reader, accept the truth of this story. Take its weight into your heart and mind. Share with us, your Black sisters and brothers, the gut-wrenching, heartbreaking horror. This too is part of the Black experience of death.

The Maafa That Never Ends

W. E. B. DuBois publicized Jesse Washington's story. The photographs of the boy's death confronted Americans with the visceral reality of Black death, much the same as when we watched the recording of George Floyd's murder. The anti-lynching movement grew stronger; activists, both Black and white, raised their voices louder. But the "great disaster" of racism did not come to an end. As we have seen in our own time, when the forces of justice push forward, the forces of hatred and racism push back. "We seem to be in a continuing feedback loop of repeating a past that our country has yet to address," wrote Isabel Wilkerson. "Our history is one of spectacular achievement . . . followed by a violent backlash that threatens to erase the gains and then a long, slow climb to the next mountain, where the cycle begins again."[136]

I'm now about to tell you another ugly story. The year after Jesse Washington died, Mary Turner, who was eight months pregnant, spoke out against the white mob that had lynched her husband the day before. Later, the Associated Press wrote that Mary had made "unwise remarks" about the death of her husband, and "the people, in their indignant mood, took exception to her remarks, as well as her attitude."[137]

The next day, they came for her. "The mob tied her ankles, hung her upside down from a tree, doused her in gasoline and motor oil and set her on fire," the NAACP reports. "Turner was still alive when a member of the mob split her abdomen open with a knife and her unborn child fell on the ground. The baby was stomped and crushed as it fell to the ground. Turner's body was riddled with hundreds of bullets."[138]

That happened. This isn't a horror movie that intends to titillate you with violence. I'm not telling you these stories because I like the thrill factor. I'm telling you because we need to remember brave little Mary Turner, her husband Hayes, and their baby, who all died in the most monstrous way possible. We need to remember not only their deaths but also their lives, for they too are part of this vast, interdependent organism Jesus referred to as his Body. Each of us needs Mary, Hayes, and their unnamed child. We not only mourn them, but we also celebrate them. As God does with each of us, we take delight in their reality.

But even so, how can Blacks make sense of these stories? How can we bear it? How can *you* bear it, dear white reader?

And there's more. But first, let me tell you a little incident that happened while I was writing this chapter. I had asked a white friend—another author, whose opinion I value—to read what I'd written so far. When she got to this page, she shook her head and looked up at me. "No, no, you can't keep bashing your readers over the head with stories like this. You need to be strategic with what you tell. Pace yourself. By the end of the Jesse Washington story, your readers are tired of horror stories. They don't want to hear any more, not in detail."

I looked at her for a moment. "Do you mean my white readers?" I asked her finally.

She looked a little uncomfortable. "Well, yeah. But your Black readers too, of course. Like you said, this could be triggering for them. You don't want to do that."

"No, I don't," I said, and we left it at that.

But I kept thinking about what my friend had said, that white readers would be tired of reading stories about Black people's murders. I do understand the need to pace a story; I grasp that good narrative has rhythms the human brain responds to. But as I thought about rewriting this portion of the chapter, I realized I was angry.

The lives and deaths of Jesse and Mary and all the others are not useful inflection points for a piece of writing. They were real human beings—as real as you and me—and we should honor and respect them. They had to bear the horror of their deaths; the least we can do is spend a few minutes sharing just a taste of that horror.

Okay, I'm done with my little aside. Let's move on together as we look more closely at the Maafa that never ends. I'll hold your hand, you hold mine; we'll do our best to listen to these stories, and then we'll grieve, opening tender places inside us where we can learn, where we can grow.

Two years after the deaths of Mary Turner, her husband, and their baby, another seventeen-year-old Black boy, this one named Eugene Williams, was swimming in Lake Michigan on a hot July day, when he accidentally drifted into one of Chicago's "white beaches." The white swimmers and sunbathers threw stones at him. A rock struck him in the head and knocked him unconscious; he dropped into the water and drowned.

During that same summer of 1919 (which was an earlier age of pandemic, when about fifty million people around the world died from influenza), so much blood poured into America's streets because of racial violence that people called it "Red Summer." From New York to Tennessee, from Nebraska to Connecticut, white mobs hung, burned alive, shot, or beat to death Black men, as well as women and children. Thousands of Black-owned houses and businesses burned to the ground. In at least twenty-five separate riots across the country, hundreds of Black people died, and thousands more were injured, struck down by whites who were never punished for their crimes. "Ethnic cleansing was the goal of the white rioters," said historian William Tuttle. "They wanted to kill as many black people as possible and to terrorize the rest until they were willing to leave and live someplace else."[139]

But Blacks fought back. Out of the racist violence of that summer, the NAACP grew stronger, gaining about 100,000 new members. Black journalists told their people's stories, so that white Americans could no longer ignore what was happening. Blacks became activists; they filed lawsuits; they pressured Congress.[140] And the children of those Blacks were the ones who began the Civil Rights Movement.

But as is always the case, racism did not lie down quietly and disappear. As the Civil Rights era dawned at the beginning of the 1960s, a crowd of angry white people in Alabama attacked a Greyhound bus carrying Freedom Riders (protestors against segregationist laws). The mob threw rocks and bricks through the windows. They tossed a firebomb inside the bus, and as smoke and flames filled its interior, the attackers barricaded the door. "Burn them alive!" someone in the crowd shouted.

And still the killings did not end. Although now no longer publicly celebrated and photographed, lynchings continue in America. In 1998, in Jasper, Texas, three white men encountered a Black man named James Byrd, a husband and father who worked as a salesman; the white men dragged him behind their pickup truck for three miles, until he was dead. In 2011, ten white teenagers in two cars intentionally ran over James Craig Anderson in a Jackson, Mississippi, parking lot (but first they beat him, shouting, "White Power!"). In 2020, three white men shot and killed twenty-three-year-old Ahmaud Arbery who was jogging near Brunswick, Georgia. The men claimed they thought Arbery was a burglar.[141]

In 2022, lynching was finally made a federal hate crime. After signing the law, President Biden said, "Hate never goes away, it only hides under the rocks. If it gets a little bit of oxygen, it comes roaring back out, screaming. What stops it? All of us."[142]

Freud spoke of what he called the *repetition compulsion*: "These repetitions are the silent summoning of our unhealed injuries and unexamined failures," as we seek to find resolution from the original wound.[143] In a similar way, slavery repeats itself again and again in America, finding new forms but always reopening that original mutilation of America's soul. Economic and educational inequities are another expression of slavery; police killings are a form of lynching.[144]

And the Maafa's destruction repeats itself in America in still more ways:

- While Blacks make up 12 percent of the U.S. population, 33 percent of the prison population is Black. (White people make up 64 percent of the U.S. population, but only 30 percent of the prison population is white.) In many places in the United States, if you're a Black man, odds are good (one out of three) that you'll spend some time in prison at some point in your life (versus one in seventeen if you're a white man).[145] Black women are similarly impacted: one in eighteen Black women born in 2001 is likely to be incarcerated sometime in her life, compared to one in 111 white women. This is not because Blacks are more inclined to criminal behaviors than whites are. Bias by decision-makers at all stages of the justice process disadvantages Black people; for example, while rates of drug use are similar across racial and ethnic groups, Blacks are arrested and sentenced on drug charges at much higher rates than white people. Studies have also found that Blacks are more likely to be stopped by the police, detained pretrial, charged with more serious crimes, and sentenced more harshly than white people.[146]

- More Black people die early from heart disease, hypertension, diabetes, lung disease, asthma, and obesity than white people do. And it's not because

Black people are genetically predisposed to get sick (any more than they're genetically disposed to be criminals). "Black culture" is also sometimes blamed for the Black community's health inequity, the implication being that we are susceptible to so many diseases because of our lifestyle—but this theory fails to look at reality: low-income Blacks often live in areas where exercising outdoors is dangerous, and gyms are not financially possible; Blacks don't go to the doctor as often as whites because many of them lack health insurance; and Blacks eat food high in sugar, fat, and sodium because these are the most affordable options in the areas where they live. On top of that, a 2022 study found that Blacks who have encountered racism in their lives are more likely to have early-onset memory loss, and another study found that Black women who experience the highest levels of interpersonal racism (such as racial slurs directed at them or discrimination at work) were nearly three times more likely to have memory loss than people who had not been exposed to racism.[147] Black people also encounter additional risk factors: prejudiced health-care providers who don't treat them with the same attention they show to white patients; dangerous workplaces; unsafe housing; inadequate educational opportunities; and communities where the air, water, and soil are polluted with industrial waste.[148]

- Blacks' health disadvantages are also transmitted intergenerationally. Studies have found that Black children are more likely to have experienced the death of a close family member, which has an impact on their emotional and physical health later in life.[149] The transmission between the generations also goes both ways: other studies have found that discrimination against their children significantly impacts Black mothers' health.[150]

These are just a few examples of the disaster that never ends. Racism keeps dealing out death, generation after generation. As psychiatrist and philosopher Frantz Fanon wrote, "Hate demands existence, and he who hates has to show his hate in appropriate actions and behaviors; in a sense, he has to become hate. That is why the Americans have substituted discrimination for lynching."[151]

The Afterlife of Slavery

I have heard white people say (and read similar comments on social media), "But I never enslaved anyone. I never lynched anyone. I didn't create a system that denied opportunities to Black people. I hate that all those things happened—but they're over. Can't we just move on now? Can't we start living in the present instead of the past?"

No, we can't. We are forever clad in mourning, not because we are living in the past but because the past has never ended. The peril to Black lives is still here. As Saidiya Hartman wrote: "If slavery persists as an issue in the political life of black America, it is not because of an antiquarian obsession with bygone days or the burden of a too-long memory, but because black lives are still imperiled and devalued by a racial calculus and a political arithmetic that were entrenched centuries ago. This is the afterlife of slavery—skewed life chances, limited access to health and education, premature death, incarceration, and impoverishment. I, too, am the afterlife of slavery."[152]

Yes. Like Hartman, I too am the afterlife of slavery—and so are you. It doesn't matter whether you are Black or white. We all carry the reality of slavery (as well as the death that is racism) within our minds and bodies. It is a little like long COVID, that ongoing disease millions are now suffering; although the virus is no longer visibly present in their bodies, it continues to sap their energy and strength.

In his book *Afropessimism,* Frank B. Wilderson III described slavery as a permanent condition: "Every Black person is always a slave and, therefore, a perpetual corpse, buried beneath the world and stinking it up."[153] I agree that the corpse is there, buried within America, fouling our world with its stench—but I refuse to claim "slave" as my identity. My perspective is more in line with sociologist Jared Sexton's, who describes "walking the fine line between optimism and pessimism, between life and death" by affirming Blackness, "inhabiting Blackness" and refusing to distance ourselves from it.[154]

Amen, brother. Let us stop denying who we are—but let us do that as Blacks and whites together. Together, let us affirm the beauty of Blackness, let us glory in its many gifts, even as together we continue to wear this heavy cloak of mourning. If we do not, we will all still be slaves, for, as Fanon wrote, "the Negro enslaved by his inferiority, the white man enslaved by his superiority alike behave in accordance with a neurotic orientation."[155]

The Neurosis of Death

Neurotic is a psychological term that's not used as much as it once was, and it's no longer a diagnosis a practitioner like me would use when working with a patient. But the old meaning of the word, the one Fanon would have been familiar with, is an appropriate term for the racist world we share. Being neurotic meant you were unusually sensitive to perceived threats and likely to experience intense emotions like anxiety, fear, moodiness, worry, envy, frustration, and jealousy. Psychoanalyst Karen Horney believed that neuroses are soothing illusions that keep us from not only seeing the truth but also from moving toward the goals we truly value. An even worse characteristic of neuroses, according to Horney, is that they create relationships that are "devoid of the value of reciprocity," relationships that lack "mutual understanding, tolerance, concern, sympathy."[156] Isn't that where we find ourselves today when it comes to the death that is racism? Instead of uniting in this shared sorrow, owning it, and carrying it together, it divides us.

Once mourning was a communal experience. It drew communities together, tightening the bonds that connected its members, even as the community's shared strength helped individuals bear the sorrow. Together, we found ways to give meaning to death. Today, our unwillingness to admit death's reality is one more life-sapping gash in the mesh of our society. It asks Blacks to mourn on their own, without the support of their white sisters and brothers—and it denies whites the wisdom, strength, and resiliency of the Black community.

In the confrontation with death, we need each other—and we need the past. Within our single tessellation of life, Blacks and whites together must not only affirm life in the valley of death but also, together, give birth to a new hope. But we cannot do that until we face the trauma of the last five hundred years. We cannot heal if we continue to hide the imprint of death we all carry.

Today I see more clearly than yesterday
that the back of the problem of race and color
lies a greater problem which both
obscures and implements it:
and that is the fact that so many civilized persons
are willing to live in comfort
even if the price of this is poverty,
ignorance, and disease
of the majority of their fellow [humans].

—W. E. B. DUBOIS[157]

MEDITATION PRACTICE

Racism and death are two topics that are difficult to talk about. They're particularly difficult if you're Black talking with a white friend or vice versa. We tend to tighten up physically in response to these topics, and we also tighten up mentally, often becoming defensive or resistant to hearing other points of view. In Rhonda V. Magee's book *The Inner Work of Racial Justice*, she speaks of the "don't-know mind" as essential for accepting "our own ongoing need to learn, and to live with inevitable uncertainty."[158] She's talking about a mental attitude that can engage openly and freely with racial issues, rather than a mindset that's tight with resistance and defensiveness. We can learn this attitude toward others by practicing it first with ourselves.

Begin by sitting comfortably. Then focus on your breathing—in, out; in, out—for several moments. When you feel present in your body, mentally picture your heart or mind as an open hand held out in friendliness and trust. Now notice what you are feeling, both emotionally and physically. As you notice each sensation, do not judge it; do not try to make a story that explains it; and most of all, do not turn away from it. Whatever it is, greet it with a friendly curiosity. Listen to it. Pay attention to it. Take its hand.

If you practice doing this for even five minutes a day for the next forty days, you will begin to lay down new neurological pathways in your brain, creating new habits of thinking. This attitude of friendly curiosity toward things you don't understand and topics that make you uncomfortable will spread out from yourself. You can begin also practicing it when talking with others who may have different experiences and ideas than you do.

You and your body are important
parts of the solution. . . .
Your body—all of our bodies—are where
changing the status quo must begin.

—RESMAA MENAKEM[159]

Once you start approaching your body with curiosity
rather than fear, everything shifts.

—BESSEL A. VAN DER KOLK[160]

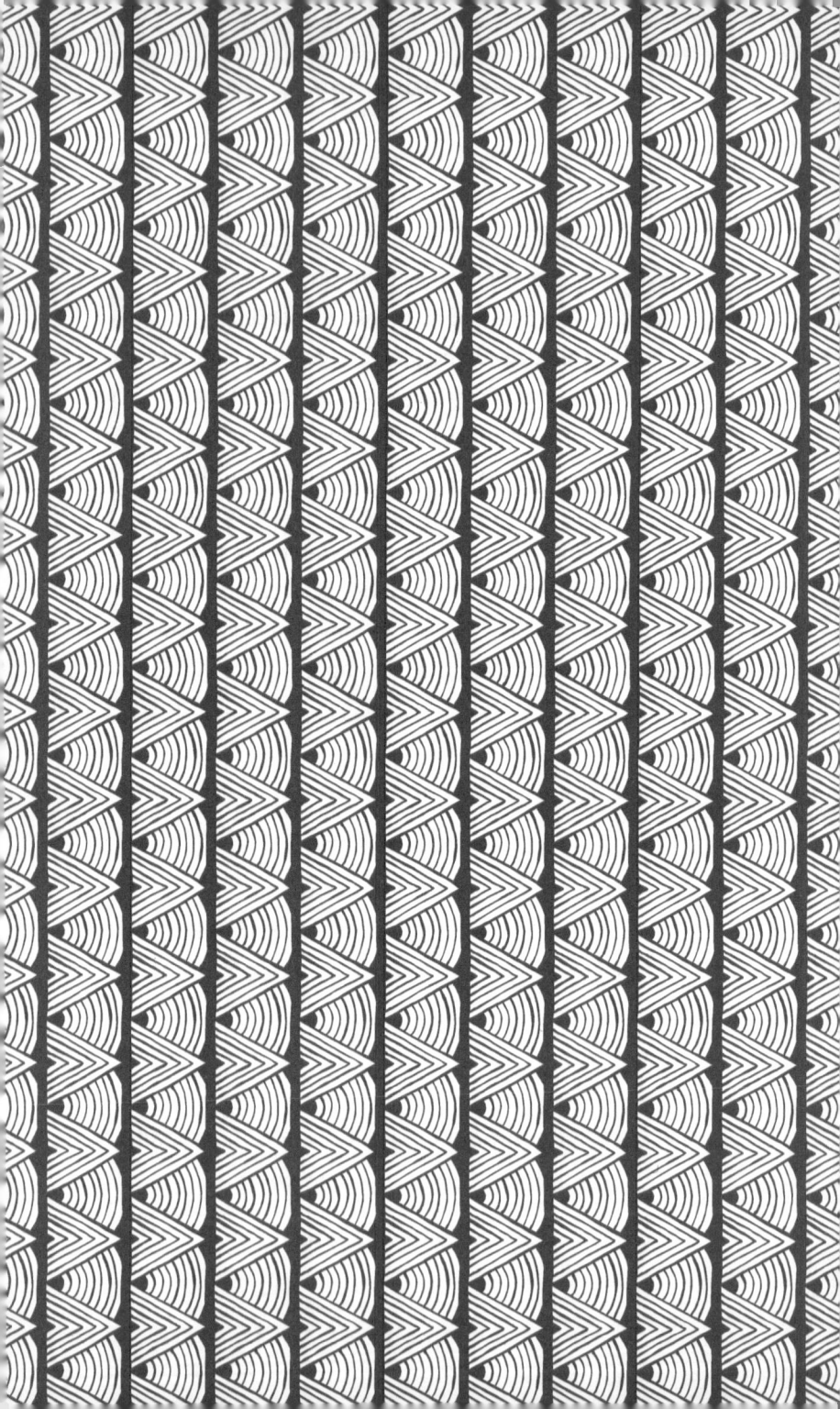

4

RACISM AND TRAUMA

DEATH'S LASTING IMPRINT

*We carry the memories of our
deepest experiences
in our bones and skin and teeth,
in our families, communities,
and societies. . . .
Trauma's legacy weaves and
wires our very world,
informing how we live in it, how we see it,
and how we see and
understand one another.*

—THOMAS HÜBL[161]

It doesn't matter what we look like. . . .
If we were born and raised in America,
white-body supremacy and our adaptations to it
are in our blood. Our very bodies house
the unhealed dissonance and
trauma of our ancestors.

—RESMAA MENAKEM[162]

MY GRANDMOTHER'S ENERGY USED TO AMAZE me. She seemed to spring into each day, eager to fully engage in life. But sometimes, while we were cooking together in her kitchen, I saw her cry.

This usually happened when she was in the middle of telling me a story. Though she was a wonderful storyteller, her narrative would become broken and confused. The tone of her voice frightened me, and I did not want to listen.

"No," she would say, "you must listen. Then you will understand why I have to work so hard." At this point, she would often need to sit down, rubbing her left leg as though it pained her.

I would shift the conversation to easier stories about our family's past, stories that would not make her cry. She would stand up again, and we would go back to our cooking, laughing and talking as we always did while we worked together.

Tatie's kitchen was her favorite place in the world, and it was mine as well. I loved to be there with her, surrounded by the good smells of roasting chicken and boiling beans. One day, though, she suggested we leave the house and go outside for a walk. Perhaps she did not want her kitchen's walls to be tainted by the story she was about to finally tell me.

And so, as we walked, she told me about the two white men who had tried to kill her brother, my great uncle. As that story flowed into another, I noticed she had begun to limp a little, and she interrupted herself to say, "I have to sit down." We found a bench, and she sat, then rubbed her left leg as she went on with her story.

It was not a pretty story. She told me about one of our enslaved ancestors, two generations ago, who had been beaten nearly to death by the white overseer. Our ancestor recovered, but his left leg had been badly broken; although the bone mended, it healed crookedly. He walked with an agonizing limp for the rest of his life.

Tatie rubbed her own left leg. "And now," she said, "this leg of mine pains me whenever I think of his story." As we walked back to her little house, she told me, "My mother and my grandmother had this same chronic pain. No one has ever known why, since none of us ever injured our legs."

"Have you talked to your doctor about it?" I asked.

She nodded. "But he never listens. Sometimes he tells me that all Black folks have aches and pains. Other times he implies I'm just looking for attention."

The persistent pain in her leg bothered my grandmother for the rest of her life. Until the day she died, no doctor ever took her complaint seriously.

Recently, as I was doing field research on trauma, I remembered again my grandmother's leg pain, and I became angry with the white physicians who had dismissed her, not seeing who she truly was, not listening to what she was saying. In the doctors' eyes, she was simply another easily forgotten Black body, "and all Black folks have aches and pains." No one cared enough to see that my grandmother—like so many Black people—was a victim of intergenerational trauma.

Intergenerational Trauma

According to the American Psychiatric Association, trauma is "an emotional response to a terrible event like an accident, rape, or natural disaster. Immediately after the event, shock and denial are typical. Longer-term reactions include unpredictable emotions, flashbacks, strained relationships, and even physical symptoms."[163] When these long-term reactions continue for months or even years after the initial event, psychologists refer to it as post-traumatic stress disorder (PTSD). *Intergenerational* trauma passes these ongoing reactions down from mother to son and father to daughter, from grandparent to grandchildren, and on and on.

This passing from generation to generation can be understood in part from a psychosociological perspective. A woman who survived a Nazi concentration camp, for example, might have learned to cope with the violence and cruelty by numbing her emotional responses; she remained physically alive, but part of her psyche died inside that camp. After the war was over and the prisoners released, she married and had children. Although her life was physically secure now, part of her continued to be frozen in time, forever trapped in the concentration camp, and she found it hard to express affection for her children. Her cold and distant mothering style wounded her children. When they grew up, they passed these wounds on to their children, who in turn grow up to do the same with their children. Without intervention, the psychological chain of trauma between the generations may continue on forever.

But psychology alone cannot explain intergenerational trauma. "We have learned," wrote trauma expert Bessel A. van der Kolk, "that trauma is not just an event that took place sometime in the past; it is also the imprint left by that experience on mind, body, and brain." This imprint has ongoing consequences for how the human organism manages to survive in the present. Trauma results in a fundamental reorganization of the way mind and brain manage perceptions. . . . Being traumatized means continuing to organize your life as if the trauma were still going on—unchanged and immutable—as every new encounter or event is contaminated by the past."[164]

Trauma also, some scientists now believe, leaves its imprint on our DNA, that spiral code that shapes our individuality.

The Epigenetics of Trauma

In the 1960s, researchers became interested in the descendants of Holocaust survivors, wondering if these children and grandchildren shared any common traits that set them apart from the rest of the population.[165] The studies that followed were inconclusive. Some showed that the descendants of Holocaust survivors shared a distrust of the world, chronic sorrow, an inability to communicate feelings, an ever-present fear of danger, separation anxiety, unclear boundaries, and overprotectiveness of their family systems.[166] Other studies, however, indicated that the children and grandchildren of Holocaust survivors were more resilient, with a stronger appreciation of life.[167]

Then, in the 1990s, Maria Yellow Horse Brave Heart studied the effects of colonization, relocation, assimilation, and boarding schools on generations of the Lakota people. She defined these effects as the *historical trauma response* (HTR). Her research indicated that HTR can be expressed in self-destructive behaviors such as alcoholism, violence, and suicide, particularly when it is connected to the unresolved grief of trauma that is both historical and ongoing.[168]

Researchers continued to follow this investigative path. In the early twenty-first century, scientists found that individuals who had been *in utero* during the Dutch Hunger Winter (a World War II period of famine) shared a particular chemical mark on their genes, one that is linked to having higher-than-average body weight, as well as diabetes and schizophrenia.[169] Additional studies, with both animals and humans, have supported the idea that trauma leaves a chemical mark on genes, which then is passed on to subsequent generations. We're not talking about a mutation here, for the "mark" doesn't damage the gene, it merely changes how the gene is expressed—or you might say, how it is turned on or off—depending on environmental factors.[170]

According to this theory, the descendants of enslaved people would still bear the genetic imprint of our ancestors' trauma. Researcher and educator Joy DeGruy coined a term for this: *post-traumatic slave syndrome*. The past constantly contaminates—or enlightens—our present, even at a micro-cellular level.

Post-Traumatic Slave Syndrome

"American chattel slavery," Dr. DeGruy wrote, "represents a case of human trauma not comparable in scope, duration, and consequence with any other incidence of human enslavement."[171]

People who survived slavery endured countless forms of trauma. They were threatened with death and witnessed the deaths of family members and friends. They were survivors of sexual assault and physical assault. If this had happened just once in an enslaved person's life, that could easily have been enough to trigger PTSD symptoms, but in fact, violence reoccurred over and over in the average enslaved person's life.

Rape was an all-too-common trauma Black women endured. A white enslaver might rape a Black woman for a range of reasons: pleasure, punishment, to breed more Black children to enslave, or a combination of all three. Often, a white man would father multiple children with different enslaved women. In her autobiography, Harriet Jacobs wrote, "My master was, to my knowledge, the father of eleven slaves"[172]

Enslaved people also experienced soul-scarring psychological trauma. As we've already described, the first Africans who crossed the Atlantic in slave ships not only lost their homes but also their sense of who they were within the culture and system of spiritual beliefs that had shaped them. Dr. Marimba Ani wrote, "The systems and circumstances of slavery in New Europe sought to destroy African value, African self-image and self-concept." She goes on to say: "Family, language, kinship patterns, food, dress and formalized religion were gone. What replaced them was the order of slavery. The objective of the new order was to demonstrate our lack of value. It turned our humanity into weakness. . . . And instead of the security of a kin-based society that imparted emotional strength and self-image to its members, the slave order created and depended on a constant state of terror."[173]

The separation of families was another trauma many enslaved people were forced to endure. In Solomon Northup's autobiography, he described his experience in the slave market as he watched a mother being separated from her child:

> All the time the trade was going on, Eliza was crying aloud, and wringing her hands. She besought the man not to buy him, unless he also bought her self and Emily. She promised, in that case, to be the most faithful slave that ever lived. The man answered that he could not afford it, and then Eliza burst into a paroxysm of grief, weeping plaintively. Freeman turned round to her, savagely, with his whip in his uplifted hand, ordering her to stop her noise, or he would flog her. He would not have such work—such snivelling; and unless she ceased that minute, he would take her to the yard and give her a hundred lashes.[174]

(Stop here for a moment. Take a moment to *be* Eliza, to feel what she felt. Can you bear it, the loss of your child? Now, can you step back and put your arms around Eliza? Step outside linear time and lend her your strength; wrap her in love. Help her to bear this sorrow.)

Enslaved Americans carried from Africa a legacy of song and faith, and they used both to endure their pain, including the separation of mother and child.

> *Mother, is master going to sell us tomorrow?*
> *Yes, yes, yes! O, watch and pray!*
> *Going to sell us in Georgia?*
> *Yes, yes, yes! O, watch and pray!*
> *Farewell, mother, I must leave you.*
> *Yes, yes, yes! O, watch and pray!*
> *Mother, don't grieve after me.*
> *No, no, no! O, watch and pray!*
> *Mother, I'll meet you in heaven.*
> *Yes, my child! O, watch and pray!*

But no faith, no song, can eradicate the agony of saying goodbye to a child. Jungian analyst Fanny Brewster writes, "I believe that all of the children who were lost due to slavery continue to have the archetypal potential for sharing grief intergenerationally with Africanist women of color." Black women still today carry within their hearts and bones the endless loss of their children.

Mothers and children were not the only ones who slavery brutally separated. So were husbands and wives, brothers and sisters, friends and other kinfolk. Even if the separation never happened, the constant fear of it would have been traumatic in and of itself—and all too often it *did* happen. Let me tell you about Augustine Queen.

In the mid-nineteenth century, Augustine, an enslaved man, fell in love with Mary Hoppins, an enslaved woman. Augustine had grown up on a mission in Missouri, enslaved by the Jesuits, but Mary's enslaver was a prominent white man named James Lucas. Augustine and Mary wanted to get married, but according to Jesuit records, Augustine and Mary "were not permitted to marry without the permission of their respective owners, and as long as they remained enslaved to different owners, they faced the possibility of having to live apart, or even possibly being separated, should one of their owners relocate or sell them."[175]

Now, once again, take a moment, to put yourself in Augustine's and Mary's positions. Imagine you could not choose to marry the person you love without the permission of someone who claimed to "own" you. Imagine how you would feel, knowing that even with that permission, the two of you could never be secure in the knowledge that only death would part you.

Eventually, Augustine and Mary were able to convince their owners to let them marry, but their fears of being parted turned out to be well-founded. Only five months after their marriage, Mary's enslaver sold her to a military man who was currently stationed in the area. Augustine and Mary knew when the man was restationed, he would take Mary with him, so they appealed to the Jesuits for help.

The Jesuits agreed to come to their aid—but to get the funds to buy Mary, the Jesuits sold Augustine's friend, Peter Queen. Augustine was the godfather of Peter's son, but now, he was forced to sacrifice his friend's family and happiness so he could keep his wife. It's unlikely Peter saw his family ever again.

Pretend for a moment that you are Augustine. Imagine you are Peter Queen. Can you feel the trauma of never having control over your own life ? Or of knowing your happiness was bought at the expense of a close friend's? Of never being able to feel secure within the love of your family? Now imagine your parents and grandparents also underwent the same experiences you are enduring now. As trauma is passed through the generations, it grows and expands. The descendants of Mary and Augustine, Peter and his wife, consciously or unconsciously, still carry their ancestors' trauma within their minds and bodies. They endure the post-traumatic slave syndrome Dr. DeGruy described.

DeGruy found that the long-term expression of this condition—the effects on descendants—can be grouped into three categories:

1. *A loss of self-esteem*. Down through the generations, negative racial stereotypes have been absorbed from the surrounding culture, not only by whites but by Blacks too. Evidence of this is the 1940s study, conducted by Black psychologists Mamie and Kenneth Clark, which found that when given the choice between a Black doll and a white doll, most Black children preferred the white dolls, saying that the white dolls were "nicer," "cleaner," and "prettier." Whenever the experiment has been repeated over the years, the results haven't changed.[176]

   Learned helplessness is also a possible product of low self-esteem. It's a coping response that says, "There is no escaping from this situation, so there's no point in trying." Learned helplessness creates an interior enslavement that spreads through an individual's life in the form of frustration, hostility, anger issues, and depression.[177] Members of Black communities may be taught to set low goals for themselves, educationally and professionally, and many Black men have little hope for their futures, since so many of them end up either in prison or dead before they reach the age of twenty-five.[178]

2. *Impaired health and medical treatment*. Racism damages health. Black women age faster than white women.[179] Blacks as a whole experience higher stress than whites, leading to higher rates of heart disease and high blood pressure; Blacks are more

likely to have hypertension than any other racial or ethnic group.[180] Blacks have more problems sleeping than whites do.[181] When Black women give birth, their babies are more likely to have complications, including pre-term deliveries, low birth weight, and stillbirth.[182] The American Academy of Pediatrics (AAP) recommends screening Black children and adolescents for depression, stress, grief, and PTSD, and points out that Black families also face disparities in their access to health care, grocery stores with healthy foods, educational opportunities, and juvenile justice protection. The AAP further stresses that "these health inequities are not the result of individual behavior choices or genetic predisposition."[183] In other words, as we said in the previous chapter, we cannot blame Black people's health issues on their "poor choices," nor are medical problems written in the DNA shared by all Black people around the world.

One factor that *does* contribute to poor health in Blacks is inadequate treatment and diagnosis from white physicians. Doctors frequently underprescribe pain medication and other pain-management treatments to Black patients, including Black children.[184] Black adolescents are overdiagnosed with conduct disorder, and Black men are overdiagnosed with schizophrenia, when both groups might be more therapeutically assessed and treated for trauma.[185]

3. ***Internalized oppression***. Like the Black children who chose the white dolls over the Black ones, Blacks may internalize negative perceptions of their hair, skin, and facial features, believing that the closer their appearance is to a white person's, the more attractive they are. Internalized oppression can also show up as *respectability politics:* the belief that if Blacks only behaved better and presented a better image to the outside world, their lot in life would improve. An example of this would be Black parents who tell their teenagers not to wear hoodies but to dress more like white adolescents. Another example would be Black mayor Michael Nutter scolding Black churchgoers for their poor parenting skills, out-of-wedlock birthrate, clothing styles, and vocabulary.[186]

Of course, not every Black person experiences these traits, and we must be careful that the concept of post-traumatic slave syndrome (PTSS) doesn't feed into racist stereotypes. Author Ibram Kendri goes so far as to say that PTSS is a racist idea. "Unlike the more conservative and liberal racist theorists who root 'dysfunctional' Black behaviors in biology or culture," he wrote, "these more progressive racist theorists root 'dysfunctional' Black behaviors in the history of oppression." Kendri also claims that historically, "Black people certainly had the physical scars from slavery, but mentally, they were not scarred. . . . Black people as a group do not need to be healed from racist trauma."[187]

While I hear what Kendi is saying—and I agree up to a point—my reading of the psychological research as well as my professional and personal experience don't support Kendi's claim that we bear no mental scars. How could we not, having endured centuries of horrific oppression? Nor does the historical evidence indicate, as Kendi says, that Blacks were able to "strut" straight off the plantation into a successful and creative society.

"The answer to why so many of us have difficulties," writes Resmaa Menakem, author of *My Grandmother's Hands* (which focuses on trauma's aftereffects on the body), "is because our ancestors spent centuries here under unrelentingly brutal conditions. Generation after generation, our bodies stored trauma and intense survival energy, and passed these on to our children and grandchildren. Most of us also passed down resilience and love, of course. But . . . resilience and love aren't sufficient to completely heal all trauma. Often, at least some of the trauma continues." [188]

What I would also say in answer to Kendi's comments is that both Blacks and whites are traumatized by slavery's ongoing legacy. None of us in America can escape the legacy of death that slavery leaves in our hearts and minds and bodies. That traumatization may look differently in whites, but it is just as real, just as damaging, and perhaps even more deadly. Harriet Jacobs wrote, based on her time as an enslaved person, "I can testify, from my own experience and observation, that slavery is a curse to the whites as well as to the blacks." [189]

I find myself thinking about the word *loss* again. If we say that intergenerational trauma takes something away from

Black people, proving them once again to be unequal to whites, then yes, that is racism. But trauma does not make us *less*. It can shape our behaviors in ways that are unhealthy and unproductive—but it can also be an opportunity for creative transformation. Black musicians turned their pain into music; Black artists and authors used their trauma to inspire works of art and literature; and Black people everywhere expressed their trauma with their stance and their dance. Trauma triggered our jokes; we cooked trauma over barbecues and stovetops, and then we smacked our lips as we ate the fine food trauma had served up. Trauma made us pray harder and love more. It made us sing while we wept. But it did not lessen us.

Psychologists Richard Tedeschi and Lawrence Calhoun have identified *post-traumatic growth* as the ability to rise higher than ever after adversity.[190] Their work doesn't deny the deep pain of trauma, but they found that post-traumatic growth and post-traumatic stress disorder can coexist in the same individual.

Based on their research data, Tedeschi and Calhoun identified five broad categories of growth that can develop and expand alongside the pain of trauma:

- The ability to recognize and embrace new opportunities

- The capacity for stronger and more loving relationships

- A sense of deep inner strength

- A knack for appreciating and savoring life

- A commitment to deeper and evolving spiritual beliefs

Looking at those categories, I would say that Black people as a whole are excellent examples of all five.

Meanwhile, our white sisters and brothers (yes, you, dear white readers) still struggle to recognize their own intergenerational trauma from slavery. Blacks have endured centuries of physical and psychological oppression and injustice—but whites have carried the soul-deadening weight of their guilt, their need for power, their loss of meaningful culture, their paranoia and insecurity. "As long as you keep secrets and suppress information, you are fundamentally at war with yourself," wrote Bessel A. Van der Kolk. "The critical issue is allowing yourself to know what you know. That takes an enormous amount of courage."[191] The refusal to acknowledge slavery's festering wound is itself a form of ongoing spiritual trauma.

Spiritual Trauma

I was born in Haiti, and then spent most of my young-adult life in France. Growing up outside America's particular brand of racism, I was able to absorb from my African roots a strong foundation for my perceptions of the world and myself. (It was a shock to me when I came to the United States, where for the first time I experienced racism as a personal reality.) Nevertheless, I always feel slavery's centuries-old shadow as it falls across my life. I am alive today because my ancestors found ways to survive slavery. I believe the memory of their pain is imprinted on the cells of my body.

In the summer of 2022, while I was doing my annual silent eight-day retreat down in Bay St. Louis, Mississippi, I went outside to pray as I wandered through the beautiful grounds around the retreat house. Making my way between thick oak trees dripping with Spanish moss, prayer came very easily, as easy as the wind in the trees.

But then I noticed a grove of ancient trees surrounded by a cleared space. As I came closer to the trees, a chill came over me. I sensed lynchers waiting in the shadows, looking for a runaway slave . . . or waiting to teach an uppity Black man a lesson. Sweat sprang out on my skin, and my breathing came fast. I looked around me, but I was still alone. And yet I seemed to hear the growing clamor of a gathering crowd. When I looked up at one of the trees' spreading branches, I saw a rope hanging from it.

I swallowed back a scream. I was a Black man in a small white town in Mississippi. I did not want to call attention to myself, so I turned my back on those terrible trees and made my way to the safety of the retreat house.

There, I later learned that those trees were, in fact, lynching trees; my reaction to them had not been pure imagination. Now, I could not shake images of lynching from my mind. The branches of the trees seemed to reach inside my mind, groping for me, laying claim to me. The peace I had felt at the retreat house shattered, leaving me uneasy and restless.

And then, after a few days, my thoughts about those trees changed. I began to see America's lynching trees as victims who had also been traumatized. Now, in my mind's eyes, the trees were noble, innocent beings who had not asked to participate in racism and violence. I felt sorrow for them, and I spent the following day praying for the trees . . . for the men and women who had died hanging from them . . . and finally for the people who had committed such atrocities in this country. I left the retreat with a feeling of immense freedom, energy, and joy.

How do I explain this experience? Purely my imagination (with the assumption that the products of our imagination are "not real")? Or did something profoundly *real* happen to me because of the presence of those trees and the memory of the past? I believe both psychology and epigenetics explain some of the intergenerational trauma we experience, but I also believe other factors are at work.

Neuroscientists have proposed a theory of consciousness that suggests that the human brain is not the producer of consciousness but the receptor. Cardiologist Pim van Lommel theorized that the brain is much like a television set, which receives waves of invisible information it decodes into sounds and pictures. When you turn off the television, reception ends—but the flow of information is still there. Dr. van Lommel also proposed that consciousness is "nonlocal," an idea based on quantum physics that would mean that although the body (including the brain) has limitations in time and space, consciousness itself is limited by neither.[192] "Local realism" is the lens the Western world has used for centuries, which sees the physical world as the only *real* reality, a reality that can only be influenced by its immediate (local) surroundings. When we look through the local-realism lens, we see the individual inanimate parts of a dead physical universe. There is growing evidence, however, that a nonlocal universe, where everything is interconnected in a net of eternal relationship, is a more accurate lens through which to perceive reality.[193] If the *real* universe consists of relationships that exist across space and time, my "spiritual" perception of a historical trauma becomes more credible.

Our nervous systems—our ability to receive messages from the outside world—take shape within the matrix of other nervous systems, a context that includes all time, all places. As Dr. Gabor Maté puts it, "Our brains are really wired together."[194] This is also part of the African Ubuntu understanding: *I am because you are.* Your reality has shaped mine, as mine has yours. I would not be the same without you, and you would not be the same without me. The vast mesh of life to which we all belong includes both past and present.

Dr. van Lommel described a reality that is far more compatible with the African mindset than it is with the Euro-American: "One cannot avoid the conclusion that endless or nonlocal consciousness has always existed and will always exist independently from the body, because there is no beginning nor will there ever be an end to our consciousness. For this reason we should seriously consider the possibility that death, like birth, can only be a transition to another state of consciousness. According to this idea death is only the end of our physical aspects, and during life our body functions as an interface or place of resonance for our nonlocal consciousness."[195]

My experience with the lynching trees affirms this perception of reality. That experience also taught me something important about spiritual trauma: as we seek to heal past trauma, we have the potential to change the present. Or is it the other way around: when we change the present, we heal the past?

Thomas Hübl, the founder of the Academy of Inner Science, refers to this as *retrocausality*. He wrote: "If proven, the theory of retrocausality could mean that influences from the present or future are able to act on, and thereby *change*, the past. From the mystical perspective, this is an essential principle of grace and is always true. The future indeed has the power to rewrite the past. In fact, when we integrate shadow or trauma, we're utilizing this principle because healing past energy creates a forward ripple effect. This releases light and energy that was previously held in shadow, offering greater movement and freedom of will in the present."[196]

Coming from the materialistic science of the Western world, this concept may seem like woo-woo nonsense—but once again, some uncanny ideas in the field of quantum mechanics lend credence to the possibility of retrocausality. Quantum physicist Dr. Peter Evans, for example, suggests that events do not need to proceed in only one direction; instead, time may flow in both directions, meaning that an event in the past might be influenced by an event in the future.[197]

While the Euro-American mind struggles to grasp how this could be possible, the indigenous African concept of time focuses not on the future but on the past. This means that instead of time's "arrow" flying ever "forward" into the future, time is rooted in the past, with the African community facing toward the ancestors. John Mbiti, a prominent African theologian, explains that it's not so much that time itself moves "backward," but that events do. (We cannot rightly use the words *backward* and *forward,* however, because that implies the Western perspective is the "correct" one, while the African concept of time is "wrong" and "backward.")

Time itself is a very different concept for the African, Mbiti says. It is not something that passes, it is not something that can be wasted or saved, and it is not something that can be measured—nor is the future like an empty container of time waiting to be filled with events. In the mind of the traditional African, time consists only of being and doing, and since as yet neither is taking place in the future, the future has no substance. Only the past and the present exist constantly in active relationship with each other, with the present always facing toward the past.[198] While our Western minds may struggle to make sense of this, the African worldview quite comfortably accommodates all that to us may seem irrational or paradoxical.

The Euro-American outlook has difficulty uniting the spiritual and the material into a single perspective, which means we often carry within our mental maps two separate and contradictory belief systems. William James, the great nineteenth-century American psychologist, noted that the human psyche lives in both a material and a spiritual world; the model he implies is that we are physical beings inhabiting "an invisible spiritual environment from which help comes, our soul being mysteriously one with a larger soul whose instruments we are." James indicated that traumatic experiences can open the door into the invisible, spiritual world.[199] Jungian Donald Kalsched agrees, saying that the spiritual world often becomes "suddenly visible through a gap created by trauma."[200]

Traditional African wisdom sees only a single reality, not two, but it also recognizes the spiritual power of trauma. According to African spiritual teacher Malidoma Patrice Somé, when a person in African indigenous culture is going through a period of emotional or psychological brokenness, that person is believed to be in intense interaction with the Spirit. The person may appear dysfunctional, even crazy—but with healing and resolution comes the release of vital spiritual gifts to the community as a whole.[201] This is the hope I hold on to even as I acknowledge my own trauma. In order to heal, I know I will need the participation of the entire community, both Blacks and whites—and if you want to heal, you too will need that broken but still-possible unity.

We can no longer "whitewash" the past, refusing to see its truth. Jungian psychologist Fanny Brewster has written that the trauma Black people carry is magnified by unresolved ancestral pain, "because we as an American collective have been largely unwilling to permit remembrance of this cultural trauma. In the attempt at suppression, everything gets pushed back into the shadows and any attempt to bring to light the darkness of racism that caused the cultural trauma is also critically forbidden or avoided. . . . Until this shifts towards the direction of acknowledgement and awareness, our collective racial healing is delayed and each new generation is born into the repetitive cultural trauma of previous generations."[202]

So then, let us no longer "choose the dirty pain of silence and avoidance," which only makes the wound grow deeper and more infected. There is no hiding from the centuries of trauma, no way to truly avoid it—but we can choose to accept the pain honestly, openly, "cleanly."[203] This ancient pain we carry in our bodies can even, in some way, become our gift to a world that would deny the reality of racism. "The embodiment [of trauma]," wrote Jenny Escobar, "becomes a crucial tool of truth telling when there are not mechanisms that recognize, honor, and assure" that the truth will be "kept alive and integrated into the social fabric."[204] Our trauma is a scream for justice.

The forces of spiritual death and destruction are strong—but the forces of love and life are stronger. Trauma need not destroy us—and, as members of the African diaspora have always known, *death cannot kill love.*

Death is not the extermination of life. That is the Western perspective, but Christ's message of endless love tells us that death is not the end after all. From an African perspective, death can even be a call to a greater sense of community.

We want to forget all the hatred, grief, and pain
of the American slavery plantation system.
It can be too much to think on—even now.
However, it is a past that will not go away
without the allowance of the truth
of those slavery times.

—FANNY BREWSTER[205]

Ideally, America will grow up and out
of white-body supremacy;
Americans will begin healing their
long-held trauma around race.

—RESMAA MENAKEM[206]

PRAYER PRACTICE

For this practice, you will need to get together with a partner or even a group of friends. If you belong to a small church group, you might suggest that you undertake this practice at one of your meetings, and if, by chance, you are reading this book in a discussion group, this practice is a good way to conclude your discussion.

Begin by sitting in a circle, and for a few moments simply breathe in unison: in . . . out; in . . . out; in . . . out. When you sense that the group has quieted, one of you can begin singing, with the others joining in. Sing something simple, that you all know, such as "This Little Light of Mine," "We Shall Overcome," "Amen," or "We Shall Not Be Moved." (The group should agree on the song before beginning this practice.) Sing the same song softly and slowly, again and again.

Then, after a few moments, stand up and join hands as you sing. Speed up the tempo and allow your bodies to sway and move. Lift your voices louder; dance, stomp your feet, and clap your hands. Smile. Laugh. Embrace.

Then gradually lower your voices again and slow the tempo. Sit down once more, and once again join hands. As it feels natural, let the song fade into silence. Rest together in silent prayer until you sense it's time to move on. Then, if possible, you might share a meal, a snack, or even just a drink of water. As you eat and/or drink, talk with each other and process the experience you have just shared.

Research on trauma treatment has found that when people move together as a group—such as singing in a choir, dancing, or doing yoga—it helps to heal the trauma we all carry in our bodies.[207]

*In order to change,
people need to become aware of their sensations
and the way that their bodies interact
with the world around them.
Physical self-awareness is the first step
in releasing the tyranny of the past.*

—BESSEL VAN DER KOLK[208]

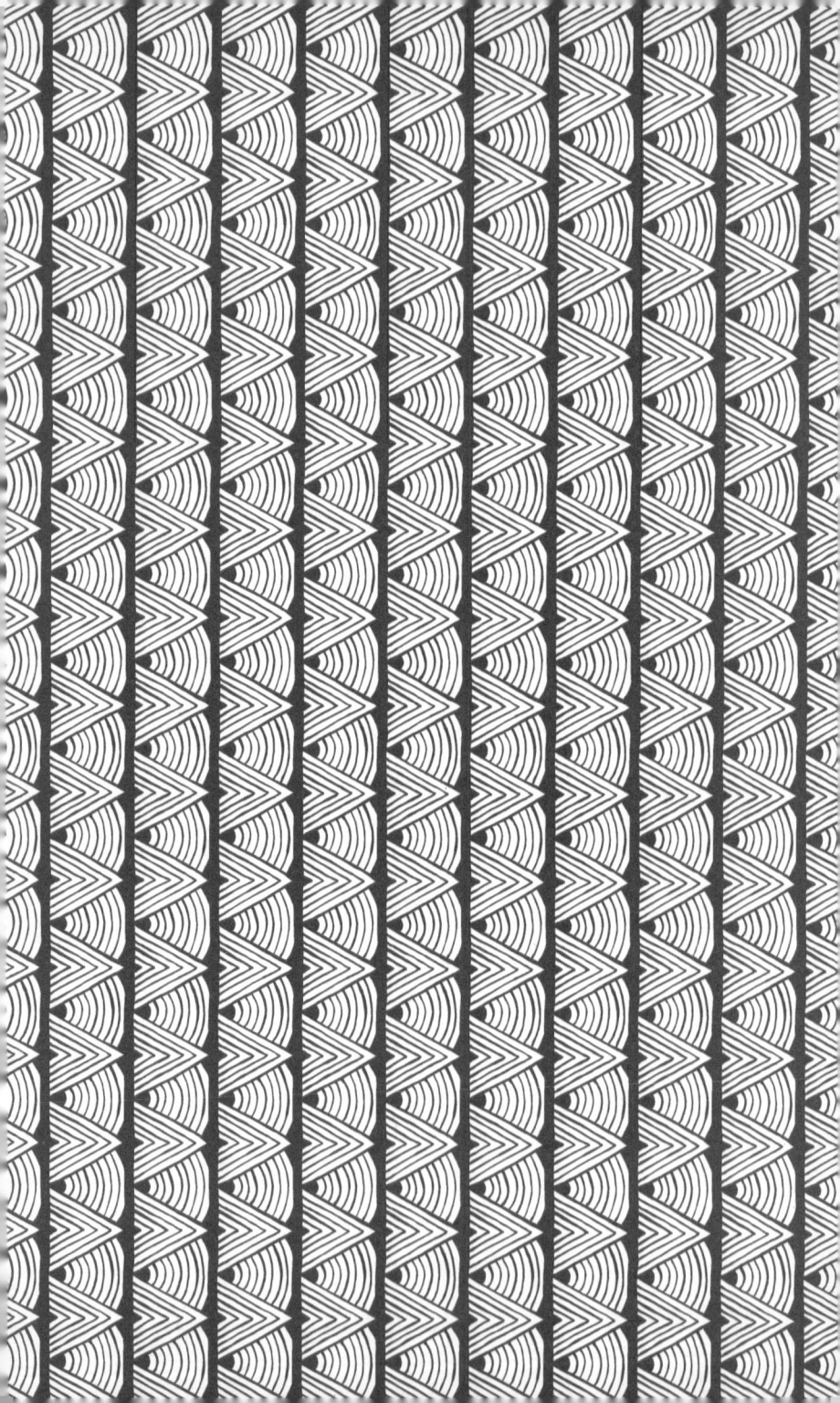

5

GRIEF AND RAGE

DEATH AS A SHOUT
FOR JUSTICE

*To be a Negro in this country and
to be relatively conscious
is to be in a rage almost all the time.*

—JAMES BALDWIN[209]

*We were aware of the fact
that death walks hand in
hand with struggle.*

—STOKELY CARMICHAEL[210]

I'M SORRY, DEAR READERS, BUT I NEED TO begin this chapter with another ugly story, one that hurts to read, to remember. But we dare not forget it. This story must be held in our hearts forever. As you read it, remember—your reactions, whatever they may be, are not the point. Please, bear witness to the pain in this story without trying to shift the focus to your own response.[211]

The Story of Emmett Till

In 1941, in Chicago, Mamie Till gave birth to a beautiful baby boy she named Emmett. He grew up to be a bright child who helped his mother around the house, loved to pull pranks, and was often the center of attention in his group of friends. The early years of his life were not always easy—he had polio when he was six, which left him with a stutter, and he saw his father and then his stepfather abuse his mother—but for the most part, Emmett was a happy child whose life had always been cushioned by his mother's and grandmother's love. He thought well of himself, as all children should, and by the time he was a teenager, he was dressing up in fashionable clothes and flirting with the girls. He was a charming, cocky, sweet boy, comfortable with both Blacks and whites.

When Emmett was fourteen, his great-uncle Mose came to visit. Mose was from the Deep South, and Emmett loved listening to his uncle's stories about life on the Mississippi Delta. Emmett longed to visit the land where his family had roots, and his mother agreed to let him go with a couple of older cousins.

"Be careful down there," Mamie warned him. "It's a whole different world from what things are here in Chicago. You gotta mind yourself around white folk. You need to be careful. You understand, now?"

Emmett promised he understood. But how could he? He had never lived in the Deep South.

Emmett arrived in Mississippi on a hot day in August. A few days later, while his great-uncle Mose was preaching at a church prayer meeting, Emmett and one of his cousins decided to skip the service and go buy candy. No one knows for sure exactly what happened next.

According to one of his cousins, Emmett pulled out a school picture of his class in Chicago and showed it to some other Black teenagers who were standing outside the store. "See all those white kids?" he said. "Up in Chicago where I live, Blacks aren't separated from whites like down here. Those white kids are my friends just as much as the Black kids."

To the other boys, Emmett's claim seemed as unlikely as if he had said, *I'm friends with the President of the United States.* They assumed he was lying.

"If you're such good friends with white folk," one of the other boys said, "I dare you to go inside the store and talk to that white woman in there." The white woman was Carolyn Bryant; her husband owned the store, but she was alone behind the counter that day.

Emmett grinned and accepted the challenge; the other boys followed him inside to see what would happen. Instead of speaking to Carolyn, however, Emmett gave her a wolf whistle.

Another of his cousins said later, "I think he wanted to get a laugh out of us or something. He was always joking around." The cousin, who had grown up in Mississippi, went on to say, "Well, it scared us half to death. You know, we were almost in shock. We couldn't get out of there fast enough, because we had never heard of anything like that before. A black boy whistling at a white woman? In Mississippi? No."

Later, Emmett's mother theorized that her son hadn't intended a wolf whistle at all. Because his speech was often unclear, she said, she had taught him to whistle before he spoke; it was a method she'd discovered helped him to articulate his words.

At the time, Carolyn Bryant told a completely different story. According to her, Emmett came into the store, grabbed her hand while she was stocking the shelves, and said, "How about a date, baby?" When she pulled away from him and retreated behind the counter, he followed her, she said, and grabbed her around the waist. "What's the matter, baby, can't you take it?" Carolyn again pulled away from him. "You needn't be afraid of me, baby," she reported that Emmett said, using an "unprintable word" as he "mauled" her.

The other boys there at the time insisted none of this happened. They said Emmett simply picked out some candy, paid for it, and left the store. In any event, after the boys left the store, they saw Carolyn Bryant come out and get a gun from her car. This may have been the moment when Emmett whistled (according to some of the eyewitness accounts), but it was an expression of amazement and not intended as a wolf whistle. The terrified teenagers ran away.

Emmett was afraid to tell his great-uncle what had happened. He didn't want to get in trouble—but he was no longer having a good time in Mississippi. He was ready to go back home.

Unfortunately, before arrangements could be made for his trip back to Chicago, Carolyn Bryant's husband heard what had happened. Early in the morning of August 28, Roy Bryant and his brother John barged into the small cabin where Emmett was staying with his family.

Emmett's great-aunt offered the men money if they would go away and leave them in peace. Mose told them, "The boy's from up North. He don't know no better."

But the white men did not listen to their pleas. They dragged Emmett out to their truck, where they tied him up, tossed him into the back, and drove him to a barn. Then they clubbed him with their guns, again and again and again.

Three days later, two boys found Emmett's body while they were fishing in the Tallahatchie River. The corpse was naked, wrapped in barbed wire, and tied to a seventy-five-pound metal fan. Emmett had been shot in the head, his eye was dislodged from its socket, his back and hips were covered with bruises, and his face was nearly unrecognizable. His great-uncle Mose could only identify him because of the silver ring he wore.

Later, in an interview with *Look* magazine, Roy Bryant's brother John said, "Well, what else could we do? He was hopeless. I'm no bully; I never hurt a n – – – – r in my life. I like n – – – – rs—in their place—I know how to work 'em. But I just decided it was time a few people got put on notice. As long as I live and can do anything about it, n – – – – rs are gonna stay in their place. N – – – – rs ain't gonna vote where I live. If they did, they'd control the government. They ain't gonna go to school with my kids. And when a n – – – – r gets close to mentioning sex with a white woman, he's tired o' livin'. I'm likely to kill him. Me and my folks fought for this country, and we got some rights."

When her son's mutilated body was returned to her, Mamie insisted on opening the casket. She wanted to see her son one last time—but she could not recognize him.

Stop for a moment here. *Be* Mamie. Feel what she feels as she looks at her once-beautiful baby boy. Can you imagine the trembling in her legs, the sickness in her belly, the terrible fist of pain in her chest? Can you feel them as though your own son was the one lying in a casket, beaten beyond recognition, simply because he was a happy-go-lucky kid with black skin?

Now, I ask you to just be *with* Mamie. Allow yourself to enter a timeless space of eternity, where you share with her the terrible sorrow, the helplessness, the rage she feels. Support her with whatever strength you can offer her. Know your *real* connection to her, a connection that exists outside time and space, within the wounded Body of Christ. You need Mamie—and she needs you. That is not an abstraction, not a pretty idea. Your need for each other is real.

I believe in that moment, as she looked down at her dead son, Mamie did draw strength and courage from what Africans think of as the "abode of the ancestors," the place where time does not matter, and we are all connected. Drawing on that spiritual power, she made a decision.

"Keep the casket open," she told the undertaker. "I want everyone to see what I see"

The Transformative Power of Grief

"I believe that the whole United States is mourning with me," Mamie said, inviting us all to enter her terrible grief. She challenged the media to photograph her son's body and then share the pictures with the public. In doing so, she made white Americans realize her sorrow was something they *could* share. They could identify with a Black mother. Black deaths were no longer a distant, abstract reality; whites were forced, at least for a moment, if they were capable, of feeling the hideous pain of a Black mother's anguish. In a letter to the NAACP, Mamie stated that she had set out to "trade the blood of my child" for the "betterment of my race."[212]

Mamie Till-Mobley, wrote historian Simon Stow, "understood that mourning was not simply an act of grieving, but also of grievance. Revealing the brutalized body ensured that the deceased boy would also become . . . a body of knowledge, a body that would have *a power beyond death*." Mamie, Stow went on to say, made "mourning a transformative act," one that pushed back "against the seeming totality of fear, dehumanization, and death."[213]

Grief can give birth to new life. Mamie Till-Mobley proved it.

Grief and Anger

According to Merriam-Webster's online dictionary, our primary modern-day understanding of grief equates to a "deep and poignant distress caused by the loss of a loved one." The word *grief* grew, however, from older roots that meant "afflict, burden, oppress, wrong, injustice, make heavy." This older understanding, connecting grief to oppression and injustice, is what Mamie Till-Mobley experienced, just as generations of Black mothers and fathers, aunties and uncles, siblings and friends have.

As we mentioned in chapter 1, anger is one of the stages in Elisabeth Kübler-Ross's grieving model. We often think of this anger as being directed against God or the Universe or simply circumstances. "Why did this have to happen to my loved one?" we cry. "How could you allow this to happen, God?" We don't really expect an answer to our questions, and eventually, we conclude that this is a futile anger, one we must set aside so we can more fully process the meaning of our sorrow.

Black Americans, of course, experience all five stages of grieving (sometimes simultaneously), just like anyone else—but for us, often the anger of grief takes on special meaning. It is not something we send out randomly into the universe, hoping a distant Deity may hear us; our anger is directed much more closely to home. All too frequently, we *know* what caused our loved ones' deaths: racism.

From an evolutionary perspective, all emotions serve a survival function, sending us messages that our attention needs to be directed in a particular direction. Anger's message has to do with injury or mistreatment. "It's not fair!" we shouted as children when someone got a larger share of something than we did, stamping our feet and then bursting into tears of rage. As adults, our anger can send us the message that we need to defend ourselves and our loved ones against oppression. It energizes us to take action. This is the form Mamie Till-Mobley's grief took (even as she also mourned her son in all the other ways a mother sorrows). By sharing her grief with all Americans, she opened the floodgates to the activism and resistance that became the Civil Rights Movement.

Emmett Till's death was not the first time Black grief became the channel for the generative flow of justice. Since funerals were one of the rare occasions when Blacks were allowed to gather during slavery days, these rituals of sorrow sometimes also became opportunities for anger to crystalize into revolt. Back in Richmond, Virginia, for example, at the turn of the nineteenth century, a man named Gabriel (often referred to as Gabriel Prosser because of his enslaver's surname) used a child's funeral to help trigger what might have been the largest revolt of enslaved people in America. (Unfortunately, bad weather and betrayal caused the rebellion's failure, and Gabriel and many of his followers were hanged.)

More than a century and a half later, in 1963, when the Ku Klux Klan bombed the 16th Street Baptist Church in Birmingham, Alabama, twenty-two people were injured. Four little girls—eleven-year-old Denise McNair and fourteen-year-old Cynthia Wesley, Carole Robertson, and Addie Mae Collins—were killed.

Again, I'm going to stop here for a moment and ask you to spend some time with those four girls. Their names are more than historical facts; they represent warm, breathing, joyful children who had their entire lives ahead of them. Little Denise McNair had a composed, ladylike demeanor; she loved to perform on stage, where she acted in plays, did dance routines, and read poetry, often on behalf of muscular dystrophy fundraising. Cynthia Wesley had a friendly smile and wore her hair in bangs; she was a studious girl who did well in math and reading, and she loved playing in the band. Carole Robertson often wore her hair in a single, long braid, and when she smiled, her eyes narrowed into mischievous slits; she loved to sing, play her clarinet, and read. And Addie Mae Collins was an artistic, sweet-faced girl whose glasses gave her a serious air that didn't represent her true outgoing nature. In the moments before their deaths, the four girls were giggling and chattering, dressed in fancy white dresses for Youth Day at their church. Can you see them, can you hear them? Can you smell the scent of their skin, feel the texture of their hair between your fingers, hear their quick breaths of excitement? Can you remember they are part of you, that you need them, that our world would not be complete without each of these unique, precious girls? Can you love them? Can you grieve them?

In his eulogy at the girls' shared funeral service, Dr. Martin Luther King Jr. said: "In a real sense they have something to say to each of us in their death. They have something to say to every minister of the gospel who has remained silent behind the safe security of stained-glass windows. They have something to say to every politician who has fed his constituents with the stale bread of hatred and the spoiled meat of racism. They have something to say to a federal government that has compromised with the undemocratic practices of southern Dixiecrats and the blatant hypocrisy of right-wing northern Republicans. They have something to say to every Negro who has passively accepted the evil system of segregation and who has stood on the sidelines in a mighty struggle for justice. They say to each of us, black and white alike, that we must substitute courage for caution. They say to us that we must be concerned not merely about who murdered them, but about the system, the way of life, the philosophy which produced the murderers. Their death says to us that we must work passionately and unrelentingly."[214]

Something about a child's death gets past even the most cold-hearted defenses. The nation's outrage galvanized the civil rights and desegregation movements. It led to the passage of the Civil Rights Act in 1964 and the Voting Rights Act in 1965.

Again, in the summer of 2020, after we watched George Floyd be murdered, his breath choked from him beneath the knee of a white police officer, our grief ignited us to action. The protest movement that swept across the United States (and even around the world) was the largest ever, sending 15 to 25 million people into the streets.[215] Some people may have been titillated at some level by the constant replaying of his death; the ongoing exposure to the footage may have triggered trauma reactions in others; but above and beyond these responses was a unity in sorrowful rage that spurred us to take action. As Judith Butler noted, "open grieving is bound up with outrage, and outrage in the face of injustice or indeed of unbearable loss has enormous political potential."[216] George Floyd's murder convinced many whites that racism was not a thing of the past. As a result, the Minneapolis police department was defunded, and the Black Lives Matter movement swelled in size and influence.

The Instincts of Death and Life

Freud believed humanity is driven by dual instincts: the death drive and the life drive (or the pleasure principle). The drive toward death and destruction, he said, was expressed through behaviors such as aggression, repetition compulsion, and self-destructiveness.[217] I see this clearly at work in the mindset that took control after 9/11, as Americans engaged in wars that achieved nothing but more human sorrow and suffering.

I am not saying Blacks are less prone to this compulsion than whites are, but in my people's history, I also see what Jacques Lacan described in his own version of the Freudian drive concept. Instead, of creating polarity between the drives of life and death, Lacan merged them. The "will to destruction," he said, becomes the "will to make a fresh start," a will to create something different, something better, from what has gone before."[218]

White folk often acknowledge the creativity and richness of the Black community (spiritually, musically, and athletically, in particular, as well as in the realms of literature, fashion, cooking)[219]—but still they deny Blacks the right to the other element in Lacan's equation: the rage that seeks to destroy in order to create something better. I often hear white acquaintances make comments like these:

> "Blacks want to be put at the head of the line—and in the process, white people are getting shoved to the back."

> "Every other group that came to America has been able to achieve the American Dream—there's nothing holding Blacks back from doing the same. They shouldn't demand special treatment."

> "Blacks keep insisting on their so-called rights—but they're forgetting that whites have rights too."

"The past is in the past. Why can't Blacks just get over it?"

"Blacks have a chip on their shoulder."

When I hear people say things like this, I confess it's a struggle to not express my anger. As a member of a religious order, however, I'm expected to rise above negative emotions. Most of all, I do not want to be perceived as an "angry Black man." Whites fear Black anger; they also refuse to acknowledge its legitimacy.

The Western world allows white men to express anger; it may even admire them for their forcefulness. Research studies have found that in a job setting, people tend to see a white man's anger as an indication of his strength, competence, and higher social status. Meanwhile, a woman's or a Black person's anger, the same studies concluded, indicates weakness, lack of self-control, and unprofessionalism.[220] The message is: *Your anger is wrong, and you should either hide it or get rid of it as soon as possible.*

These cultural expectations are not rooted in the psychological definition of anger, however. While what we do with anger can be constructive or destructive, anger itself is neither right nor wrong.

The Meaning of Anger

Psychologists refer to anger as a "secondary emotion"; in other words, we usually have another emotional reaction that comes first, before we experience anger. Emotional pain, including grief, can trigger anger. Many times, however, anger is the first emotion of which we're aware. The primary emotion—fear, hurt, disappointment, sorrow, frustration—hides beneath the anger. Often, we may never be consciously aware of the primary emotion at all.

The Western world, seeing through the lens of dualism, classifies emotions as positive and negative. Joy, affection, and courage, for example, are considered positive emotions, while sadness, anger, and fear are thought of as negative. These categories are ancient: in the first century of the Common Era, the Roman philosopher Seneca wrote that anger is the most "hideous and wild" of all emotions, "a short madness" that is the cause of all wars, slavery, theft, arson, murder, and genocide.[221] Most classical philosophers agreed with Seneca, and early Christian theologians also described anger as a type of mental illness. In the seventeenth century, at the beginning of what the West knows as the *Age of Enlightenment,* René Descartes wrote that anger was a subcategory of hatred,[222] the opposite of love. The obvious conclusion? Good people don't get angry.

But there were cultural exceptions to this. After all, the Hebrew scriptures spoke of God's anger, so clearly, anger couldn't be all bad. Consequently, there was a largely unspoken cultural rule that people in authority were allowed to get angry with those who occupied subjugated roles.[223] Royalty could express anger at their subjects; parents could get angry with their children, husbands were permitted to verbally and physically abuse their wives, and whites were entitled to punish enslaved Blacks. Meanwhile, obedient children did not get angry in response to their parents' anger, pure and righteous women did not fight back against their husbands, and "good Negroes" most definitely did not show anger.

Western society, in one way or another, tends to assign morality (or lack of it) to anger, even anger that is unexpressed—but in reality, anger is amoral. At its most basic level, it is simply a physiological reaction, one aspect of the human fight-or-flight response. While fear prepares our bodies to run away from danger, anger gets us ready to fight. This is why anger is so often equated with aggression. (And why an angry Black man is perceived as dangerous.)

Anger and aggression are not, however, the same. As clinical psychologist Harriet Lerner wrote, "Anger is a signal and one worth listening to. Our anger may be a message that we are being hurt, that our rights are being violated, that our needs or wants are not being adequately met, or simply that something isn't right. . . . Just as physical pain tells us to take our hand off the hot stove, the pain of our anger preserves the very integrity of our self. Our anger can motivate us to say no to the ways in which we are defined by others and 'yes' to the dictates of our inner self."[224]

In 1949, pediatrician and psychoanalyst Donald Winnicott, famous for his study of child development, wrote that our earliest experiences of anger happen when we are newborns screaming our outrage at being thrust from the comfort of our mothers' wombs. Those infant cries were our first self-assertion, our expression of a "clear aim, to live one's life one's own way and not reactively."[225] A decade later, Neo-Freudian

Jacques Lacan said that anger is our response when the real world fails to conform to our idea of what the world *should* be.[226] Psychologically speaking, at the most fundamental level, anger is directly related to our sense of justice.

Yes, anger can make us act in crazy and destructive ways. But isn't that also true at times of joy, love, excitement, courage, and other so-called positive emotions? Unrestrained emotion, of any sort, can be dangerous.

Anger, even rage, has the potential to be a force for positive transformation. Philosopher Myisha Cherry, author of *The Case for Rage,* defines a type of rage that is "focused on what we can do to make things better," that "brings motivation to do something productive: to join an organization, to give money, to sign a petition, to protest in the streets. That's the kind of anger that I believe is virtuous. It's the kind of anger that I see as necessary to really bring about a better world."[227] Back in the thirteenth century, Thomas of Aquinas recognized the same truth, writing, "He who is not angry when there is just cause for anger is immoral. Why? Because anger looks to the good of justice. And if you can live amid injustice without anger, you are immoral as well as unjust."

Black Anger

This was the moral and virtuous rage of Mamie Till-Mobley; it was the rage that inspired the Civil Rights Movement; and today, it is the rage that drives Black Lives Matter. And still, Black anger is not accepted. It is not seen as either an inescapable aspect of Black sorrow or as a necessary and constructive agent of change. As Frederick Douglass wrote in the nineteenth century, "Those who profess to favor freedom, and yet depreciate agitation, are men who want crops without plowing up the ground, they want rain without thunder and lightning. They want the ocean without the awful roar of its many waters."[228]

I recognize, of course, that not all Black anger is transformative and constructive. In Winnicott's discussion of primordial anger, he noted that when an adult responds to a baby's cries, the baby learns the purpose of anger: anger's function is to help her get her needs met. When, however, no one consistently comes to her when she cries, Winnicott wrote, "the individual is always left with some confusion about anger and its expression."[229] Myisha Cherry commented on this distinction, saying, "anger promotes growth and helps define selfhood when it attains the satisfaction it demands—that is, when the needs it expresses are fulfilled. But when those needs go unanswered, it has the opposite effect, implanting confusion and despair in the heart of the self. . . . When a claim for justice is dismissed, anger is liable to take on a life of its own."[230]

I believe this is what has happened all too often within the Black community. Our cries of sorrowing rage have often been ignored. Instead, our righteous anger was demonized, made into something evil and threatening. And so we swallowed our anger. But we could not digest it.

In her book *Killing Rage*, bell hooks described what Black life was like when she was growing up in the South during the days of Jim Crow: "We learned when we were very little that black people could die from feeling rage and expressing it to the wrong white folks. We learned to choke down our rage. This process of repression was aided by the existence of our separate neighborhoods. . . . Within the comfort of those black spaces we did not constantly think about white supremacy and its impact on our social status. We lived a large part of our lives not thinking about white folks. We lived in denial. And in living that way we were able to mute our rage. If black folks did strange, weird, or even brutally cruel acts now and then in our neighborhoods (cut someone to pieces over a card game, shoot somebody for looking at them the wrong way), we did not link this event to the myriad abuses and humiliations black folks suffered daily when we crossed the tracks and did what we had to do with and for whites to make a living. To express rage in that context was suicidal. Every black person knew it. Rage was reserved for life at home—for one another."[231]

Many Blacks seldom express their anger at all. Instead, we experience the effects of chronic stress. When the fight-or-flight response is something we live with constantly rather than a reaction to a specific crisis, the constant flood of adrenaline and noradrenalin no longer does the job it was intended to do. Instead, it becomes destructive, causing elevated heart rate and blood pressure, tense muscles, interruptions in the function of the digestive and immune systems, and difficulties with mental focusing. This is what happens when we are not allowed to process or express our anger: it eats our own bodies.

When society denies Black young people, especially our young men, the right to be angry, they too become vulnerable to a host of physical and psychological symptoms that interfere with their well-being. These include self-defeating attitudes, poor school and job performance, and self-destructive behaviors.[232] Drug-dealing and gang membership are consistently condemned as "evil"—by whites, as well as by many Blacks—but given the realities of many Black men's lives, these may seem to be the only practical answers to their need for income, self-respect, and a sense of belonging.

But this doesn't have to be the case. Studies have shown that when Blacks are able to use their anger to improve a situation or as a form of accepted social communication, they have higher levels of cardiovascular health; they have a greater sense of personal agency and control over their lives; and they experience more stability in their family and job lives.[233] Black students who participate in programs where they are encouraged to express anger in ways that contribute to the well-being of their communities have higher reading scores and tend to obtain better-paying (and legitimate) jobs after they graduate. [234] As Iya eh-hee-may Ehimeora posted on Facebook, speaking to the Black community, "Your body is not a coffin for pain to be buried in. Put it somewhere else." The same applies to our anger (for our anger and our pain are one and the same).

Still, the fact remains that we are entitled to our anger. It is our privilege and our right. It is as much our ancestral birthright as our spirituality, our creativity, and our physical strength.

"My response to racism," said Audre Lorde, "is anger. I have lived with that anger, ignoring it, feeding upon it, learning to use it before it laid my visions to waste, for most of my life. Once I did it in silence, afraid of the weight. My fear of anger taught me nothing. Your fear of that anger will teach you nothing."

But Audre Lorde also believed that anger can be useful. "Focused with precision it can become a powerful source of energy serving progress and change. And when I speak of change, I do not mean a simple switch of positions or a temporary lessening of tensions, nor the ability to smile or feel good. I am speaking of a basic and radical alteration in those assumptions underlining our lives."[235]

When our rage is "metabolized"—in other words, processed into something that can be *used* in a constructive way—it can, according to Myisha Cherry, be a "virtuous channeling" of the power and energy of anger "without the desire to harm or pass pain."[236] South African poet Vuyelwa Maluleke speaks of the "softness" of rage, a rage that is both powerful and vulnerable.[237] This, I believe, is a sacred rage. It is the rage that Mamie Till-Mobley demonstrated. And it is a rage Jesus would have understood.

Rage and Justice

Picture this: Jesus and his friends have just arrived in Jerusalem to celebrate Passover. The streets are so crowded with pilgrims from around the world that it's nearly impossible to get anywhere, but Jesus patiently makes his way through the throng until he reaches the Temple, the center of Jewish worship. He goes inside, longing to spend a few quiet moments in communion with his Father.

The Temple, however, is filled with the noise of people buying and selling, bartering and bickering. It's just as crowded in here as it is outside. Jesus stands for a moment, listening to the bleating and lowing of animals intended for sacrifice. He overhears a conversation between a merchant and a customer; the merchant is clearly cheating the other man.

And Jesus gets mad.

I don't mean he gives a little sigh or rolls his eyes in saintly exasperation, nor does he choke back his anger with a few murmured words of prayer. Nope, Jesus, the Son of God, the One who came to show us what God is like, is royally pissed.

"Get out!" he yells. He runs through the Temple, knocking over the tables where people are exchanging money. "Get out! Get out!"

The Temple is now a mess of overturned tables and people milling about and shouting. Merchants and moneychangers scramble around on the ground, trying to collect their spilled coins.

Then Jesus climbs up on one of the tables still standing and shouts, "This is a house of prayer! A place for communion with God—not a place for greed and cruelty. You have turned my Father's Temple into a house of death. It is meant to be a house of love and life. You have set up barriers against people who worship my Father differently from what you do. You have shut out the women. You are making money from the lives of frightened animals. This should be a place where everyone is welcome, where everything is safe—not just one more place of oppression and death."

Jesus' friends are as startled as anyone else in the crowd; they've never seen their Teacher get so angry. And he's not finished. He leaps from the table and grabs one of the merchants by his robe, dragging him out into the street. Like a madman, Jesus whirls through the Temple, shoving and hitting. Pigeons flutter free from their cages and fly outside into the sunshine. Cattle scatter, their hooves clattering on the stones, and then they too escape through the Temple gates.

Finally, the Temple is almost empty. Only Jesus and his friends remain, along with a few people with physical challenges who were unable to flee from Jesus' anger. Pigeon feathers drift through the air. Jesus is panting. His face is red, and sweat drips from his forehead. He shakes back his hair, takes a deep breath, and says, "All right then. I'm going to pray now. Does anyone here need healing?"[238]

This is not how we expect the Son of God to act. Theologians have struggled to make sense of his behavior since the earliest days of Christianity. Third-century theologian Origen said the story was purely metaphorical: the Temple represents the human soul, while the buyers and sellers symbolize sin. Origen's colleague, John Chrysostom, disagreed, insisting that Jesus acted this way in order to prove his power and Divinity (since God is allowed to be wrathful, while humans should not be). In the eleventh century, Bernard of Clairvaux used the story to justify the violence of the Crusades, and in the sixteenth century, after John Calvin helped burn a "heretic" alive, Calvin said his actions were the same as Jesus' performance in the Temple; Calvin was merely purifying the world of evil. Then, when I looked online to see what modern theologians and preachers are saying, I found these interpretations:

- *We need to cleanse and keep our bodies spiritually pure (so don't practice New Age blasphemy).*

- *Jesus was ending the old Jewish system of animal sacrifice.*

- *Jesus wasn't angry; he was just filled with zeal.*

- *Jesus needed to fulfill the prophecy in the Book of Psalms: "Zeal for your house has eaten me up."* (Do people believe, I wonder, that Jesus had a list of prophecies he kept in his pocket? "All right then," he would have said, "I can check off that one. Now let's see, what's left? Oh right, I have to bruise Satan's head" [Genesis 3:15].)

- *Jesus wanted us to understand that Christianity should not be commercialized.* (Amen, brother.)

- *Jesus was demonstrating that God does not tolerate sin, and all who are sinful will be treated as harshly as Jesus treated the moneylenders.*

- *Jesus didn't actually hit human beings, just the animals.* (Really? Come on.)

- *Money, power, and politics should not be mixed with worship.*

I agree with that last interpretation (and a couple more as well), but I think it is interesting that no one says, "Jesus simply got mad. He was a human being, and he lost his temper." Remember, also, that this incident took place only a few days before his death. If he knew what was coming (and I believe he did), he would have been understandably on edge, his emotions more volatile than usual. At the deepest level, he may even have been angry about death itself, his own as well as the entire setup of human life. He knew that death is not the end, but no one, including Jesus, has ever said it was easy.

But we're uncomfortable saying anything that might imply Jesus had a temper tantrum—because we have so long equated anger (especially the violent rage that Jesus demonstrated) with sin. We believe "good" people need to censor their emotions.

"I'm not convinced," wrote Cole Arthur Riley, "we can tell the truth alienated from the truth of our own emotion." She went on to say, "Apathy is giving up, a surrendering to what is. And it's inherently a disconnecting force. It moves you away from a person. . . . Rage is inherently relational. It might come with fire, but it's still moving toward something, and in proximity, there is hope for reconnection. In this way, anger itself is a form of reconciliation. It is a bringing together." But, she pointed out, "There is a difference between an anger that dominates and an anger that liberates."[239] Jesus' anger liberated. It set animals free from bearing the burden of human sin. It welcomed those who had been previously excluded.

Anger is a finger pointing to injustice. We are not meant to linger there, allowing our anger to turn into hatred, but anger is often the place where we begin. It is the flashing light, the blaring alarm, and the shrieking siren. "Pay attention!" anger shouts. "There's something wrong here! It needs fixing—and it can't wait! For God's sake, there are people *dying*. Don't just sit there shaking your head. *Do* something!"

Our responses to anger's call can divide us—but they can also unite us.

Anger and Unity

As I've said before, Western society is all about dualism—and dualism separates things into opposing pairs. You can't be both black and white or good and bad. You have to be either a man or woman but never both; if you're dead, you can't be alive; and if you're a liberal, you can't be a conservative. You have to choose your side (or accept the "side" given to you) and stick with it. In the twenty-first century, this sense of division is widening, becoming deeper and uglier than ever before. Meanwhile, African culture has always understood that in fact, we *can* be many things at the same time. Reality is not binary.

And justice isn't about taking sides. If I win, you don't have to lose. Instead of competing for resources and attention, we can join forces and cooperate. Instead of pushing and shoving, we can embrace. I don't need to humiliate you in order to feel good about me. The affirmation of my goodness and beauty does not negate yours; instead, we can bring out the best in one another. And I can be angry and still forgive you.

Justice, wrote Cole Arthur Riley, "communicates that . . . [offenders], too, were made for beauty. In justice, everyone becomes more human, everyone bears the image of the divine."[240] She went on to say: "It is easy to think that in injustice only the oppressed have their freedom to gain. In truth, the liberation of the oppressor is also at stake. Whether it's the privilege we've inherited or the space we've stolen, what began as guilt will mutate into shame . . . which is more sinister and decidedly heavier on the soul."[241]

Some of Jesus' last words on earth were a prayer for us all: "may they all be one as You are in Me and I am in You; may they be in Us."[242] This is not a unity that's enforced by power and subjugation. Instead, it's a constantly spinning, readjusting, and course-correcting swirl of creativity that can contain and utilize our anger as it works to repair all that is broken in our world and affirm all who have been oppressed.

"If some have cause to celebrate, join in the celebration," wrote the apostle Paul to the church in Rome. "And if others are weeping, join in that as well. Work toward unity, and live in harmony with one another" (12:15–16 TV). I believe Paul's words also mean that when others are angry at death and injustice, we must share their anger. If we want to affirm Blackness, we cannot distance ourselves from what it means to be Black. We must rage against the Black reality of living under the constant shadow of death. We must no longer evade the past. We cannot pretend that critical race theory is a myth or deny that our racist history still shapes our present reality.

"What unbinds our past is what opens up our future," wrote theologian James Alison.[243] When our identities no longer rely on the binary categories the West offers us, then it becomes possible to face the past in such a way that it no longer restricts our present lives. Instead, something new happens. Our anger finds its purpose. It builds rather than tears down. Life expands with possibility. This is the abundant life Jesus described in the Gospel of John, a life of such fullness and richness that no dualism can divide it, and no linear concept of time can interrupt it. The overflowing bounty of this life sweeps death into life, and transforms anger into love.

Anger and Love

"The opposite of love is not rage," wrote activist Valarie Kaur in her memoir, *See No Stranger*. "The opposite of love is indifference. . . . Anger is the force that protects that which is loved. We cannot access the depth of loving ourselves or others without our rage."

Mamie Till-Mobley's grief and anger would not have existed without the anguished depth of her love for her son. She was strong enough and generous enough that her love cracked open the boundaries that once enclosed her as a private individual—and she invited us all to enter and share her terrible experience of anguish. Her anger created hope where none had existed before.

It is impossible to romanticize the terror and violence of Emmett's murder; rage is the proper response to this hideous narrative of racism. And yet, as Mamie's sorrow became a shout for justice, she created a pathway for love to follow: a pathway to lead us to our true identities, a pathway to lead us home.

Anger is energy—nothing more, nothing less.
It is an energy that, exactly like nuclear energy,
can be used for destruction or to power an entire city.
It is just a question of what we choose it to serve.

—RIENZO COLPO[244]

PRAYER RITUAL

First, create a safe space where you can access your anger without fear it will hurt anyone. To do this, find a time and place where you can ensure you won't be interrupted by anyone's need for help or attention. (If you live in a family or a community, you may need to ask someone to stand guard, helping you protect this time.)

Next, fill a bath (or turn on the shower, if you don't have a bathtub). As the water runs, take a few moments to meditate on the force of its flow. Think

---

of all the ways water can be both destructive and creative. Remember that even when floods destroy farmland, they also bring with them the potential for increased soil fertility once the waters recede. Finally, say these words from the prophet Amos: *Let justice run down like water, and righteousness like a mighty stream* (5:24 NKJV). Place your hands in the flow of water and repeat the verse several times.

Now, step into the bath or shower. As you feel the water on your body, identify any places that feel tense. To identify the sources of your anger, spend a few moments pondering these questions:

> *What do I value that is being threatened?*
>
> *What must be protected and repaired?*

Consciously release the hidden anger your body has stored in its muscles. Imagine your anger flowing into the water, being transformed into a force for justice. Now ask, *What positive action can I take? How can my anger become an expression of love?*

As you step out of the bath or shower, repeat again the words from Amos: *Let justice run down like water, and righteousness like a mighty stream.*

Continue to meditate on the questions you asked—*What do I value that is being threatened? What must be protected and restored? What positive action can I take? How can my anger become an expression of love?*—bringing them with you as you dry yourself, get dressed, and return to your ordinary life. If the answers do not come easily or immediately, don't be concerned. In the days that follow, set aside a few moments each day to return to these questions, allowing them to unfold within you in their own way and time.

When you feel anger building inside you, repeat this ritual. You may even want to practice it daily in your morning shower.

Righteous anger is a tool of justice,
a scythe of compassion, more
than a reactive emotion.
Although it may have its roots deep
in our fight-or-flight desire
to protect those in our family or
group who are threatened,
it is a chosen response and not simply
an uncontrollable reaction.
And it is not about one's own besieged self-image,
or one's feelings of separation,
but of one's collective responsibility
and one's feeling of deep, empowering connection.

—DESMOND TUTU[245]

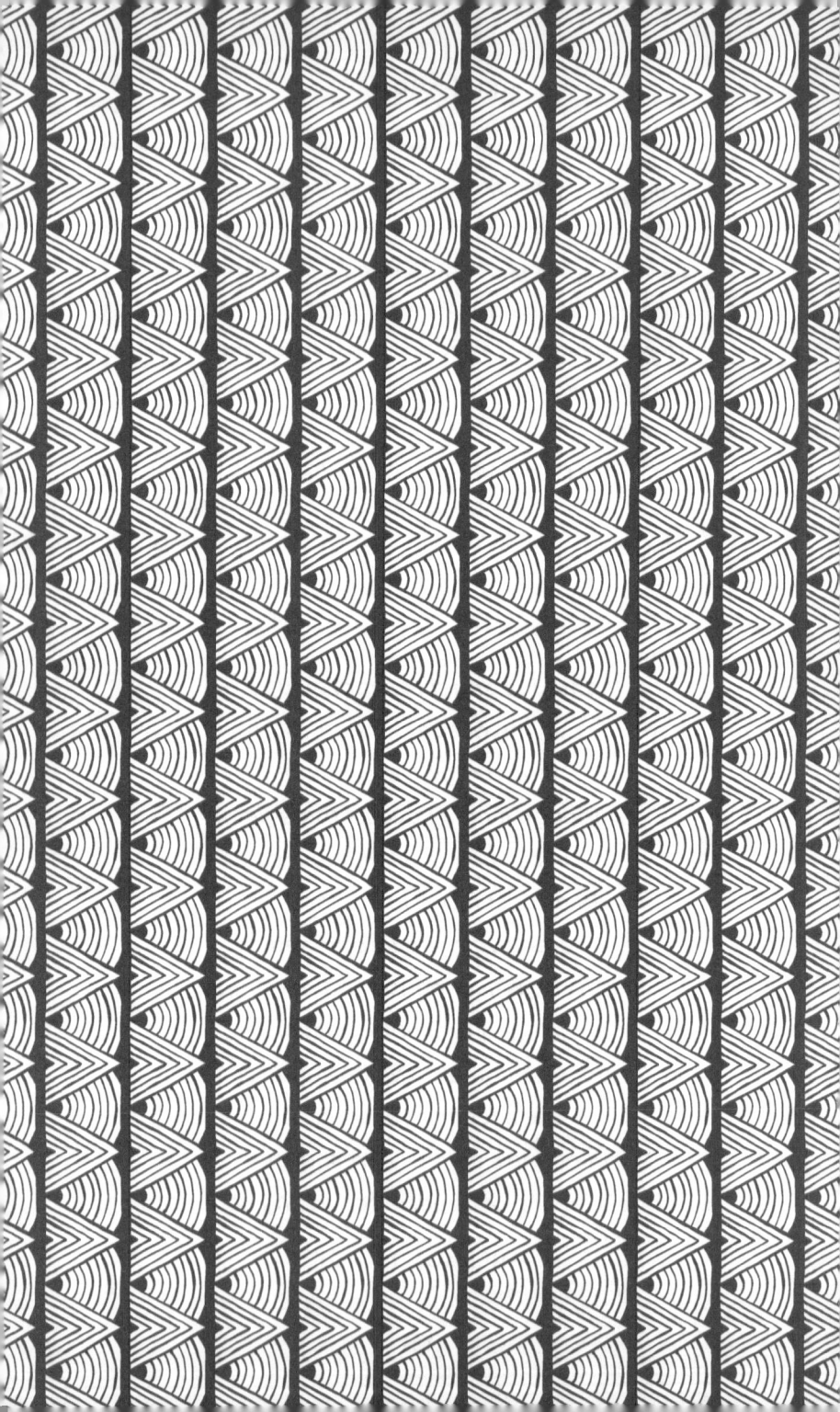

6

CROSSING THE WATERS

DEATH AS AN AFFIRMATION OF IDENTITY

Our aim, even in the face
of the brutally imposed
difficulties of black life,
is cause for celebration. . . .
Celebration is the essence
of black thought.

—FRED MOTEN[246]

Of death the Negro showed but little fear,
but talked of it familiarly and even fondly
as simply a crossing of the waters,
perhaps—who knows?—
back to his ancient forests again.

—W. E. B. DUBOIS[247]

IF YOU'VE NEVER BEEN TO A BLACK FUNERAL— what we call a *homegoing*—you have missed out on one of my people's peak experiences of faith and community. Black funerals celebrate life. They're noisy, lively affairs: we sing, we cry, we dance, we pray, we clap. The old ladies sway their arms, and younger folks move their feet to the beat of the music. There are plenty of tears but few solemn silences; in fact, there are barely any moments when only a single voice is heard. The church overflows with a constant murmur that swells and falls like ocean waves, punctuated by shouts of "Amen!"

There's a popular African proverb that everyone knows these days—*It takes a village to raise a child*—and, as journalist Danielle Broadway has pointed out, "it also takes a village to bring God's children home."[248] Another African proverb, this one from the Twi people of Ghana, is equally applicable: *Death's ladder cannot be climbed by one person.* At a Black homegoing service, everyone works together—with their arms, their legs, their voices, and their hearts—to support the one who is climbing the ladder home. This sorrowful-yet-joyful ritual lasts for hours, creating a "gigantic work of persuasion that affirms that the dead are not dead."[249]

The Homegoing Service

In 2017, when I was in the early stages of my life as a Jesuit, I undertook a journey rooted in the life and teachings of our founder, Ignatius of Loyola: I went on a thirty-day pilgrimage. My superior gave me thirty-five dollars and a one-way bus ticket, and then he sent me on my way with his blessing. For a month, I had to trust God's providence to help me survive. I traveled from Saint Paul, Minnesota, all the way to Key West, Florida. On my way, I stopped in New Orleans, a city so full of black faces that I felt more comfortable than I had in many years.

While I was there, I made friends with a man named Everest Chante. Everest lived on the streets; he lacked four walls and a roof, but he had much to share with me in terms of wisdom and insight. And so, when he invited me to come with him to a funeral, I was happy to go along.

Although I knew no one at the funeral except Everest, I felt instantly at home. I could have been back in Haiti, where I was born. There were differences, of course, but the essential spirit of the New Orleans funeral was the same as I had experienced in my birthplace, as well as in Congo, Cameroon, South Africa, Uganda, and Benin.

The order of the service listed on the program was forgotten, and time was suspended. For those hours that we sang and danced, wept and prayed together, somehow we were in eternity. As theologian James Alison wrote, time itself can be redeemed, transformed into something "capable of participating in the endless abundance of God's life."[250] In that timeless space, we affirmed not only the life of the one who had died but also our own eternal life.

> *Steal away to Jesus,*
> *Steal away, steal away home!*
> *I ain't got long to stay here!*
> *My Lord calls me!*
> *He calls me by the thunder!*
> *The trumpet sound it in my soul!*
> *I ain't got long to stay here!*

Sitting in the pew beside Everest, singing the familiar song about home-going, I realized that in many ways, death is as much a transition point as a wedding or a graduation. During my visits to African countries, I noticed the funeral rites there often contained many of the same symbols as initiation ceremonies. As Kongo teacher and spiritual leader Kimbwandende Kia Bunseki Fu-Kiau explained, "Death is not the end: . . . we die in order to undergo change." He went on to say that dying is an active process that "permits life to flow and regenerate its power/energy."[251] That renewed energy and power were clearly visible in the people gathered here in this church. At this very moment, each song and prayer proclaimed, their loved one was entering a new phase of his life. He was in the momentous passage into his truest home, the home Jesus had prepared for him (John 14:2).

And so, even as his friends and loved ones wept and sometimes groaned in sorrow, they also celebrated the achievement of his life, and they rejoiced in the certainty of his ongoing existence. They understood "that for God death is not"—or at least it does not exist in the way we so often imagine it. "God's loving and sustaining . . . is not interrupted or diminished by death."[252] Their loved one was not dead, because God's love cannot die. Instead, his death was a new beginning, an entry into a deeper relationship with God and with all creation.

As I listened to the memories that were spontaneously shared and the songs that burst from the mouths of loved ones, I took a moment to leaf through the funeral program. I looked at pages of informal photographs that gave me a sense of who this man was; I read about the date and place of his birth, the names of his parents and grandparents and great-grandparents. Unlike whites, who can sign up for Ancestry.com and trace their family line back for many generations, we Blacks seldom have a family tree with deep roots and many branches; slavery eradicated even the memory of those trees. To compensate for this lack, funeral programs record the kinship network that is known. They are another way to connect the past to the present.

I looked up from the bulletin as a woman stood up and sang another familiar song, tears in her eyes:

Swing low, sweet chariot,
Coming for to carry me home,
Swing low, sweet chariot,
Coming for to carry me home.

I looked over Jordan and what did I see
Coming for to carry me home,
A band of angels coming after me,
Coming for to carry me home.

Goosebumps made my arms prickle. I almost thought I heard the rustle of angel wings, and I knew I was in one of those moments when time and eternity intersect. A homegoing service is truly a powerful space, a place for affirming identity and memory, community and faith.

Hours later, when the service was done, Everest and I went outside. He turned to me and said, "Let's make a libation now for our brother."

He pulled a plastic water bottle from his pocket, unscrewed the cap, and then took my hand in his. With his other hand, he poured a little water on the ground, while saying the name of his deceased friend. "Ashé," we both said.

For the Black community, the ancient practice of libation has many meanings. It represents the water that sustains all life upon the Earth, as well as the spiritual water that flows out from a source that will never run dry. According to the West African cosmology I explained in the introduction, water is the medium of connection between death and life, the vehicle that allows us to pass between the worlds. In recent years in America, a libation has also become a way to say, "This Black life matters."

Ashé is a West African word that's often spoken at Black libations. Sometimes used interchangeably with "amen," *ashé* refers to the lifeforce that streams through all reality, a power that makes things happen and produces change. It is the eternal energy that fills both the cosmos and every atom of the physical world. When we say *ashé*, we affirm reality is bigger than what we can perceive with our senses, and we call for the mighty wind of God's Spirit to blow from that world into ours.

Everest and I stood for a moment longer, our hands clasped, our heads bowed, and then he said, "Let's go on down to the repast."

So we joined the line that led down to the church hall in the basement, where a literal feast waited. Aluminum trays filled with barbecued ribs, barbecued chicken, green beans, okra, sweet potatoes, casseroles, baked beans, and macaroni and cheese lined a long table, along with platters of oysters, shrimp, and fried fish; bowls filled with home-baked rolls, fresh greens, potato salad, and cornbread; and a crockpot of steaming gumbo. At the far end of the table were the desserts: red velvet cake, sweet potato pie, banana pudding, and peach cobbler.

Dancing and singing work up a healthy appetite, and we were in need of sustenance—but this homegoing meal satisfied more than physical hunger. As we ate together, we created a circle of fellowship and comfort around the bereaved family. I watched as folks moved around the hall, greeting each other. A flurry of movement centered on an older woman, the widow of the deceased. People held her in their arms, rocking; they wept with her; they shared stories that made everyone laugh, including the widow. And all the while, everyone was eating. Food was the balm that eased their sorrowing hearts; it nourished them with a rich form of love that could be tasted and swallowed.

The bountiful food was also a way to express love and respect for the one who had died. I was reminded of something Tashel Bordere, a University of Missouri professor who studies bereavement, said about Black funerals: "You spare no expense. ... The broader culture may have devalued this person, but the funeral validates this person's worth in a society that constantly tried to dehumanize them."[253]

Although I did not know the deceased, in that moment I felt my kinship with him. I knew that in some way, he was there with us. I experienced what historian Robert Farris Thompson called "the flash of the spirit,"[254] and I knew I was participating in a community who were supporting the deceased as he "crossed the river"—the waters of Kalunga—and entered into the unseen, unknown aspect of the universe.

I looked around the church hall, filled with the noise and laughter of Black people comfortable in their own space, and I sensed I was part of something far larger than this particular gathering, something that stretched back in time through the days of slavery and then all the way to Africa. As anthropologist Melville Herskovits noted, "the funeral is the true climax of life" for those of us who share an African heritage. He went on to say that "no belief drives deeper into the traditions of West African thought." Whatever else we in the Black diaspora have lost of our homeland's customs, our attitudes toward the dead have survived.[255]

This homegoing service, like all other Black funerals I have attended, affirmed life. Sorrow was not denied and plenty of tears were shed, but underneath the sadness lay the certainty that death is not the end. These folks knew their loved one had gone home. Like their African brothers and sisters, they affirmed, in the words of Senegalese philosopher Souleymane Bachir Diagne, that this "human being is alive and strong in his ties to the divinity, to his clan, to his family, to his descendants, as he is strong and alive with his heritage."[256]

What It Means to Go Home

For enslaved Blacks, home meant freedom,[257] the escape from slavery. They had been free back home in Africa, and they trusted they would be free again in an eternal home on the other side of death's life-giving waters. Living in a cramped and hurtful world where whites controlled nearly all aspects of their lives, the thought of going home was more than a wistful daydream. It helped them endure by expanding the "boundaries of their restrictive universe . . . upward until it became one with the world beyond."[258] Home meant hope.

This did not mean enslaved Blacks meekly surrendered to the injustice of this world. Instead, their hope was an energizing force. Belief in home-going restored enslaved Black folk's dignity and identity. It empowered them to escape, to rebel, and to practice tiny daily acts of resistance.

Remember the story I told you in the introduction about the Igbo who flew home to Africa? The Euro-American world dismisses stories like these as mythology or metaphor (at best) or simple-minded superstition, figments of uneducated and ignorant minds (at worst). Either way, such tales are obviously not *true*.

Or are they? Historian Jason Young points out that Black Americans' stories about literal home-going create a tension "between the rise of scientific rationalism, on the one hand, and the persistence of what might be regarded as a spiritual counterculture, on the other." He goes on to say, "For enslaved Africans and their progeny, this counterculture included a wonderfully rich epistemological worldview that insisted on dynamic notions of human agency and possibility. . . . In the flying African, Blacks are proposing not only the existence of a mythic culture hero capable of escaping from slavery and racial oppression, but also the primacy of new worlds and possibilities away from the constraints of slavery and racial oppression."[259]

And, as another historical scholar, Timothy Powell, put it, "The greatest challenge in summoning the ancestors within the margins of the white page of academic discourse is overcoming conventions that inhibit the ability to speak of the spirits of the dead as being active agents in the story."[260]

Once upon a time, whites were also at home in a world of magic and miracle, a world rich with meaning and promise. The Celtic people of the British Isles, for example, knew full well that the world of spirits, including the ancestors, was but a thin membrane away from our world—and in certain circumstances, the membrane could easily be crossed from either direction. The Scientific Revolution, however, led the Western world to different wonders, ones that were achieved through the power of technology. What the Scientific Revolution began in the sixteenth century, the Industrial Revolution furthered in the nineteenth, severing Euro-Americans' relationship with a larger, more mysterious world. The human realm expanded exponentially in some ways, but it also was flattened. We assumed reality was only that which could be perceived by our five senses; any reference to an invisible, intangible world was considered fantasy.

Western society traded wonder for what it called knowledge—and most Westerners lost their sense of belonging to a many-layered reality, a reality rich with possibility and connection. No longer aware they were enmeshed in a vast, breathing network of life, they found themselves instead in a lonely, sterile environment. The multidimensional world of connection and hope was no longer their home.

What Is Home?

As part of my graduate-school research, I spent eighteen months working in a community clinic in the Republic Democratic of Congo. On my last day there, early in the morning, a group of twenty-some women came to my office. (My office was also my bedroom, my dining room, and my living room.) I woke up to the sound of their laughter and their singing.

"P'tit Doc," they called to me through the window, "we see you in there! Come out now!"

I smiled, got out of bed, and still in my pajamas, went outside into the early-morning light.

The woman formed a circle and placed me at the center. They prayed, sang, danced, laughed, and hugged me. They told all sorts of stories about me, which caused even more laughter.

Finally, they asked one of the girls to go next door and borrow five francs to buy a gallon of water.

When the girl came back with the water, the women's leader poured a little on the ground, a libation that affirmed our connection to the Earth and to the Spirit. Then each one of the women took a sip; when it was my turn, I did as well. All twenty-some of us shared the gallon of water, affirming the life-giving bonds of relationship between us. I realized this was the exact same ceremony they had enacted a few days earlier for an older woman as she was dying. In Africa, saying goodbye to the dying is no different from saying goodbye to someone who is leaving for another country. Life continues in both cases, affirmed by the sharing of water, even while the separation causes sadness.

After the gallon jug was empty, one of the women said, "P'tit Doc, you are leaving us—but you will always be with us. You are ours. You are always welcome here. This is your home, and you will always be here."

This experience has warmed my heart ever since. Despite the immense geographical distance that now separates me from the community where I worked in Congo, I still carry this home with me wherever I go. It continues to support me; it assures me I am strong and capable, even when my surroundings try to tell me otherwise. It tells me I am connected; I belong; I am loved. As a Jesuit, I cannot own a house. I will likely live in many different places during the course of my lifetime. And yet now, I still experience a deep sense of home.

The word *home* can mean different things, of course, to different people. Researchers who studied the African meaning of home found that it included these definitions:

- *Home means the cradle—the source of deepest identity.*

- *Home means the abode of the ancestors, the place that roots people and gives them stability.*

- *Home means comfort and safety; it's a space where people experience peace.*

- *Home is the place where physical and emotional needs are met.*[261]

From an African perspective, a home is not necessarily four walls and a roof. Nor is it a place to store one's personal possessions. Those ideas about home express the Euro-American emphasis on individuality and materialism. Instead, from an African perspective, you could take the four definitions listed above and replace the word *home* with *community*: community is the source of deepest identity; community roots people and gives them stability; community creates a space where people are safe and comfortable; and community is what ensures that physical and emotional needs are met. (I am reminded now of my friend Everest Chante: he lacked a roof, but he did not lack a home, for he was comfortable in the fierce exuberance of New Orleans' streets.)

What does home mean to you? French philosopher Gaston Bachelard wrote that the home is "the topography of our intimate being . . . how we take root, day after day, in a 'corner of the world'; a "dream" that "deepens to the point where an immemorial domain opens up for the dreamer of a home beyond [humanity]'s earliest memory."[262] Our sense of home, psychologists say, begins with the womb, the site of our deepest identity, our most primitive experience of security. As adults, many of us long for a physical space where we can reexperience that primeval sense of safety and selfhood.

We can never return to a physical womb, of course, nor can we return to Eden, the idyllic home of humanity described in the Hebrew scriptures. Nevertheless, the yearning for home twines through many of the Western world's stories. In Homer's *Odyssey,* for example, the entire plot focuses on Ulysses' difficult journey home. *The Wizard of Oz* has a similar storyline: Dorothy's adventures take place along a linear path homeward, which she finally reaches as she chants, "There's no place like home." In the children's book and movie *The Incredible Journey,* the struggles of two dogs and a cat focus on the same home-going motif, and the novel *Cold Mountain* by Charles Frazier describes the dangers a wounded Confederate soldier encounters on his way home to his wife. The movie *Vivarium,* an odder and more pessimistic version of this archetypal pattern, tells the tale of a young couple looking for the perfect home who find themselves trapped in a labyrinth of identical houses.

According to Jungian psychology, the archetype of the home symbolizes the self, and so the journey home is actually the story of the search for identity and individual selfhood.

"This crucial connection between finding oneself and finding a home in the universe," wrote Jungian blogger Brian Collinson, "is a perennial, archetypal theme in human storytelling."[263] But is it a human archetype—or merely a Western archetype? The women in Congo welcomed me into a home I carry with me wherever I go. This sense of home does not depend on either linear time or three-dimensional space, for it exists in a larger reality. In the African mind, the symbolism of home has nothing to do with establishing and protecting one's individuality, for home is about connection and community.

James Baldwin wrote that home is "not a place but an irrecoverable condition."[264] In other words, home has little to do with a geographical space. Instead, home may be whatever gives us a sense of spiritual and psychological rootedness. "Go back to where you started," Baldwin wrote, "or as far back as you can, examine all of it, travel your road again and tell the truth about it. Sing or shout or testify or keep it to yourself: but *know whence you came*."[265]

In *Song of Solomon* by Toni Morrison, the protagonist, Milkman Dead, does exactly what Baldwin recommended: he seeks out his ancestral roots. Milkman's character is stunted by racism. As a child, he was teased and beaten, and now, as an adult, he bears the generational scars, physical and emotional, of centuries of oppression. Western materialism has infected his soul, he is alienated from his loving family, and he is so different from the rest of his community that he even walks against the flow of traffic on the sidewalk. When he heads South to seek his roots, at first, he is motivated only by greed. Along his journey, however, he encounters many dangers and adventures, and gradually, he begins to change.

So far, this story sounds a bit like the Western world's archetypal *Odyssey*—Milkman even encounters a woman named Circe—but the ending of the story is far different. In his ancestral home in Virginia, Milkman learns he is descended from an African shaman who was able to fly. This knowledge fills him with joy and a sense of purpose he had previously lacked. In the final scene, Milkman claims his own ancestral power—and leaps into the air, "for now he knew . . . : if you surrendered to the air, you could ride it."[266]

Morrison does not tell us what happens next. Like the story of the seventy-five Igbo, the ending depends on your own beliefs: Did Milkman fall to his death—or did he soar through the sky into a more joyful reality? Is his story one of tragedy and futility—or triumphant hope?

Home and Death

Ultimately, how we think of home is related to how we think of death. If our home is a physical place, then we are constantly at risk of losing it. A fire may burn it down, or financial difficulties may force us to surrender it to the bank. Thieves may invade it and rob us of our possessions. Eventually, death will take us forever away from our homes, casting us vulnerable and afraid into a dark void, while our homes are left behind, like the inanimate, empty shells of dead sea creatures.

In the Gospel of Luke, Jesus tried to explain the emptiness of this attitude:

Someone in the crowd said to Jesus, "Teacher, my father died, but now my brother is claiming the family home as his own. Tell him to divide the inheritance with me."

Jesus said, "Be careful! Real life has nothing to do with possessions." Then he told them a story. "Once upon a time, there was a rich man who just kept getting richer and richer. He used his wealth to buy fine furniture, expensive artwork, and closets full of fancy clothes. His house soon was crowded with his many possessions.

"'Hmm,' he said to himself one night while he lay on his bed. 'I have so many things but nowhere to put them all. What am I going to do?' After he had thought for a moment, he said, 'I know—I'll tear down my house and build an even bigger house in its place. Then I will have space enough to store all my things.' He chuckled. 'When I lie on my bed then, I'll say to myself, "Look at all your things! Lay back now and take it easy. Be as lazy as you want. For the rest of your life, you can eat, drink, and be merry."'

"But then, out of the silence of his bedroom, he heard the Creator's voice speaking to him. 'Foolish man!' the Creator said. 'Tonight your breath will be taken from you. And then what will happen to all these things you're hoarding? What good will they do you? Your home won't be yours anymore—because you'll be dead.'"

Jesus looked out at the crowd. "This is what happens to people who cling to their wealth. They think that material things can enrich their souls, but all the while, their souls are poor and empty. They don't understand that all true riches are contained within the Creator."

After the crowd had gone, Jesus said to his friends, "Did you understand what I was saying? I'm telling you—stop being so worried about the physical details of your lives. You spend so much time thinking about what you will eat and what you will wear. But life is more than that, and your bodies are far more beautiful than the clothes you put on them. Look at those birds over there. They don't earn money, they don't buy things, and they don't build houses where they collect belongings. And yet the Creator gives them everything they need."[267]

When enslaved Africans heard this story, they understood what Jesus was saying far better than their white enslavers did.

Africans and those of us in the African diaspora are not immune, of course, to the lure of material goods and this-world wealth. Nevertheless, in the extravagant celebration of a homegoing service, we acknowledge that our real wealth comes from our community. Within that collective warm embrace are contained everything we truly need: laughter, music, dancing, shared food, and most of all, love. This is a home we will never lose, for the community exists outside time and space. In this world's phase of existence, we suffer pain and sorrow and injustice—but at the same time, we are held safe within the community that is our home. Death cannot sever our connections to the network of life.

Why? Because death is merely the pivotal moment when we learn to fly. Then, as we leap into the air—naked, trusting only in the Creator—our wings unfurl, ready to carry us into the Mystery that lies ahead. As Sojourner Truth said as she approached her death: "I am not gonna die, honey. I'm going home like a shooting star."

The cause for [Black] celebration
turns out to be the condition of possibility.

—FRED MOTEN[268]

Some glad morning when this life is over, I'll fly away!
To a home on God's celestial shore, I'll fly away!
When I die, hallelujah, by and by, I'll fly away!
Just a few more weary days and then I'll fly away
To a land where joy shall never end, I'll fly away.
I'll fly away, oh Glory, I'll fly away!
When I die, hallelujah, by and by, I'll fly away!

—AFRICAN AMERICAN SPIRITUAL

MEDITATION EXERCISE

Ironically, most Christians, despite their belief in eternal life, tend to avoid the thought of death, but Buddhist teaching has always recognized that meditation on our own death can have powerful spiritual and psychological benefits. The exercise that follows is based on Buddhist meditation practices.[269]

Find a quiet place where you will not be disturbed, and sit in a comfortable chair or on the floor with your legs crossed. Dim the lights. Set a candle and matches or a lighter near to you on the floor or table, but do not light the candle at this time. Instead, close your eyes and focus on the sensations in your body. Feel the pull that gravity has on your entire body, connecting it to the Earth. Then shift your attention to specific parts of your body:

- Feel the heaviness of your legs and hips as they rest on the floor or chair; acknowledge that gravity pulls at the bones and muscles of your legs and buttocks. Rest here in this heaviness for a few moments.

- Now shift your attention to your abdomen. Sense the Earth's pull on the inner organs within your belly—your intestines, your bladder, your sex organs, your kidneys, your liver, your stomach.

- Let your attention rise into your chest cavity. Focus on the breath that enters and leaves your lungs, expanding and contracting your ribcage. Notice that gravity pulls at your heart and lungs as it does the rest of your body.

- Next pay attention to the bones in your arms and shoulders. Feel the heaviness in your arms; notice that gravity is urging each part of your body to move closer to the Earth.

- Finally, feel the muscles in your neck supporting your skull. Feel the density and weight of your cranium as it rests on the spinal column.

Dwell for a few moments in the awareness that your body is a physical substance connected to the Earth, pulled by gravity toward the Earth's center.

Now ask yourself: *What is it within me that perceives these sensations? What is the receptor that coordinates these perceptions? Is there something within me that stands separate from the physical body?* Some Buddhists refer to this separate thing as the "light body" (as opposed to the "heavy body" that must be obedient to gravity). The light body is the part of you that recognizes sounds and sights, scents and flavors and textures, and makes sense of them, finds meaning in them.

Now return your attention to your breath. As the air moves in and out of your nostrils, think of it as a silken strand that stitches your heavy body to your light body. Your breath allows an invisible awareness and identity to remain in the solid material of your body. Each breath is precious, creating a delicate balance between the visible world around you and the invisible world of perception and meaning that's "within" you.

Focus on each breath individually, as though it were the one-and-only breath, as though no breaths preceded it, and no breaths will follow it. Take the dimensions of life and spirit and sensation into your body as you inhale; welcome this single breath, delight in it, celebrate it. And then, let each breath go. Surrender this connection between the physical world and the larger, mysterious, invisible world. Imagine that each breath is your last; accept that as you surrender each lungful of air, your connection between the heavy body and the light body is severed.

Let go of the breath. Don't hold on to it. Don't be attached to it. Don't think about the previous breath, and don't anticipate another breath. Consciously surrender your desire to focus on breath as something linear, something that happens again and again throughout time, and instead, let yourself "die" into the space at the end of your exhale.

If fear or anxiety rises into your consciousness, let it go as well. Let go of your plans, your regrets, your hopes. Don't hold on to anything. Float free. Feel the vastness of the space between each breath. Sense that you are not alone here in this immense Mystery; even as you escape gravity's grip on your flesh, you are held and cherished.

In the tiny space between breaths, acknowledge that this could truly be your last breath. As any fears, resistance, or sorrows arise in reaction to this thought, let them gently fall away. Other thoughts will emerge, but again, dismiss them, with firm courtesy. Those thoughts belong to the heavy body. Any thought that comes to your mind is not relevant in this bright, timeless space between breaths. Here, all is Mystery. The only certainty is Love.

Now, shift your focus away from the breathless space of surrender that comes after each exhalation and turn your attention to each inhalation. Imagine that each one is the first breath of life. Each one attaches body and spirit, heavy body and light body. Each one is completely new. With each inhalation, let yourself be born anew into your body. Awareness is joined to form. Spirit submits to gravity.

With each inhalation, follow Jesus' commandment: be born again. Be born into this physical world of pain and oppression, and bring with you the light and healing from the "spiritual world." You are being born to bring kindness and peace, healing and justice into the world. This is why you were born: to learn and to teach, to love and be loved, to help others and to accept others' help. Each breath empowers you for this work.

Now open your eyes. Light the candle and look straight into the flame. This flame represents the Divine light you carry within you. As you look into the flame, reorient yourself within your body. Claim your own Divine identity. Thank God for the light She sheds into your heart and mind. As you blow out the candle to end your time of meditation, say out loud, "I thank you, Spirit of Life, for my light, my life, my identity. I trust you to hold me in life and in death and on into still more life."

In the hours and days ahead, whenever your sense of your sacred identity wavers, whenever it feels attacked or diminished by the world's sorrow and suffering, take a moment to once again focus on your breath. Reground yourself in the awareness that each breath opens into both life and death. Each breath stitches your physical identity to your spiritual identity. Each breath affirms that God is both within you and without.

When I discover who I am,
I'll be free.

—RALPH ELLISON[270]

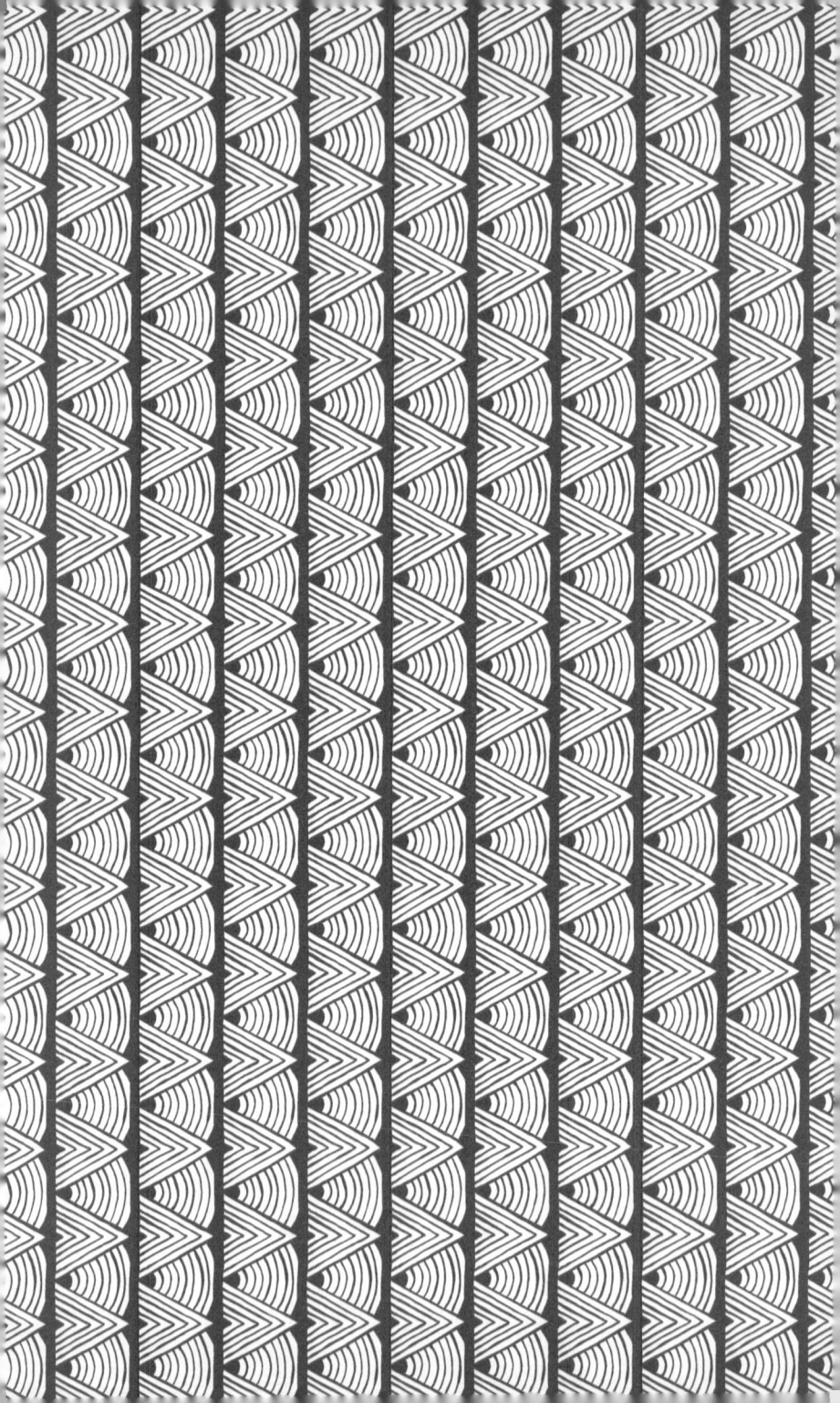

7

THE FEAR OF HELL, THE HOPE OF HEAVEN

DEATH AND THE CALL TO COMMUNITY

When I get to heaven,
going to be at ease.
Me and my God gonna do as we please.
Gonna chatter with the Father,
argue with the Son.
Tell 'em 'bout the world I just came from.

—AFRICAN AMERICAN SPIRITUAL

I WAS RAISED IN A GOOD BAPTIST FAMILY (both my mother and my grandmother were ministers), and I grew up with the assumption that people who follow Jesus will end up in heaven after they die, while people who don't will most likely go to hell. This view of the afterlife is based on the Western schema of dualism: good versus bad, white versus black, life versus death, heaven versus hell. There's no room for ambivalence within this schema. There's also no room for tolerance, hospitality, and inclusion. It never occurred to me this might be a racist way of thinking.

Then, during my time in the Republic Democratic of Congo, I encountered a different understanding of the afterlife. Instead of the either-or structure of life and death, heaven and hell, the BaKongo people see life as being like the spiral of a conch shell. This spiral contains what we consider to be "death," but the BaKongo define death differently than we do. For them, the realm of life and the realm of death are both equally "alive," illuminated by the same sun, though they are separated by the great sea that is both a barrier and a passageway. At the rising and setting of the sun, the two realms exchange day and night, just as at the "death" of our bodies, we exchange the realm of life for the realm of death. Meanwhile, life itself—the state of active being—never ends. What we in the Western world see as death is merely a transition point in life's cycle.

There's a problem here in what I've been trying to write: I'm using Western vocabulary to explain African thinking, but in doing so, I squeeze African concepts into definitions that are contrary to their true meaning. A word like *afterlife,* for example, makes no sense in a worldview where life never ends. Words like this also reveal that while Euro-American Christianity claims to believe in eternal life, it nevertheless sees death as the destroyer that ends life as we know it.

In the dualistic Western world, you can be dead, or you can be alive, but you can't be both. Meanwhile, in the African mindset, reality has a simultaneous unity: an individual can be both "dead" and "alive." When Simon Bockie, an African researcher, interviewed a BaKongo woman who had had a near-death experience, he found that since "her existence was never interrupted, she rejected the use of the verb 'to die' in our talk because, as she often put it, 'How can I claim that I was dead when in reality I never was? I moved from one place to the other without any interruption.'"[271]

And so, we need to define our terms more clearly. Death and racism are synonymous, we have said, just as life and community are. The type of death we are referring to here separates people, severing the connections between them. It annihilates communities. This is not the death that is a doorway into new life, for racism = separation = death = destruction. Community, however, according to the African understanding, gives life, a life that never ends, even if it changes locations. The cessation of a physical body's life process, while it may be painful for those who are still embodied, is not destruction. The essence of each person can never be destroyed. It is held safe within the community.

This is not to say that African spirituality leaves God out of the picture. A common assumption of Western Christianity might be that the human community (the "world") and the Divine are at odds; we must leave the one in order to reach the other. For the African, however, a community cannot exist outside God—and God cannot exist outside community.

"God does not die, so I cannot die," is an African proverb that points to the understanding that the apostle Paul expressed: In God, we live and move and have our being (Acts 17:28). In God, we *live.* Community = life = God. Since God cannot die, neither can I.

And neither can you. No one is excluded.

Heaven and Hell as Racist Concepts

If heaven is a reward for being good in this life, then by its very nature, it's exclusionary. The "good people" go to heaven, the "bad people" are kept out. It's a strictly segregated structure— and since this structure was built by white men, it's pretty easy to guess what the good people look like. A sign hangs over heaven's door: "No bad [Black] people allowed." Is this a biblical concept? Generations of Christians have believed so.

It wasn't always this way, however. Origen, a third-century Christian theologian from Africa, described human life in a very African way: as a spiral. According to Origen, God creates us, we fall away from unity with God and others, and through Christ, we return to unity. We go through this cycle over and over, following a spiral path that returns us again and again to the same spot, while always taking us higher with each cycle. Origen called this cycle *apokatastasis*—moving away from a state of ruin toward renewal (Acts 3:21). Just as all things were one at creation, so shall all things return to oneness. Heaven is all-inclusive.

Humans, however, have an ancient tendency to form in-groups, while viewing others as belonging to out-groups. People in an in-group identify with each other, while they often perceive those outside their group as threats. They don't feel the same empathy for out-group members that they do toward those in their own group. They may even feel justified in treating those in the out-group with cruelty.[272] Jesus said he had come to put an end to in-group–out-group thinking, opening the door from one ethnic group—the Jews, who called themselves the *Chosen People*—and inviting the rest of the world to enter. "There is neither Jew nor Gentile, neither slave nor free, nor is there male and female, for you are all one in Christ Jesus," wrote Paul (Galatians 3:28 NIV). And yet, very quickly, Christians began to think of themselves as the new Chosen People, the in-group, while all others fell into the out-group.

Only a century after Origen, Augustine of Hippo (sadly, another African) sent the Western church off on a tangent that would eventually lead it far from the teachings of its founder. As part of his theology, Augustine envisioned the connection between humans and the Divine as being like the master-and-slave relationship. Jesus, Augustine wrote, "is the true and eternal slavemaster," and he went on to say, "What a debt of gratitude rich people owe to Christ for bringing peace to their households!"[273] The peace he was speaking of required that Christian women obey their

husbands, while Christian enslaved people had to be obedient to their enslavers. God, according to Augustine, sure
did love him a good hierarchy.

Following this line of thinking, Divine reality is not
a mesh of life, where all are equally valued and needed. It's
a lot more like a henhouse where the pecking order rules.
According to the logic of the henhouse, some individuals
are expendable. Augustine endorsed this belief, but it was
not enough for him that some people might be destroyed;
he also wanted them tormented. God will keep the bodies of
the damned from disintegrating in hell's fires, he wrote, so
that they "can persist in the torments of everlasting fires." He
added, "It is possible for living creatures to remain alive in
the fire, being burnt without being consumed, feeling pain
without incurring death; and this by means of a miracle of
the omnipotent Creator."[274] This very strange understanding of God's nature is predicated on the need to keep some
people out of heaven. Heaven is the ultimate in-group, and
hell is the supreme out-group (people who deserve to be
eternally punished). Since members of the out-group were
destined for eternal destruction, Christians believed they
were also justified in fighting and killing them—and enslav-
ing them. This, in their minds, was the world as Divine
justice willed it to be.

This concept of justice may have made sense within the
medieval European model of human life, but it makes no sense
within most twenty-first-century definitions of justice, where
condemning even the worst criminal to endless torment is

clearly cruel and inhumane. And yet, even as Christians speak of God as being infinitely merciful, they continue to describe a petty, angry Deity who needs to be appeased with offerings and sacrifices. As an Ignatian, I have learned to read the Bible as an invitation to intimate relationship (with Christ and with his Body, a community that is not limited by time or space). From this perspective, "hell" is not a place of permanent punishment but rather the consequence of separating ourselves from the interwoven bonds of relationship. Meanwhile, the invitation to connection remains forever open.

And yet I still read some Christian ministers trying to justify hell by squirming their way through the following evasions:

- *We may not understand, but our faith requires us to accept without question.*

- *God loves us so much that he gives us free choice, which means we must be free to choose hell.*

- *God's concept of justice is different from ours, and we just have to accept that in faith.*

This circular reasoning goes nowhere, of course. I almost prefer those ministers who come right out and admit there's no love in their version of hell. "There is not a drop of love of God in the pit of hell," said one of these ministers. "It is filled up with the wrath and the vengeance of the almighty God."[275]

In Dante's *Paradise Lost*, we find a sign over the gateway to hell that reads:

Through me is the way to the city of woe,
Through me is the way to eternal pain,
Through me is the way to a lost people.
Justice moved my great Creator
Divine Power made me,
the Supreme Wisdom and the Primal Love.
Before me, nothing else was created
nothing, but the eternal and I last eternally.
Abandon all hope, you who enter here.

We owe much of our modern-day notion of hell to Dante. The imprint of his imagery is far deeper in the Euro-American mind than is the relatively vague biblical concept of *sheol*—and entrenched within this imagery is the idea that *segregation* is essential to the Divine plan for humanity. Before anything else was created, according to Dante, God's "love" created a place where "lost people" could be warehoused, a place of eternal oppression and suffering, a place where hope cannot survive. In my mind, it's an oxymoron to say Divine love could make a place of hopelessness, and yet somehow, generation after generation has managed to believe Christian love can exist hand in hand with division, oppression, and exclusion.

Nietzsche, I believe, saw things more clearly when he said the sign over the gate of Dante's heaven should have announced: "I too was created by eternal hate."[276] The traditional Christian idea of heaven is so "pure," so homogeneously "good," that there is no room for black sheep and outcasts, no space where refugees and exiles can be accommodated, no room for hospitality, no room for love. (In fact, it's rather like some Americans' idea of the United States.)

Back in slavery times, when enslaved Blacks converted to Christianity, whites were reluctant to think they would have to share heaven with them. Consequently, whites grudgingly came up with a segregated concept of heaven, where Blacks were tolerated in a separate, inferior region of the celestial grounds. One white minister told a Black congregation: "You slaves will go to heaven if you are good, but don't ever think that you will be close to your mistress and master. No! No! there will be a wall between you; but there will be holes in it that will permit you to look out and see your mistress as she passes by. [277] (Apparently, this man truly believed a glimpse of the white woman who had enslaved them would comfort deceased Blacks.) Even after slavery ended, white Christians assumed they would not have to look at black faces in the after-life. To make sure Blacks weren't confused about their proper destination in the heavenly realm, they were usually buried in separate burial grounds. Racism was so embedded in the white mindset that many people could not imagine a world where it did not exist, even in the afterlife.

Blacks, however, knew better. Whites, they said, had "turned heaven inside out."[278] Despite the slavery-endorsing version of the Bible that white men preached to them, enslaved Blacks discovered for themselves the *real* meaning of the gospel. When they spoke of the coming judgment, they knew exactly who required judgment—their enslavers.

I'm a-gonna tell you 'bout the comin' of the judgment,
Fair thee well, fair thee well.
I'm a-gonna tell you 'bout the comin' of the judgment,
Fair thee well, fair thee well.
There's a better day a-comin',
Fair thee well, fair thee well.
In that great a-gettin' up morning. . . .
So glad, chariot's a-comin'
And I don't wanna be left out!
In that great a-gettin' up morning,
Fair thee well, fair thee well.

Instead of acquiescing to the white man's convoluted and purely "spiritual" Christianity, Blacks simply took Jesus at his word.

I've been 'buked and I've been scorned,
I've been 'buked and I've been scorned,
Children, I've been 'buked and I've been scorned,
Tryin' to make this journey all alone.
Jesus died to set me free,
Jesus died to set me free,
Children, Jesus died to set me free,
Nailed to that cross on Calvary.

Already-and-Not-Yet Reality

When enslaved Blacks sang about their freedom in Christ, they were not singing about something abstract and intangible. Jesus died to set them free—and they saw no difference between the "spiritual" and "literal" meanings of freedom.

I often read that enslaved Blacks used "heaven" only as a code word, to hide their true beliefs and their rebellion. But this assumption fails to understand the African mindset. For enslaved Blacks, the white man's attempt to separate the tangible world from a transcendent realm seemed utterly nonsensical. Instead, Blacks firmly grasped the unity of Christ's *now-but-not-yet* realm of heaven. From a Western perspective with its linear model of time, now-but-not-yet theology is a paradox; for those who shared an African heritage, it was a familiar reality. They understood that time can participate in eternity.

Race in the World to Come

The Christian heaven is usually thought of as a place of harmony. According to this line of thought, somehow, when we die, all differences will be automatically wiped away. In our modern image of heaven, neither race nor racism exists there; they simply disappear, along with all other forms of pain and suffering.

I once performed an experiment where I asked people to draw their idea of heaven. I was interested to see that most white people imagine heaven (even the liberal ones who pride themselves on their antiracism) populated only by white faces. When I asked questions about this, the conclusion I reached was that these whites accepted that Blacks would be allowed in heaven—but they assumed that everyone would look the same (and although they did not verbalize this, the assumption was that black skin gets painted white in heaven). Ellen G. White, the founder of Seventh Day Adventism, came right out and said this in a sermon she intended to comfort and encourage oppressed Black folk: "look forward to heaven," she told them, "because there we will all be White."[279]

Glory hallelujah!

Nathan Placencia explained why this is not an accurate understanding of the eternal realm: "Races might not exist in the afterlife, but racial identities do. . . . [This] is required because racial identities facilitate the forgiveness and reconciliation needed to realize the vision of harmony promoted in the Christian tradition. . . . This preservation is preferable, because the existence of racial identities in the afterlife avoids identity erasure and homogeneity."[280]

Wiping racism away in heaven, without the hard work of reconciliation, restoration, and forgiveness, is a little like whites who think racism can be solved by being "color blind." (It's also a little like a child who thinks she can't be seen because her head is inside a paper bag.) This understanding not only denies the reality of the Black experience, but it also allows whites to believe they can escape a confrontation with the life-sapping wounds racism has dealt their own hearts.

Artist Nick Cave's installation at the Massachusetts Museum of Contemporary Art titled *Until* also poses the question: *Is there racism in heaven?* A reviewer of the piece said this: "If in our idealized imagination, we think of ourselves as beings who have [in heaven] forgotten racialized police violence and its precursors in Jim Crow and slavery, then we are imagining

beings who are not us—ones that do not resemble us suffi-
ciently to count as continuous with ourselves. To project ourselves in heaven without the memory of racism is to think of the
effects of racism as something detachable, something that could
fall away, leaving our identity intact. Could one live in heaven
and not remember Sandra Bland[281] and the circumstances that
ended her life? What is at stake in wanting to imagine oneself
as such a being?"[282]

Exactly. We cannot use modern Christianity's understanding of a spiritual life-after-death as an excuse to avoid the
cost of racism. Instead, we need the firm African conviction
that death is only a transition point into more life, greater life.
If anything, more will be asked of us then, not less—and it
will be *real,* not an ethereal fantasy; a continuation of this life's
challenges, not a remote and hazy escape from life.

Most of all, it will be community, a place where we are
each seen, and *no one* is overlooked or excluded.

The Community of Heaven

The people I encountered in Congo were suffering from years of
war, a war that in large part was caused by the divisive greed of
Western industry. Meanwhile, the rest of the world was barely
aware that four million people had died in Congo since 1998.
This was just another example of the death that is racism: *Black
lives don't matter.* They matter so little they aren't even seen, and
their deaths do not register.

As I worked with the people of Congo—women who had
been widowed and raped, children who had been orphaned,

people who were being forced to encounter death every day thanks to a never-ending war—I sometimes felt I was drowning in a monstrous sea of death. How could I help these people who had lost so much?

Then, after I had been in Congo for about six months, one of the women in the community called to me: "P'tit Doc, come here! We want to pray with you and receive you into the community."

"After all this time, hasn't the community already accepted me?"

"No," she said. "You need to be seen and received by all of us. Everyone needs to see you, as we see God in you."

What this woman was talking about is similar to a concept endorsed by humanist psychologist Carl Rogers: *unconditional positive regard*. In order to be truly ourselves, we need to be *seen* with total acceptance. This is one of the gifts of community, one we each need if we are to come into a full realization of our own identities. Along similar lines, psychologist Jacques Lacan described an infant's sense of sight as the first witness to her own existence, while at the same time, through sight, the infant is invited into relationship with the world around her; it is only through seeing and being seen by other that she develops a sense of "I." Lacan concluded that ultimately, we are who we are only in relation to other people.[283]

Ubuntu: *I am because you are.*

This understanding opened in me a space where I could continue to grow. I realized I had been assessing the people of Congo from a Western perspective: as people who had "lost" so much because death had "stolen" it from them. These people were suffering immense physical and emotional pain, this was true, but they were not diminished. Their identities were held strong and safe by the community that still contained them, despite the years of war and death they had endured.

I almost wrote, "Their *spiritual* identities were held strong," but then again, I would be thinking with a Western mind, separating spiritual from psychological or sociological. The African mind sees no such distinction, *for all of life is spiritual.* The idea that our spiritual identity might be different from our social identity would make no sense to the African way of thinking. It would be a little like saying that breathing is not just as much a life process as digestion and blood circulation.

When theologian and scientist Ilia Delio describes the community of life using the language of quantum physics, she might very well be also describing the African understanding: "Each particular person may be likened to a 'particle' in which our 'radiating centers' are 'waves' of relatedness. At the most fundamental level, we are webs of energy, fields within fields, which means we are always connected to everything that comprises the 'world.' We never act alone or think alone because the fundamental stuff of life is intrinsically relational; in our cosmic roots we are already one. . . . We are not simply human beings; we are interbeings interacting in the great cosmic evolution of the Whole."[284]

And that, I believe, is what Jesus meant when he talked about the realm of heaven.

The Realm of Heaven

In the Gospels, when Jesus spoke of heaven, he was not refer-ring to our image of golden streets in a celestial city where all is perfection. The "realm" he described (Matthew 13) was in many ways much closer to the African concept of community: something that is both now and coming-into-being, a reality that exists both within and outside time. The realm of heaven is like a tiny seed, Jesus said, which holds within it the mystery of immense growth. Physical size and other measurements have no meaning in the divine realm, which is why Jesus said it is also like yeast: something tiny that nevertheless causes our reality to expand and be transformed. The divine realm is like a buried treasure, Jesus said, which is already there and yet must be sought and found; and it is like a net, that sweeps up everyone, without regard for good or evil.

Euro-Americans have often had a romantic notion of community. Again and again, those who were besotted by this notion have formed intentional communities. The track record of these communities is not good, however; sooner or later, human imperfection raises its ugly head, members become disillusioned, and the community falls apart. Just as Westerners imagine heaven to be a place of unflawed perfection, their understanding of community is much the same.

Meanwhile, the African concept of community has very little to do with perfection or harmony. It is simply the matrix of reality in which we all live—and reality is messy. It offers challenges and difficulties, as well as joy and opportunities. Jesus' depicted the realm of heaven as being a similar sort of place: disruptive and disturbing, challenging our habits and priorities, even as it embraces us in a world of active love. And perhaps there we have it: love is not a state of easy, automatic, and static harmony but rather an interactive way of being that is often difficult, even painful.

Jacques Lacan, who is considered a Neo-Freudian, suggested that there exist not one but two deaths: the physical death of the body and symbolic death. Freud had taught that the death drive is central to human life (see chapter 5), but Lacan understood that "to embrace the death drive is to paradoxically die symbolically in order to return to living; . . . the drive is given the name of death and its work is life!" The Lacanian understanding of the death drive is not a negative acceptance of destruction but rather "a literal life beyond death."[285]

"Unless a kernel of wheat falls to the ground and dies," said Jesus, "it remains only a single seed. But if it dies, it produces many seeds" (John 12:24 NIV; remember, according to Jesus, *seed = the realm of heaven*). This kind of death—Lacan's second death—is essential to community. As we "die" to our individual egoic selves, we bring to life the fruitful possibility of community. Unfortunately, this is contrary to our cultural way of thinking (which is perhaps why the West's intentional communities have been so unsuccessful). Contemplative Beatrice Bruteau describes our situation accurately: "*If we cannot love our neighbor as ourself, it is because we do not perceive our neighbor as ourself.* We perceive the neighbor as precisely *not* ourself, but as a potential threat (or potential aid) to ourself. This perception in turn is based on other assumptions and ways of ordering the world that have to do with how reality is differentiated into separate objects and events and how these are organized into groups or unities. It is not a matter of the exhortation being an ideal that is difficult to attain; it is a contradiction of our culture that is strictly *impossible* to realize, so long as we see the world the way we do."[286]

The African mindset (and the nonlocal-reality model), on the other hand, experiences a world so tightly knit together that what hurts you hurts me and vice versa. As human beings, we exist within this interconnected world at many simultaneous levels of reality, allowing us to communicate within the *spirit village,* the place where, according to the Beng people of Africa, we are all present, no matter where we are on the continuum of birth, life, and death.[287]

The Call to Community

From the perspective of both the African worldview and the Gospels, we live in a community where nothing excludes or divides—even space and time. Death does not remove us from this community; instead, it is a transition point into a still deeper communal experience from which we can continue to serve and be in relationship.

Meanwhile, Lacanian psychology calls for us to experience the "second death," dying to our limited selfish perspective so that something wider and healthier can come into being. Jesus called this being "born again"; death and birth, as Africans know, are so intertwined that we may eventually find they are actually one and the same thing.

And so, whether we're speaking of "physical" death or "spiritual," in this sense death is not the destruction of being. Instead, it is a call to more life. It is a call to community. Racism is the death that destroys—but the death that gives itself away in love is the road to life and freedom.

It is the path that will take us home.

Way down yonder in the graveyard walk,
I thank God I'm free at last!
Me and my Jesus going to meet and talk.
I thank God I'm free at last!
On my knees when the light pass'd by,
I thank God I'm free at last!
Thought my soul would rise and fly,
I thank God I'm free at last!
Some of these mornings, bright and fair,
I thank God I'm free at last!
Goin' meet King Jesus in the air.
I thank God I'm free at last!

—AFRICAN AMERICAN SPIRITUAL

PRAYER PRACTICE

Today's prayer practice is based on an Ignatian approach, whereby we use our imaginations to enter into scripture and prayer. As with other forms of meditation, if you find yourself distracted by your thoughts, simply acknowledge each distraction as you become aware of it, and then dismiss it gently and firmly as you refocus your mind.

Begin by finding a quiet place and a comfortable position. (You want to be relaxed—but not so relaxed that you're tempted to fall asleep. If by chance, however, you happen to fall asleep, that's okay as well. You can start over again; trust me, God will be there waiting for you.) Take a few deep breaths, in and out through your nose. Imagine as you breathe out that any worries or stressful thoughts are flowing from your body into God's hand. As you breathe in, be conscious of God's love entering you.

Now read from the Gospel of Matthew, chapter 13, verses 44 through 46. This is the final section of Jesus' discourse on the realm of heaven. At this point, he has dismissed the crowd and is speaking only to his closest followers. Read the verses slowly. Then read them again, and this time, notice any word, phrase, image, or idea that seems to strike you with particular clarity. Stay with that, whatever it is, for a few moments. Notice how it makes you feel. What new thoughts does it open up?

Here are some questions you might also ask yourself:

- Where and what is your treasure?

  ◦ What "field" is the site where you invest your energy, time, and other resources?

  ◦ Is your "treasure" an aspect of the realm of heaven—or is it in the realm of the ego?

- Notice the people Jesus describes in these stories feel a sense of urgency about obtaining treasure. They don't hesitate to sell what they have in order to obtain something far more precious—and they don't postpone taking action until some later, more convenient time. They take action immediately and joyfully, with excitement, not because they "should" or "ought to."

  ◦ Do you feel a similar sense of urgency when it comes to your relationship with the realm of heaven?

  ◦ What might you need to surrender if you want to "buy" the field where the treasure lies hidden? Think about this in terms of the questions you just considered. If your "treasure" is currently buried in another field (if you are spending your time, energy, and other resources on the ego rather than God's realm), what might need to change?

- Where do you already sense the realm of heaven breaking into your ordinary life? How can you nurture and encourage these moments and experiences?

- Ask Jesus to show you where he is inviting you to find new joy, excitement, and meaning in your life.

Take a few moments to talk with Jesus as though he were sitting in the room with you. Discuss with him all you have reflected on during this exercise. Share your feelings and thoughts. When you are done, ask him to come with you as you return to your daily responsibility. Invite him to point out to you when and where his realm is already manifesting in your life—and ask that he show you how to make more space in your life for these moments and activities.

When our thoughts—which bring actions—
are filled with hate against anyone, black or white,
we are in a living hell. That is as
real as hell will ever be.
While hate for our fellow humans
puts us in a living hell,
holding good thoughts for them brings
us an opposite state of living,
one of happiness, success, peace.
We are then in heaven.

—GEORGE WASHINGTON CARVER[288]

8

DEATH'S LOVE STORY

KINSHIP BEYOND DEATH

Death is not a separation
but a different form of communion,
a higher form of connectedness
with the community,
providing an opportunity for
even greater service.

—MALIDOMA PATRICE SOMÉ[289]

BACK IN 2006, I STAYED WITH A family in Baringa, a village in the Tshuapa Province in Congo. One of the first things I noticed was that something was always going on—and not just one thing but many things, all at the same time. People were constantly coming and going, working and eating, playing with children and cooking food, laughing and talking, caring for animals and tending gardens; and all the while, countless conversations were taking place at the same time, overlapping and interweaving. It was a noisy, confusing, but mostly happy place.

And then, suddenly, all that busyness came to a halt. Justin Kaduala, a well-respected man in his sixties, had died. Now, the entire community had only a single task: to prepare for Justin's funeral. In the weeks that followed, everyone in the village had a role to play.

Visitors from out of town began to show up; some of them had come hundreds of kilometers, either on foot or on the back of a donkey. Each visitor brought provisions Justin's family would need in the days ahead. Now the busyness resumed, as people came and went, everyone getting ready for the funeral.

As I participated whenever and wherever I could in all this commotion, I overheard a sentence that caught my attention: "This is a new page in a love story." At first, I thought I might have misheard, but then I heard someone else again refer to their relationship with Justin as an ongoing love story.

Justin's family and community mourned his death with a depth that was obvious and sincere—but at the same time, I sensed a certain joyful anticipation as they prepared for his funeral, almost as if they were getting ready for a wedding. The story of their love for Justin had not ended; it had merely entered another phase. When the day of the funeral finally arrived, it was not only a celebration of the past they had shared with Justin; it was also a celebration of the future, as they entered into a new relationship with him.

Death as an Ongoing Relationship

When my grandmother died, despite my sorrow and the sense of disequilibrium (as though the very floor I walked on had suddenly disappeared), I experienced for myself the meaning of death's love story. Even as I raged against death, allowing my grief to drive my thoughts and actions, I slowly became aware Tatie had not left me. Moving around the house, I felt she was still there, always just in another room. I couldn't see her, but only because I can't see through walls; she was no more absent or lost than she would be if she were merely in a different part of the house.

My experience is shared by many Black people. A twenty-four-year-old gang member, for example, reported, "I lost most of my homies to violence in the 'hood. I know I got their spirits watching over me, got my dead homies watching over me."[290] Filmmaker Richard Fung confessed that his sense of relationship with his deceased mother "connects me to a past I would have no other way of knowing. And in this sea of whiteness, of friends, enemies, and strangers, I look at her and know who I am."[291] After the death of Maya Angelou, Oprah said, "Now that she's gone, I think I value and love her even more. Without the density of her body, I can better feel the intensity of her spirit. I feel stronger. More awake and more alive and ready to carry on her legacy."[292] José Esteban Muñoz wrote that for Blacks, the connection to the dead is "a mechanism that helps us (re)-construct identity and take our dead with us to the various battles we must wage in their names—and in our names."[293] After author Haoua Diatta's husband died of COVID-19, she believed he continued to guide her, even helping her to get back to her writing.[294]

For Blacks, clearly the ongoing connection we experience with our dead has nothing to do with being tied to the past in a way that keeps us stagnant, unable to move forward into the future. Instead, these relationships empower us and give us identity. Our deceased loved ones are with us, though not in the same way they once were. When we ask them for help, they respond.

This connection with the dead is not unique to the African diaspora, of course; many other cultures have similar beliefs. For Euro-Americans, however, society-wide assumptions and traditions do not support or validate these beyond-death relationships. Instead, such experiences are often dismissed as something only "primitive" and "superstitious" cultures take seriously.

Perspectives on the Dead

"At night, I sometimes feel my father and mother are in the room down the hall," a white friend told me recently, speaking of her parents who have been dead for several years. "It's like they're right there in my life, close by, where they have always been, ready to help me and support me." She paused and then said, "But this is the first time I've ever told anyone that. I don't talk about it to people." When I asked her why that was, she said, "Talking about it would make it seem less real. People would either doubt my experience—or they'd make it seem like something else. Something weird or scary."

Her comments made me realize that modern-day Western culture has very little room in it for the living dead. In fact, for most white Americans, the phrase *living dead* speaks of zombies and terror, rather than relationship and love. From this perspective, death is such a terrifying force that anything that passes through it will be transformed into something horrifying, no longer familiar or beloved.

The psychoanalyst Hans Loewald wrote about turning ghosts that haunt and persecute into ancestors who guide and encourage[295]; he was speaking metaphorically, but his words, I believe, are also accurate when applied to the cultural differences between Euro-Americans' understanding of the dead and those of us in the African diaspora (as well as in many traditional Asian, Pagan, and Indigenous cultures). Our ghost stories are love stories.

Those of us guided by the scientific Western perspective do not believe in ghosts, of course. Instead, any perception of the dead's presence is generally considered a hallucination. The fact that there's a psychological/neurological term for this— *bereavement hallucination*—indicates this experience is not at all uncommon, even among Euro-Americans. In fact, one study found that 47 percent of all widows and widowers have "hallucinations" of their dead spouses, while another similar study found that 60 percent experienced this phenomenon, and yet another study reported 82 percent. A 2008 *Scientific American* article concluded that "only a minority of people reading this article are likely to experience grief *without* re-experiencing the dead" (emphasis mine).

The "sense of presence" both my friend and I experience is the most common "bereavement hallucination," but some people also see, hear, and even touch their deceased loved ones. Most of these people, however, like my friend, do not talk about their experiences (though women are somewhat more likely than men to tell at least one person); the most commonly cited reasons were the fear of ridicule and being "considered insane or mentally destabilised by their loss." Psychologists explain these experiences in a variety of ways—and ultimately conclude there is no "empirical evidence" indicating a "survival of consciousness."[296] Despite this, some scientists are taking quite seriously the possibility of not only life after physical death but also of the potential to communicate with those who now inhabit the invisible realm. The survival of consciousness is an idea humans have always had; it had little room to grow within the atmosphere of the Scientific Revolution, but today it is once more being studied.[297]

Cemeteries as Points of Connection

While I was working on this book, I realized I needed some data to balance theory and secondhand research—and so I went to one of the oldest and largest cemeteries in the country, the Arlington National Cemetery, to do some behavioral observation. Until 1948, the cemetery was almost completely segregated (since whites did not want to rub elbows with Blacks, even in death); section 27 was reserved for Black burials, and still today, the families of Blacks buried in Arlington often choose to have their loved ones' graves in section 27.

On my first day in the cemetery, from 9:00 a.m. to 5:30 p.m., I wandered through section 13, a white section of the cemetery, trying to be discrete as I observed the behavior of white visitors. I counted 170 white visitors during my time there; 147 of them came to a particular grave, took a picture, talked briefly to their companions, and then left. Their visits lasted ten minutes or less, and the groups consisted of two to four people. (The other twenty-three visitors seemed to be tourists, wandering aimlessly through the historical cemetery, pausing only occasionally to read a gravestone here and there.)

On another day, I went back to the cemetery, but this time, I spent the day in section 27, observing Black visitors. Altogether, 220 Black people came that day during the eight and half hours I was there; 201 of them sat down on the ground next to a particular grave—and they stayed there for a half hour or longer, praying and talking. Many of them seemed to be in a conversation with an unseen presence, and on more than one occasion, I overheard pleas for help. Often, I heard the word *remember.* Fifty of these individuals had brought food with them to eat while they sat by the grave; the impression I got was that each small group of two to seven people was also sharing a meal with the deceased person.

Based on these observations,[298] I eventually made some conclusions: White people tend to see graves as places of historical interest, which are, in effect, dead places (in the sense they are inanimate). Meanwhile, Blacks experience their graves as living sites of family closeness, expressions of *home*, as well as places to gather to renew their relationships with those who have "crossed over." I realize my sample is limited, and it may very well say more about how whites and Blacks perceive graves rather than the dead. Still, the impression I got was that for Blacks, their loved ones are not historical figures shut in the dusty closets of the past, but rather they are present beings who continue to live and interact at the sites of their graves.

Author Michael Lesy presented a different understanding of how most whites perceive cemeteries, describing the "forbidden zone" that's marked on the map of American culture, "a place every citizen knows but fears to enter. . . a place guarded by dread but surrounded by fascination. It is the zone of death." Even a century and a half ago, though, Euro-Americans were comfortable with their dead, at home in cemeteries as places of serenity and contemplation. Now, for many white folks, cemeteries have become settings for horror movies. Graves exude evil and fear rather than love and peace.

"Critically acclaimed best-sellers are written about pathological killers," Lesy went on to say; "television programs are punctuated with murder . . . ; crowds of ticket holders wait in line to see films of massacre and dismemberment, homicidal spectacles. . . . Our culture is permeated by images and accounts of death, but they are only fictions, works of imagination, counterfeits. The real thing is carefully hidden."[299] If this is true, then it's no wonder Euro-Americans might prefer to distance themselves from the graves of their loved ones. To face the broad-daylight reality of a grave would be to face the certainty of their own deaths.

For Blacks, on the other hand, our loved ones' graves are places of comfort and connection. According to Haitian death traditions, the first person to be buried in a cemetery or a private family gravesite (as was the case for Tatie) automatically becomes the guardian of that place. In the spiritual language of Vodou, we consider this person to be the manifestation of Baron Samedi, the spirit who welcomes others into the land of the dead. According to this belief, Tatie now holds the key that opens the gateway into the invisible world. As each member of my family dies and is buried in that cemetery, she will greet them and lead them on their journey home. That image always makes me smile.[300]

But do Blacks believe our deceased loved ones are literally present with us when we stand beside their tombstones? Do we think the dead spend all eternity hanging out in cemeteries? And if not, just where *are* the dead? Are they under their tombstones (trapped in their coffins)? Are they in heaven? On the "other side"? Or are they everywhere and nowhere? How can we nurture a relationship with them now?

To start with, no, I do not believe Tatie is trapped in the cemetery where her body is buried. The cemetery, however, serves as a space for ritual—and ritual is one way to sustain our relationships with friends and family who now live in another dimension.

Ritual as a Bridge Between the Living and the Dead

Frederic and Mary Ann Brussant, commentators on contemporary spiritual thought and practices, note that ritual becomes more "resonant" in the broader culture during periods of great stress and soul-searching. Today, the aftershocks of the COVID-19 pandemic, as well as its ongoing dangers, have created a space where we all need the power of ritual.

"Ritual," the Brussants explain, "has its genesis in the movements of the soul and our need to express deep emotions and intuitions in story, symbol, and action. Through prayers, blessings, rites, ceremonies, and celebrations, we honor our connections with God, others, community, nature, the world, and the whole cosmic dance."[301] Yes. That's it exactly. I would add that ritual serves as a handle by which we can "grab hold" of the spiritual world; it's a way in which we can experience with our five senses that which we cannot see or touch, hear or smell or taste. It is a bridge between this world and the Other World.

Visiting a loved one's grave can be a private ritual that allows you to continue to express your love in a tangible way. There are many ways to do this:

- Place cut flowers or a stone on the grave.

- Sit and read out loud from a shared favorite book.

- Have a picnic with friends, including the deceased member of your gathering.

- Do a libation, pouring water or wine on the grave.

- Pray.

- Speak to your loved one as though she or he were sitting beside you.

Do whatever feels comfortable and meaningful to you!

Some people, however, are simply not at ease by a grave. Others may prefer to affirm and celebrate their loved ones' lives (instead of deaths) in other ways and settings. There are plenty of other options for nurturing a relationship with the dead.

Nature

According to the Senegalese poet Birago Diop, as the wind blows through the trees, we can hear our forebearers breathing. "The dead are not gone forever," nor are they buried beneath the ground, for we can hear them in the rustling leaves, the ripple of water, and a child's cry; we can see them in plants and rock and flame; we can sense their presence when we are alone—and when we are surrounded by a crowd. "The dead are not dead."[302]

I read this poem to two white friends and asked them how they interpreted it. One said, "When we die, our cells are broken down and go back to Nature. So the poem is saying that the physical molecules that once were a person are now present everywhere." The other friend had a different interpretation: "It's not meant literally. Because the deceased person lives on in our memories, we carry them with us everywhere. Everything beautiful that we see or touch or hear can remind us and bring their memory alive."

And then I emailed these interpretations to a Black friend and asked for her thoughts. "Of course Diop meant the poem to be understood literally!" she wrote back. "Molecules and memories are all well and good—but they're not much use when you're longing for comfort. And why would we want to settle for such dry and sterile comfort, when there's so much more being offered?"

"What exactly is being offered then?" I asked her.

"The dead are not dead!" she wrote back. "How hard is that to understand? They are alive! Not symbolically alive or alive only in memory or only in their cast-off cells. *Really* alive, with juice and snap! And just as God is everywhere, breathing through everything, so now do they, because now they are with Her. They are no longer limited by time and space like we are. They are literally present in ways we can't imagine, looking after us, loving us. They are not dead!"

Finally, I happened, almost accidentally, to share my Black friend's comments with a white pastor. His response was: "That smacks of animism!"

Well, yes, it does. Is that a bad thing?

The word *animism* comes from the Latin word *animus,* meaning "spirit" or "soul"; animism is the belief that everything has a soul. Everything is spiritually alive. Nineteenth-century anthropologist Edward Burnett Tylor was the first Euro-American to give this belief an English name. Unfortunately, he went on to describe animistic societies as primitive and childish—and that condescending attitude still exists today. In reality, however, as Daniel Foor has explained, "Animism is one name for an ancient and ultimately ordinary ethic that emphasizes relationships. Animists recognize that living humans are only one kind of person in a much wider network of kinship. These others include our human ancestors, the big spirits of animals and plants, mountains and metals, fire and water, microorganisms, wind and weather, deities of many regions and temperaments, star people, nature spirits, and so on. We inhabit a responsive and relational world. This understanding is the inheritance of all human beings."[303]

In *Crossing the Threshold of Hope*, Pope John Paul II wrote, "It would be helpful to recall . . . the animistic religious which stress ancestors worship. It seems that those who practice them are particularly close to Christianity." The Pope wrote of the "common language" animists share with Christianity as a "kind of preparation for the Communion of Saints," explaining that "faith in the Communion of the Saints is, ultimately, faith in Christ, who alone is the source of life."[304]

Christianity has often misinterpreted animism, however, defining it as Nature worship, ancestor worship, or, worst of all, idol worship. In reality, animists do not worship any of these things; they do, however, reverence Nature and the ancestors. They see both as belonging to a vast spiritual reality that intersects with the visible world.

As I tried to explain this concept to the daughter of one of my friends, she said, "Oh, I get it! It's like in *Lion King*, where Pumbaa says the stars are balls of burning gas—but Simba says they're his father and all his other ancestors looking down on him."

I'm not a huge fan of Disney portrayals of Indigenous cultures, but I had to look this one up—and sure enough, she was right. There's a scene where Simba, the young lion, is talking with his father under the stars. The father says, "The great kings of the past look down on us from those stars. Whenever you feel alone, just remember that those kings will always be there to guide you. And so will I." This is what Simba is referring to when he and his friend Pumbaa the warthog are talking about stars.

Then I came across a kids' science website that said in reference to the conversation between Simba and his friend: "Pumbaa is the one who describes stars correctly—stars really are just burning balls of gas burning billions of miles away."[305] This brings us back again to the Euro-American inability to see the possibility of both-and. Something cannot be a burning ball of gas *and* the spirit of your father.

Let me tell you a story (this one is not ugly, I promise!) that a colleague of mine told me about her lonely childhood. Her siblings were much older than she was, and her parents were emotionally distant. During her childhood, the family went through several serious crises, and my friend was left to handle these on her own as best she could. And so, from the time she was a very young child, she would spend her time in the comforting embrace of an old apple tree, telling the tree all her troubles. The tree listened. And then the tree answered.

"I called her Oolah," my colleague told me. "I don't know why." She rolled her eyes. "Well, I do know—that's what Oolah told me to call her. But why my imagination grabbed onto that name, I don't know."

My friend described the way whenever she was scared or lonely, she would run to Oolah. Oolah had a definite personality: she could be cranky; she was also brutally honest, forcing my friend to confront the hard realities of her life; and Oolah's love was endless and patient. Her wisdom guided my friend through her difficult childhood, and Oolah's love made her resilient. In Oolah's branches, my friend was safe.

As my friend told me this story, she repeatedly made clear she knew she was talking about her childhood imaginary friend. She spoke of how the creation of "Oolah" allowed her to mother her own self; she used words like "imaginative play," "personified objects," and "autonomy."

I smiled and nodded, for this is vocabulary I also know well, and it is an accurate interpretation of my friend's experience. And then I asked, "So when was the last time you talked to Oolah?"

My friend hesitated, then rolled her eyes again and laughed. "The last time I visited my parents," she said. "Last week."

A tree, according to the online Merriam-Webster dictionary, is "a long-lived woody plant that has a single usually tall main stem with few or no branches on its lower part"—but while the Western mind assumes that this is *all* a tree is, the African mind believes a tree's tall-stemmed woodiness is just one aspect of its reality. Another aspect of the tree's reality might be the spiritual expression of an old woman who loves you unconditionally. Both-and.

A lonely child uses her own creativity, resilience, and innate wisdom to imagine a make-believe grandmother who guides her through life's challenges. Even today, "Oolah" is simply the name of one aspect of my colleague's personality. When she talks with Oolah, she is really accessing that wise, nearly unconscious part of herself. But—might my friend's experience also have taken place in her spirit village? Might Oolah actually be one of my friend's ancestors? These seemingly contrary understandings—one psychological and the other "woo-woo"!—can coexist in the very same space. Both-and. As Jesus said, "Spirit blows where She wishes. You hear Her voice, but you can't tell where it's coming from or where it's going."[306]

In most languages, except English, breath and spirit are the same word. The Divine Spirit breathes through a physical world that is not dead but alive. This is a totally biblical perspective, as these verses from the Psalms make clear:

> *Praise the Eternal!*
> *. . . All you, His messengers and His armies in heaven:*
> *praise Him!*
> *Sun, moon, and all you brilliant stars above:*
> *praise Him! . . .*
> *Let all things join together in a concert of praise*
> *to the name of the Eternal,*
> *Everything on earth, join in and praise the Eternal;*

sea monsters and creatures of the deep,
Lightning and hail, snow and foggy mists,
violent winds . . . Mountains and hills,
fruit trees and cedar forests,
All you animals both wild and tame,
reptiles and birds who take flight.
praise the Lord.
(148:1–3, 5, 7–10 TV)

Spirit breathes through all things. All things praise Her.

According to quantum physics, the gap we perceive between mind and matter (between ourselves and the things we perceive) exists only in our perception. In reality, we are constantly in relationship (just as animism believes), and the nature of that relationship shapes the nature of the reality we perceive. "While people are free to argue over their favorite interpretation," astrophysicist Ethan Siegal reminds us, "none can lay any more claim to being 'real' than any other.[307]" The father in the stars, the grandmother in the tree—both are just as real as the burning ball of gas and the tall woody plant. "All kinship, in the end, is imaginary," Ruha Benjamin wrote. "Not faux, false, or inferior, but . . . a creative process of fashioning care and reciprocity."[308]

A literal translation of Ephesians 3:14 reads: "The Ancestor (the one who imparts life and is committed to it; the nourisher, protector, and upholder) is the one who names and gives identity to all families (human and otherwise) on the Earth and in the sky and in Eternity."[309] Everything is alive; everything is in relationship.

I cannot, of course, tell you where or even if you will find in Nature a way to experience care and reciprocity, the sense of ongoing kinship with someone who is no longer visibly present. I merely recommend you be open to the possibility—as well as other options for writing death's love story.

Memory

We are often told that our departed loved ones will live on in our memory. As my friend expressed in her email, this may seem like meager comfort when we are longing for the physical presence of someone we love.

But we may have a narrow understanding of memory. According to the Hebrew scriptures, remembering is a spiritual activity, one that God engages in all the time. The original Hebrew word means simply to "hold in the mind," with the implication that this is a generative process rather than a static state; in other words, what is held in the mind in this fashion ultimately creates something new.[310] The Hebrew God is constantly "remembering" His people, while He calls on them to also remember.

Holding something or someone in our mind in this way enables us to reexperience them as though they were physically present, not as dead images incapable of movement but as if they were alive with the ability to touch and change us, to enter into relationship with us. Memory is like a magic power our brains possess that allows us to time travel; we bring the past into the present, and by doing so, we shape the future.

We assume that memory focuses on the portion of time we call "past"—but we may be wrong. According to philosopher Jean-Paul Sartre, "past, present, future, should not be considered as a collection of data to be added together" but as structures within a "synthesis."[311] This "synthesis" means past, present, and future are not irrevocably separated, as we perceive them, but might actually be aspects of the same phenomenon we call *time*. Theoretical physicist Carlo Rovelli believes our understanding of time is far too simplistic to do justice to time's reality. Instead, Rovelli wrote, reality is a complex web of "occurrences," which our brains sequence in terms of past, present, and future. Our perception that time "flows" (and in a single direction) is inaccurate because we perceive only a narrow slice of the fullness of reality.[312]

Can you understand that? No? Well, I can't either. Most of our brains are simply not equipped to create a mental picture of something so far outside the accepted paradigms of our reality. (It would be much the same, I imagine, as trying to picture a color not on our known color wheel—or how to feel with a sense perception other than the five we possess.) But I wonder if minds not steeped in Western thinking might grasp these ideas far better than we can. I wonder also if the concept of linear time is not, in fact, one of the impositions that colonialism imposed on Indigenous reality.

"Time is nothing," Immanuel Kant wrote, "but the form of inner sense, that is, of the intuition of ourselves and our inner state. . . . Because this inner intuition yields no shape, we endeavor to make up for this want by analogies."[313] All our analogies for time—minutes, hours, weeks, years—are not time itself; they are merely another kind of "handle" by which we try to grasp that which can never be fully grasped. The colonizers who so prided themselves on their accurate understanding of time (while Indigenous people were ignorant and uncivilized) were in fact making the same mistake they accused "idol-worshippers" of making: they were mistaking the dead analogy for the living reality.

According to the African principle of Sankofa (see the introduction), we go back to the past to bring new life to the future. In other words, at some level of reality, we hopscotch from one temporality to the next, breaking the Western image of time as a unidirectional arrow. From the African perspective, time is a spiraling circle of birth and death. My birth into this world was a death to the life I knew before, and my death in this world will be my birth into the world beyond. When we see reality in this way, death is no longer an impenetrable barrier.

One way to relate to deceased loved ones through memory is to create tangible symbols to represent their presence. In Colombia, where violence and injustice have claimed the lives of so many people, survivors often create handmade banners from fabric or paper to represent individuals who have passed from this world. These banners, which may include pictures of things the deceased person enjoyed, the dates of their birth and death, and words or short phrases that describe the individual, are usually hung prominently inside the home, creating a permanent visible reminder of the deceased family member. Again, memory goes far beyond a mere mental activity; it allows the person who is physically no longer present to still be a part of the daily routines of home. One woman, for example, whose son was assassinated, looks at her son's banner whenever she leaves the house and asks him to both go with her and also watch the house while she is gone. "I don't see [the banner] as paper," she said. "No, I feel that he is still alive, that is what helps me." The banner allows her to connect with her son's ongoing life force.[314]

Tattoos can also be memory symbols. Mental-health expert Dan Reidenberg said, "Memorial tattoos help keep someone we lost close to us. Literally, they become part of us." He went on to say, "Like other types of memorials, memorial tattoos honor, recognize and pay tribute to someone very special to us in a way that is always accessible. . . . People can look at, touch and relive a deep connection with someone who has passed." Reidenberg also noted that tattoos placed on visible parts of the body can give mourners chances to talk about their lost loved ones and "share their legacy."[315]

Other common memory symbols include photographs, scrapbooks, and items of clothing belonging to the deceased loved one. One family I know created a memorial quilt, with a separate quilt square to represent each family member who now resides in the World Beyond. Another friend planted a tree in honor of a stillborn child; the tree gives her a place to focus on the nurturing love she feels for her child—and as she participates in the tree's growth, she is empowered to imagine her child's growth in another realm. "Those who engage in living communion with the departed," said poet and philosopher

Viacheslav Vsevolodovich Ivanov, "gather strength."[316] This is strength that both comforts and energizes; it is a gift from the past that can be passed on to the future.

In the Black community, graffiti and street art are often forms of visible memorial, particularly for those who were killed by racism. "Violent streets," wrote Gabriele Lübbers, "have created an art form that not only tackles the emotional turmoil occasioned by premature death, but also produces public sites for collective memory." They are also, said Lübbers, "implicit calls for further social action."[317]

In the summer of 2021, I had the opportunity to experience how the act of remembering connected me to a larger community. In the process of doing academic research, I spent many days in the Jesuit archives in St. Louis, Missouri, and in the Old Maryland Province archive at Georgetown University in Washington, DC. As I delved into my people's history, I pieced the dry facts into a narrative I could tell and retell.

This was not an easy experience. As I read dozens of accounts of my ancestors, people who shared my skin color, my hair texture, sometimes even my last name, I had to confront the reality that many of my spiritual ancestors, the Jesuits, had participated in the abuse and oppression of my biological ancestors. The realization troubled me so much that I felt the urge to vomit. I had to take a break from my research and get some fresh air. For several weeks, I questioned my own work as a member of the Jesuits.

I turned to *The Spiritual Exercises,* the foundation of Ignatian spirituality, and there I found the answer to my pain and doubts. Ignatius of Loyola believed *remembering* is a gift from God, a gift that, as we return it to God, is transformed into a Spirit-filled tool for both contemplation and action. And so, I committed myself to the collective memories of my people, no matter how painful they were, giving them all to God to be used to build the realm of heaven here in the visible world. I believe that in doing this, I engage in God's own ministry of remembering—holding each precious human in the Divine Mind so we can grow beyond our current limitations.

For Black folk, memory continues to connect us to our ancestors, both the ones we know and the ones whose names have been forgotten. Enslaved people once "stole away" for praise meetings "where the evocation of the ancestors was central to imagining freedom. Here they would enact ancestral landscapes." In remembering things they had not witnessed or experienced themselves, they "transformed the space of captivity into one inhabited by the revenants of a disremembered past." Today, technology helps us achieve a similar goal; hashtag signifiers, like #SayHerName, act "as gathering points that make present the slain and call upon recent ancestors—Tamir Rice, Sandra Bland, Michael Brown, Ayana Jones, and so many others—as spiritual kin who can animate social movements."[318] America's collective amnesia would erase the names of those individuals murdered by racism; like the *echthroi* mentioned in the introduction, racism always denies individuals their identity and value. Through collective memory, however, Black folk affirm their identities as they reaffirm the bonds of kinship that connect both the living and the dead.

In the summer of 2022, as I continued my archive research, I created a list of the names of those individuals I felt I had come to know, individuals who had spent their lives in slavery: *Barney, Fanny Ann, Black, Emeline, Lock, Rose Philomene, Contee, Martha, Cutchmo, Celestia, Queen, Henny, Sweets, Emiliana, Joseph Henry, Nelly Bill* . . . The list goes on and on. These are people whose faces I will never see (not in this life), but through memory, I affirm their births, their lives, their deaths, and their ongoing reality in the eternal realm. These people matter. They are part of the Spirit-Body in which we all, Black and white, participate and from which we draw our life.

One way to make sure these people do not "disappear" from our world is by storytelling. As I said at the beginning of this book, stories are how we understand each other, and stories are also how we keep memory alive. They transform dry historical facts into vehicles for a far deeper heart-connection. That is why I have told some painful stories in this book, because it is important that we do not forget. Memory enriches our communities and inspires our work for justice "Eternal Memory is the root strength and lifeblood," said Ivanov, "of any constructive work that is social in spirit."[319]

In the Gospels, at the Last Supper, Jesus breaks bread and offers it to his disciples, telling them, "This is My body, My body given for you. Do this to remember Me."[320] The Eucharist—the communion meal—is a tangible narrative of Jesus' life, a memorial we not only hold in our minds but that we take and eat as well. The Greek word (translated as "memory" and "remember") that recurs throughout the Eucharist is *anamnesis*. This is a sacred form of memory, a memory that is not mere nostalgia but rather an active participation in timeless events.

When the African American spiritual asks, "Were you there when they crucified my Lord?" it is not a rhetorical question nor a form of symbolic interaction with the belief that Christ died for all our sins. No, this too is *anamnesis,* a dynamic engagement with an event that took place millennia ago, according to linear time, and yet is always happening. The enslaved folk who wrote that song understood that the crucifixion is always *Now,* and this understanding empowered them to recognize a Christ who was present with them in all their suffering and oppression. Because they *were* there at the crucifixion, they knew the white man's Jesus was a lie. As James Cone wrote, remembering the cross "inverts the world's value system with the news that hope comes by way of defeat, that suffering and death do not have the last word, that the last shall be first and the first last." Because of enslaved Blacks' active experience of remembering the cross, they "shouted, danced, clapped their hands and stomped their feet as they bore witness to the power of Jesus' cross which had given them an identity far more meaningful than the harm that white supremacy could do them."[321] That is the potential and power of memory.

In initiating the practice of the Eucharist, Jesus not only affirmed that the ties of community hold strong beyond our departure from this life; he also introduced a radical new way of living in communion with one another, a form of community built on giving and self-surrender rather than power, competition, and oppression. Through the sacred memory of his death, he calls us to recognize that we too are there at the cross, as both oppressors and oppressed, and in that recognition, lies the gateway to individual and societal transformation. The Eucharist is a ritual of memory that helps keep Jesus' presence—his unconditional love as well as his uncompromising challenge—alive in our midst.

As always, ritual is another powerful way to "grab hold" of what is intangible. There are countless rituals of memory that can nurture our relationships with those whose presence is no longer tangible. A few examples:

- Cook your loved one's favorite meal and invite close friends and family to participate in a celebration of memory, sharing stories and laughter as well as tears.

- Find a memento of your loved one. You might carry a stone in your pocket, wear a piece of jewelry that belonged to the loved one, carry their picture in a locket, or find some other small object that is easy to bring with you wherever you go.

- Light a candle each evening in memory of the one who has passed on into another realm.

- Play your loved one's favorite music on significant anniversaries.

These are just a few suggestions for turning memory into ritual. The best way to connect through memory, however, might be to simply allow yourself to spend time *remembering*, holding your loved ones in your mind as you are held in the mind of God. The lens of memory, as we all know, is subject to imperfections, and yet it is a Divine gift that hints at another way of perceiving reality. From this perspective, the dead are not dead—and they never can be. Furthermore, as African elder Malidoma Somé asked, since the bonds of community are never broken, how could *anyone* ever die?[322]

I encourage you not to be afraid that remembering will make you sad by reminding you of what is "gone" or "lost." Nothing is lost, nothing is gone; it has just passed beyond your ability to currently perceive. Nor are memories meant to be a form of amber where we are permanently embedded like insects in a dead past, doomed to never detach ourselves from a lost reality. In contrast, Argentinian sociologist Elizabeth Jelin wrote about the "labors of memory" and pointed out that while there is danger in idolizing the past, memory also has the potential to "generate and transform" our world.[323]

Don't be afraid to play with memory; engage your imagination alongside your remembering and use the full creative powers of the human mind. Think of memory as a time machine that allows you to once more enjoy the presence of the person you love—and in doing so, bring new life to both the present and the future. As you do this, you may also find your memories go with you into your sleep, becoming dreams where you can once more talk with your loved one.

Dreams

"When a person dies," said Yoruba priest Songadina Ifatunji, "part of even the funeral rite, part of the traditional thing that is said is, 'From now on, we will see you in our dreams.'"[324] Dreams are another way in which we can maintain our connection with those who have died.

Traditional Africans believe ancestors can and do visit their living relatives through dreams. This experience—dreaming of someone who has passed on—is not unique to Africans. According to several studies, about half of all bereaved Euro-Americans also have dreams where they communicate with a deceased loved one.[325] Most white folk, however, do not regard dreams as "real" in any sense of the word.

This was not always the case. Both the Hebrew and Christian scriptures contain many references to dreams, indicating they can be a form of Divine communication.[326] The ancient Greek and Roman philosophers also taught that dreams were a vehicle by which the Divine disclosed its purposes (although Aristotle warned that dreamers needed to remember that the body's condition could shape their dreams). The early Church Fathers, including Origen, Tertullian, and Clement of Alexandria, cautioned that dreams on occasion can be demonic in nature, but they still affirmed that dreams are vehicles God uses to communicate with the human soul. In the fourth century, Synesius of Cyrene, a Greek bishop of the church, wrote that dreams have the power to "open the way to the most perfect vision of reality." Furthermore, said Synesius, divine dreams cut through human elitism, for they are universally available, regardless of "gender, age, fortune, or skill," allowing even the "one who has gone so far astray as not to know whence he came" to rise into a realm where he encounters both the Divine and the other "cosmic" inhabitants of that realm.[327]

As the centuries went by, however, the church became increasingly distrustful of dreams. Saint Augustine began this trend in the fifth century, indicating that the dreaming mind can be corrupted not only by demonic influences but also by the body's sexuality. In Augustine's autobiography, dreams played a central role in his conversion, but as he grew older, he distrusted dreams more and more.[328]

After Augustine, the church's teaching on dreams became increasingly negative. "Care was taken to encourage the belief that dreams were not from God and should therefore be ignored. As the church was seen as the ultimate authority due to it being considered as the keeper of the Word of God, it discouraged any reliance on dreams for divine insight and communication as being unnecessary. Certainly, any dream-related experiences or interpretations that fell outside the strict doctrines of the medieval church were looked upon with great suspicion and even condemnation." [329]

And so the Euro-American world ceased to believe that something spiritual might be going on while we dream. In the twentieth century, Sigmund Freud said that dreams expressed our unfilled wishes, while neurobiologists dismissed dreaming as simply the ongoing activity of our brains while we sleep. Various theories arose to explain the evolutionary purpose of dreams:

- Dreaming is like a computer's offline cleanup operations, removing unnecessary material from the mind during sleep.

- Dreaming is a way to process trauma safely.

- Dreaming promotes learning.

For most of the twentieth century, few Westerners seriously thought of dreams as a way to communicate with the spiritual world. Psychologists had noticed that many people dreamed of deceased loved ones, but they interpreted this as the mind's attempt to restore a presence that had become habitual to it. Grief theorists did not encourage the bereaved to believe their bond with the deceased loved one could continue after death; psychologists thought these "imagined" bonds could impede recovery, since they allowed people to avoid facing their "loss," thus preventing them from "getting over" their grief. Psychological tests used to diagnose complicated grief implied that the ongoing bonds were in fact pathological in nature, the product of a mental disturbance.[330]

These assumptions are changing in the twenty-first century, as psychologists begin to see that "imaginary" bonds may be a healthy grief-coping strategy that actually assists in the recovery process.[331] Meanwhile, the larger culture, including most Christians, still tends to consider people who believe they contact the dead through dreams to be either "whacky" or "crazy."

African Christianity, however, went in a quite different direction when it came to dreams. According to African theologian John Mbiti, African Christians "discovered a dream culture in the Bible" that allowed them to maintain and expand their own beliefs about dreams. "The reading of the Bible in African languages," wrote Mbiti, "provides very fertile ground for inter-religious encounter. The biblical cosmology finds a ready hearing on the African soil. The biblical and African cosmologies mutually revive, discover, complement, invigorate, affirm and, maybe, modify each other in an ongoing and living process" that "is largely absent in the Western world.[332]"

This belief in the spiritual reality of dreams is shared today throughout the African diaspora. According to dream psychologist Anthony Shafton, 70 percent of Blacks sampled in a study believed their ancestors visit them in dreams, while only 34 percent of whites believed this (despite also having dreams about deceased loved ones).

Shafton records these comments from two of the Black people he interviewed:

> My mom believes that the dead pray for the living .... She'll say, "That's your grandmother. Your grand-mother's making sure that this happened to you."

> My aunt is ninety-two. And she'll say, "Your father came and sat on my bed last night, and I talked to him." ... People, when they dream about the dead, and the conversations they have, they never talk about it as a dream, they talk about it as reality. ... So it's a way that the past—well, the ancestors are still involved in the present, through the dream.[333]

Personally, I have had dreams where I see my grand-mother. In the dreams, we talk about anything and everything, just as we used to. She scolds me and gives me advice; I tease her and make her laugh. I find these dreams to be of great com-fort—and I believe that in some way, I have in fact been able to again spend time with Tatie. In the dark of night, my dreaming mind finds a portal into a place where our spirits can commune.

What do you think? If you are uncomfortable accepting this way of continuing your relationships with deceased loved ones, I have one more option to offer you.

Prayer

Growing up as a Protestant, I heard that Catholics prayed to the dead. Or that they prayed *for* the dead, which was presented as being equally futile. "It might be a comforting thought to believe that you can pray for your deceased friend or relative," says an Evangelical website, "but it is a false comfort, as it is not found in the Word of God in any way."

Really? The Bible assures us that our loved ones con-tinue to exist; why then would we stop praying for them simply because we can no longer see them? That would be like say-ing you no longer need to pray for me because I've gone to a remote area of the world that has no phone or Internet service. Although you would not be able to see, hear, or touch me, I would still be in need of your prayer.

When I converted to Catholicism, I began to see prayers for the dead in a quite different way. As Christian apologist C. S. Lewis once wrote, "Of course I pray for the dead. . . . At our age, the majority of those we love best are dead. What sort of intercourse with God could I have if what I love best were unmentionable to him?" Prayer is a way for me to continue to express my love and support for those loved ones who have crossed over into the next life. "If we love a person with all our hearts," wrote the twentieth-century Protestant minister William Barclay, "and if the remembrance of that person is never absent from our minds and memories, then . . . the instinct of the heart is to remember such a one in prayer, whether he is in this or in any other world." The ancient church also believed in praying for the dead. In the third century, Church Father Tertullian wrote, "We offer sacrifices for the dead on their birthday anniversaries." (By this he meant that the living participated in the Eucharist on the date of these deaths, which were actually births into eternal life—an understanding many Africans still share.)

Another Evangelical website has this, however, to say about praying for the dead: "The Bible says that the fate of the dead is determined in this life. Praying for them does no good whatsoever. The dead are either in heaven or hell. If they are in heaven, they have no need of your prayers. If they are in hell, your prayers will avail nothing." I'm going to leave hell out of this discussion (since we already considered hell in chapter 7), while I consider the rest of this thought. I gather this man believes that once we die, we are perfected for all eternity, passing into a changeless state of glory.

Frankly, I see no scriptural basis for this assumption. C. S. Lewis, for one, believed the dead are not done growing; he also surmised that the transition into another world might be difficult, even painful. In the fourth century, Gregory of Nyssa expressed a similar belief, saying that a person who has had difficulty learning spiritual lessons in this life, may see things more clearly "after his departure out of the body," and thus gain new knowledge that will allow him to be prepared "to partake of divinity." Even Saint Augustine agreed, writing that the soul can improve itself after death.

I believe the dead do need our prayers, just as we need theirs. Prayer is a way to continue our reciprocal relationship. After all, we still love each other, and we are still connected within the living network of Divine Life. So why would we stop praying for each other? What's more, prayer affirms our certainty that our loved ones are still alive within the eternal Breath of God—and our relationship endures. Today, as a Jesuit, I not only pray *for* the souls who reside in the invisible world; I believe I also pray *with* them. We are all co-workers in the realm of God, each in our own way continuing the tasks to which God has called us.

Recently, I have felt called to pray not only for the souls of beloved friends and family, but also for the vast company of Black folks who endured unthinkable pain over the past centuries. I have come to believe we have been morally, psychologically, and spiritually careless in our care for those souls. Christianity has long had an energetic, intentional campaign to "save souls," an intention Westerners used to justify both their deep involvement with slavery and the destruction of the Americas' Indigenous cultures. I believe we have inflicted even more intense trauma on those Black and Indigenous souls by refusing them proper respect and care, even after their deaths.

According to the tradition of enslaved Blacks in North America, the dead gather to pray together for those the living have forgotten. And in Africa, the Igbo taught that the dead intercede in prayer on behalf of the living.[334] I love imagining those heavenly prayer meetings—but I wonder why we, the living, so seldom join them. Although the Catholic branch of Christianity prays for the dead, in the more than two decades I have been a Catholic, I cannot recall a single service that mentioned a prayer intention for the souls of those who died in slavery—my ancestors' souls. Why do we never (at least in my experience) name these people in our prayers on All Souls' Day or on other occasions when we publicly pray for the dead? Why do we not hold requiems on their behalf?

Nevertheless, the Catholic Church affirms that a two-way stream of prayer still connects the living and the dead: we can pray for the dead, while they continue to support us with their prayers. This is a teaching that's seldom mentioned in the modern church, but in the fourth century, Gregory the Theologian said of his deceased father: "I am well assured that his intercession is of more avail now than was his instruction in former days, since he is closer to God, now that he has shaken off his bodily fetters, and freed his mind from the clay which obscured it."[335] Along similar lines, Saint Jerome wrote, "If the Apostles and Martyrs, while still in the body, can pray for others, at a time when they must still be anxious for themselves, how much more after their crowns, victories, and triumphs are won!"[336] Prayer is a vibration that passes back and forth across the waters of life and death, undergirding and sustaining our ongoing connections with those who have died.

Furthermore, if prayer operates in the world outside time, then why do we not send our prayers back to those who suffered so much in life, supporting them spiritually with our love and strength? As another fourth-century Church Father, John Chrysostom, wrote, speaking of the dead who died in pain, "Let us weep for them, let us assist them to the extent of our ability, let us think of some assistance for them, small as it may be, yet let us somehow assist them. But how, and in what way? By praying for them and by entreating others to pray for them."

Presence in Absence

I have come to realize that as I widen my spiritual imagination, I not only deepen my relationship with God, but I also find a gateway to connection with my grandmother and with friends who have died. Western culture has a poor opinion of the imagination, though. It's often relegated to childhood—to make-believe and fantasy. The imaginary is, by definition, *not real.*

My spiritual ancestor, Ignatius of Loyola, believed, however, that the imagination is a potent tool for prayer and contemplation. Through the power of the imagination, he said, we can see what is not present. Centuries before him, Synesius of Cyrene wrote, "If anyone believes that the [spiritual] ascent is indeed a great thing, but has no faith in the imagination," they have not paid attention to scripture, for "this too is a means by which the blessed contact may sometimes be achieved."[337] The imagination widens our perception of the spiritual realm, even as it expands our sense of possibility in the physical world. It is an open door that God has granted us.

For me, this is a spiritually "apophatic" way of living with these loved ones. The word *apophatic* is a theological term that expresses our inability to describe God with images or words. Ultimately, all metaphors and similes, all nouns and adjectives and verbs, are not enough. Even the word *love* is not enough to describe who God is, for God is always *more* than our words can say. Our loved ones who have passed over into another realm are in a similar state; they exist in a reality beyond our ability to name or describe. But they are not dead, they are not lost, nor have they lost their lives or slipped away, and they are not gone. Their lives are not finished. They have, however, voyaged beyond our ability to see them clearly. We can no longer contain their being with words, for they live in a reality we have never fully experienced—we can only grope toward it, squinting, straining our ears to catch an occasional sense of shape, a bright glimpse, or a whisper of something *beyond*.

Philosopher Jacques Derrida fought back against the Western belief that something is either here or not here; neither presence nor absence, he said, are absolute. He spoke of "traces" of presence that always remain, even in absence, referring to this as the "absently present" dimension of reality.[338] In this chapter, we have been looking at ways to perceive those traces of presence that remain, even after death.

When thinking of those who have entered the realm beyond death, our Eurocentric thinking once more falls back into its insistence on dualistic states of being. Someone cannot be both present and absent, any more than they can be both dead and alive. But again, I believe the African perspective sees a deeper reality. Those of us in the Black diaspora deeply mourn the absence of our deceased loved ones, even as we celebrate their ongoing presence. For us, death is truly a love story, one that will never end.

And so, "since we stand surrounded by all those who have gone before, an enormous cloud of witnesses, let us drop every extra weight, every sin that clings to us and slackens our pace, and let us run with endurance the long race set before us."[339] This life is but the foyer to eternal life. Love never ends.

Grief is the price of love.
Loving someone means that one day,
there will be grieving. . . . When you see
that pain coming, you may want
to throw up the guardrails,
sound the alarm, raise the flag,
but you must keep
the borders of your heart porous
in order to love well.
Grieving is an act of surrender.

—VALARIE KAUR[340]

PRAYER PRACTICE

This prayer of memory can be used either alone or in a group. If you aren't familiar with any of the names included here, please look them up; get to know your "ancestry." Feel free to add the names of individuals you consider to also be your spiritual or biological ancestors.

We call upon the Creator and Sustainer of the Universe to inspire us to live and work together in unity, love, and respect, and to illuminate our hearts and minds that we may draw from the strength of our ancestors, both spiritual and biological.

Give us the capacity to envision ourselves and the world through Marcus Garvey's eyes, so we may know our strength and our rightful place in the world.

Make us powerful peacemakers, like U Thant, that we may work together to build a safer world for our children and their children.

Grant us dedication and vision to serve others, like Harriet Tubman, Desmond Tutu, and Eleanor Roosevelt, that we may realize that freedom and goodness must always be shared.

Give us the courage and determination of Mahatma Gandhi, that we may fight without violence for the freedom of all people.

Grace us with the dignity and humility of Dr. Martin Luther King, and give us the will to fight for a moral and just society.

In the spirit of Dorothy Day, grant us the courage to integrate our faith with our actions, standing up against oppression and speaking truth to power.

Help us develop the transforming abilities of Dekha Ibrahim Abd, that we may reshape ourselves into a new and restored people.

Bestow upon us the faith, strength, and perseverance of Queen Mother Moore, Muriel Duckworth, Kwame Ture, Cesar Chavez, and Daniel Berrigan, that we may work together to repair, heal, and restore our communities.

In the spirit of Anne Frank, use our words to change the world.

May we practice the teachings of Fannie Lou Hamer by never forgetting where we came from and always building new bridges to the future.

Reveal to us the footsteps of Peace Pilgrim so that we may follow her, remaining wanderers until humanity has learned the way of peace.

Provide us with leaders who possess the wisdom and statesmanship of W. E. B. DuBois and Black Elk, that they may walk implacably upon the path of justice, truth, and freedom. Give them the will to live, work, and sacrifice for the good of the people, while never betraying our trust through self-serving agendas.

Inspire our daily thoughts, words, and actions, so they may give honor to God, to our ancestors, and to ourselves.

We pray Your eternal peace will be with those who have crossed over before us, the named and unnamed, the great ones and the small ones. May the energy of their spirits, their wisdom, and their love continue to be with us.

And may we together forever dwell within Your love, Creator.[341]

Return to old watering holes for more than water; friends and dreams are there to meet you.

—AFRICAN PROVERB

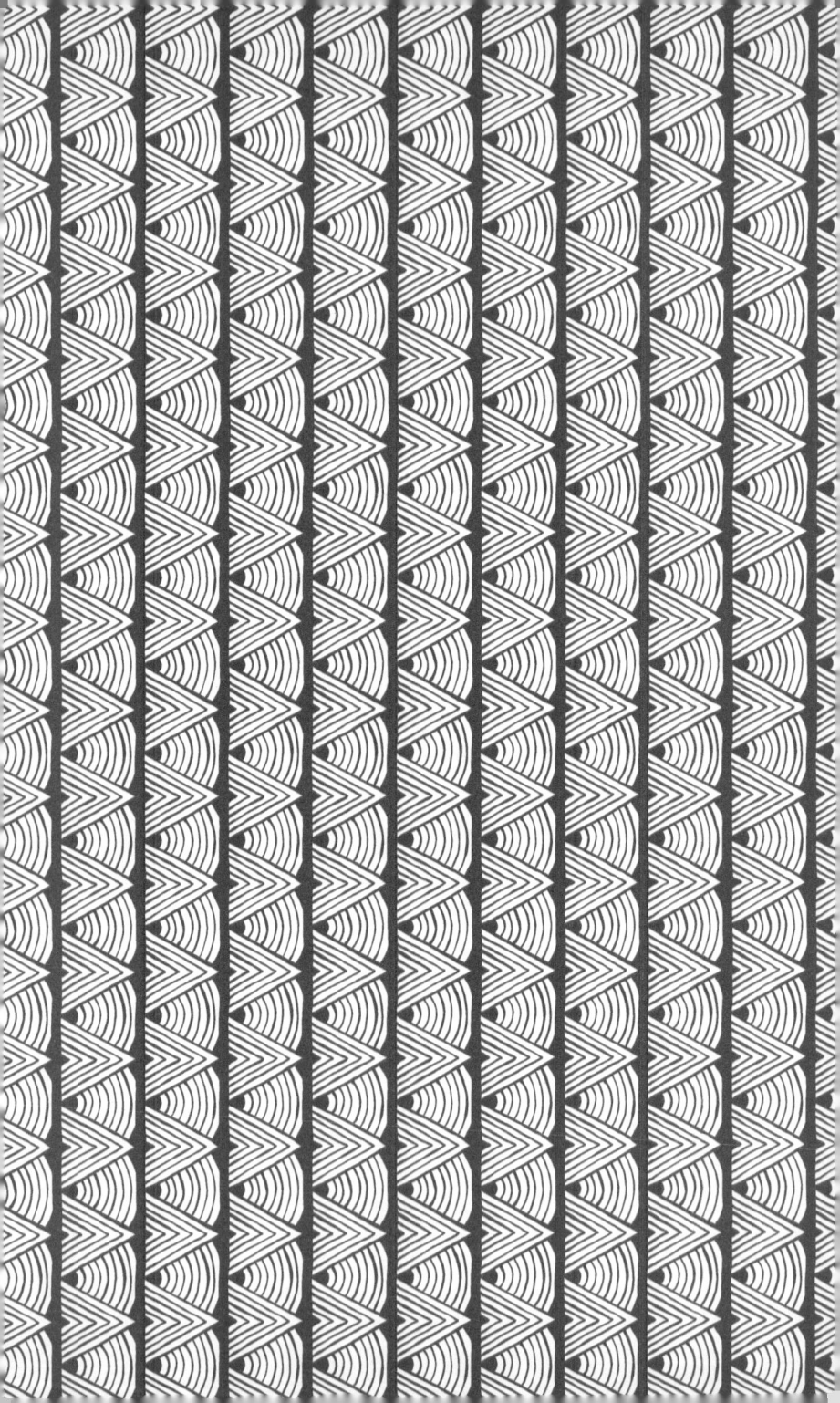

9

BEARING DEATH, AFFIRMING LIFE

DEATH AND RESILIENCE

This notion of "bearing death"
in ways that affirm life
may seem impossible . . .
particularly while
the sheer weight and scope of
death, the vitriolic rhetoric,
the political impotence, and
the stream of unjustifiable
and violent encounters imposed
onto black bodies continues.
Yet death and how we bear it
demands our attention,
calling for an unapologetic
embrace of life.

—MICHELE PRETTYMAN BEVERLY[342]

NOT LONG AGO, I SHARED THE STORY OF THE seventy-five Igbo during an online meeting. As I spoke, I watched tears of what appeared to be both joy and sorrow roll down one young woman's face; meanwhile, another woman in the group seemed indignant. Her mouth opened and closed, twitched and grimaced as I told the story; she seemed to be barely containing her words until the question-and-answer session. When the attendees unmuted their Zoom buttons, and she had her chance to speak, she said to me, "I'm sorry, but honestly, I find your story downright creepy. You don't seriously believe, do you, that seventy-five people magically sprouted wings and flew off to another world?"

I could see her perspective. I didn't want to answer her quickly or glibly, so I paused for a moment, searching my own heart and mind. *Do* I really believe the Igbo flew home to Africa? Or deep in my heart, don't I know they drowned in that dark water, thousands of miles from their home?

Impossible Possibilities

Like the Queen in Lewis Carroll's *Through the Looking Glass*, I confess I make a practice of believing impossible things. After all, as a Catholic, I believe a virgin became pregnant and gave birth to Someone who is both Divine and human—who then died, returned to life, and now lives in a dimension that is both absolutely real while being for the most part totally imperceptible to our physical senses.

But it's not only people of faith who believe impossible things, things that contradict the way we assume normal reality functions. The world is full of impossible possibilities, and I'm not talking about fairy tales or woo-woo fantasies. No, I'm referring to the scientific mysteries that are everywhere in our world. Never mind the everyday technology we've used so often that we've forgotten the mysteries that allow them to function (for example, the invisible energy that sends messages and pictures to our televisions, computers, and cell phones). That's just the beginning. The more science explores our universe, the more mysteries it discovers:

- What appears to be empty space is actually brimming with energy, as well as matter and antimatter; "virtual particles"—disturbances in the field of reality—pop in and out of existence.[343]

- Everything—including light—exists as both waves and particles. It all depends on your perspective.[344]

- Particles can become "entangled," sharing realities across unfathomable space.[345]

- Most of the matter in the universe—some 95 percent—is "dark matter," which is invisible because it doesn't interact with light; scientists have very little idea as to what dark matter really is.[346]

- The universe may have hidden dimensions concealed within it. "Imagine a mansion with a secret room," is how one journalist described it. "Now imagine that the room is vastly bigger than the mansion itself—and contains more mansions. . . .

[T]he known universe may be just one of many 'mansions' residing in the secret room—space's hidden dimensions."[347]

This is not a book about quantum physics, so if you want to learn more about any of these nonsensical realities, you'll need to do that reading elsewhere. My point here is this: *When it comes to the nature of reality, our brains' perceptions are severely limited.* "Common sense" is not always right. "There are more things in heaven and earth," as Hamlet told Horatio, "than are dreamt of in your philosophy." Or to put it another way, there are many mansions in our universe, and we have only begun to explore the entryway of just one of them.

As I tried to explain this perspective, however, I could see the woman was not convinced. She rolled her eyes and sighed. "You're talking about metaphors. No sane person confuses metaphors with reality."

I wasn't sure I understood, so I asked her to explain. "Your entire story," she said, "is a metaphor for death."

"But a metaphor is—" I started to say.

"Your story romanticizes death," she interrupted. "Even worse, it romanticizes suicide. You're talking Jim Jones craziness. You're holding up mass suicide as a symbol of hope."

"Ah." I thought about that for a moment, and then I said, "I do not see the Igbos' situation as being at all similar to that of the Jim Jones community. The Igbos did not choose death because they were under the power of a narcissistic and paranoid leader. I'm not sure you can truly understand the choices my ancestors faced when they were brought to the Americas. The Igbo in my story chose freedom. They chose life. And they were willing to die, physically speaking, in order to have life."

The woman scowled at me. "Those are dangerous ideas. You're retelling a terrible story in a way that minimizes and disguises the ugliness."

Let me be clear, dear readers. Whether we are talking about the seventy-five Igbo; the thousands of human beings who died in slave ships, on plantations, and at the end of lynching ropes; or the endless list of Black men and women gunned down by police in the twentieth and twenty-first centuries, I do not in any way intend to minimize or disguise the terror and ugliness of the Black experience of death. Nor do I think any of us has the right to look away from that ugliness, replacing it with a story that sits more comfortably in our minds.

And yet James Baldwin, who looked at racism with such honesty and courage, was able to write that "one ought to rejoice in the fact of death—ought to decide, indeed, to earn one's death by confronting with passion the conundrum of life. One is responsible to life: It is the small beacon in that terrifying darkness from which we come and to which we shall return. One must negotiate this passage as nobly as possible, for the sake of those who are coming after us." And then Baldwin ends his thought with this: "But white Americans do not believe in death, and this is why the darkness of my skin so intimidates them." Racism, Baldwin knew, goes hand in hand with the fear and denial of death.[348]

"But," I imagine that woman saying in response, "isn't that exactly what you're doing? Trying to deny the reality of death? Saying the seventy-five Igbo didn't die because instead they grew wings and flew back to Africa—that's denial."

Once again, though, this is a case of both-and reality: just as light is both a particle and a wave, depending on your perspective, death can be both a horror and at the same time a doorway into more abundant life. Both perspectives are real. One does not negate the other (though "common sense" would have it so).

Is this a dangerous idea, as the woman insisted? Maybe. It's certainly a radical idea, in the sense that it pulls up by the roots some of our assumptions about life and death. And maybe it is also dangerous because it threatens the defense mechanisms—the stereotypes and evasions—we've erected to protect us from life's fear and suffering. With those defenses shattered, we are forced to expand our assumptions. We become vulnerable to the pain of change and growth.

Telling Multiple Stories

"The single story creates stereotypes," said author Chimamanda Ngozi Adichie, "and the problem with stereotypes is not that they are untrue, but that they are incomplete. They make one story become the only story."[349]

When it comes to death, especially the violent deaths that result from racism and other forms of hatred, I believe it is essential that we do not tell a single story. If I told only the story where seventy-five Igbo grew wings and flew home to Africa, without putting the other story alongside it—the story where the Igbo drown in the swamp water—then yes, I would be guilty of covering up one reality with another. We need to hear both stories. And we need to believe both.

In Adichie's 2009 TED Talk, she described the different narratives told about Africa. "If I had not grown up in Nigeria," she said, "and if all I knew about Africa were from popular images, I too would think that Africa was a place of beautiful landscapes, beautiful animals, and incomprehensible people, fighting senseless wars, dying of poverty and AIDS, unable to speak for themselves, and waiting to be saved, by a kind, white foreigner." Adichie acknowledged that "Africa is a continent full of catastrophes"—the violence and rapes in Congo, the fact that 5,000 people apply for one job vacancy in Nigeria, and failed infrastructures and corrupt governments are a few of the examples she gave—but then she went on to affirm there are other stories to tell about Africa that are not about catastrophe. "And it is very important," said Adichie, "it is just as important, to talk about them. . . . Stories have been used to dispossess and to malign. But stories can also be used to empower, and to humanize. Stories can break the dignity of a people. But stories can also repair that broken dignity."

Telling multiple stories allows us to see a more fully faceted reality. We learn that reality—including death—is not a binary either-or proposition. This perspective counteracts both defeatist pessimism and romantic idealism. It also speaks out against the narratives that have been told by colonization, racism, and privilege. It empowers us to see a reality that is far more rich and intricate, filled with impossible possibilities.

Faithful Vision

Author James W. Coleman wrote about what he calls the "faithful vision" of enslaved Black people and their descendants. "In light of a history of oppression," he said, "only faith can contain the unfathomable evil of the past and present and project future deliverance into it." This faithful vision, wrote Coleman, is not "simplistic and otherworldly" but rather, it "sees sacred, spiritual, and supernatural agency . . . that aids individual and collective survival and salvation." It "encompasses all that human rationality can and then looks beyond that to faith."[350] It refuses to accept the stories told by colonization; it insists that there is a far vaster reality, one that even the most deeply rooted racism has no power to destroy.

This is why I suggested to the woman that she might not be able to understand the reality my ancestors experienced. I did not mean to be condescending or dismissive of her point of view—but, as Coleman put it, "The African American imagination is conceived in the individual struggle and historical travail created by the horror of the past of slavery and racism." And, as Toni Morrison reminded white readers, we Blacks "are the subjects of our own narrative, witnesses to and participants in our own experience."[351] Morrison described the Black experience of death as "unspeakable," and Coleman wrote that at the core of the Black experience "is atrocity, pain, and suffering seared indelibly on collective racial being by its unfathomable brutality . . . and intended perpetuity."[352] The living faith that has been forged out of a history of oppression is something many white people cannot easily or quickly enter into.

From the very beginning of Black folks' history in the Americas, I believe, it was our faith in the Life-Giver that empowered us to endure. Faith allowed us to shape and carry with us our music, our dances, our humor, our food, our stories, and countless other aspects of Black culture. Faith made us strong. It gave us resilience.

What Resilience Is—and Isn't

According to Merriam-Webster's online dictionary, resilience is: 1) elasticity; the capability of a strained body to recover its size and shape after deformation caused especially by compressive stress; 2) an ability to recover from or adjust easily to misfortune or change. As I try to apply these definitions to the Black experience of death, I find myself uncomfortable with them both. They bring to my mind a picture of a rubbery Black fellow who bounces through life with a good-natured smile on his face. *We've been stretched and pulled out of shape, but hey man, we just shake it off and keep on jiving.*

As a psychologist, I believe a facile, simplistic understanding of resilience is incorrect. And yet, in the ongoing wake of COVID-19, it's a word we hear and read a lot. We know resilience is a good thing to have. If we can just find the resilience we need, we can bounce back stronger than ever from whatever life has dealt us, whether that be illness, death, racism, or some other form of sorrow. That old saying from Friedrich Nietzsche—what doesn't kill me will make me stronger—is the nutshell form of this superficial understanding of resilience.

Somehow, though, it's easier to expect other people to be resilient than it is to find that bouncy, elastic quality in our own souls. We expected the millions of children who missed months of in-person school during the pandemic to return to their classrooms bright-eyed and bushy-tailed, because after all, children are naturally resilient. We encouraged their parents to have the same resilience as they adjusted to new routines and demands on their time, dealt with the ongoing symptoms of long COVID, or coped with the sorrow of pandemic deaths. The recent magazine articles on resilience are countless. Or go to Google; you'll get about 27,000,000 results having to do with resilience. So if you're not feeling particularly resilient, just take a few minutes to read one of these articles, and you'll be fine. (Or at least that's the implication.)

However, as public-policy journalist Michael Orsini pointed out, "The resilience industry is rooted in an individual model of change, one that leaves untouched the structures and systems that are responsible for the trauma in the first place." He went on to say: "Children growing up in under-served communities would not have to 'overcome' their environments if their schools and neighbourhoods had the resources they deserved. Indigenous people would not need to become resilient in the face of colonial dispossession had they not been forced into residential schools or had their land occupied." The ongoing COVID crisis cannot be as easily dissected into cause-and-effect, but the vulnerability of the Black community to COVID and other health issues is well-documented. (See chapter 1.) In light of that, Orsini reminded us: "The idea that recovery from trauma or disadvantage builds character is particularly odious because it marks certain communities as needing adversity to toughen them up while allowing others to simply go about their privileged lives."[353]

So before we talk about resilience as it relates to death and racism, I want to be clear that I am not referring to a cheap and easy bounciness, the sort of unquenchable strength we somehow expect of others, even when we struggle to find it in ourselves. As my cynical Zoom participant reminded me in regard to the seventy-five Igbo, we cannot pretend the horrors of death and racism do not exist, nor should we. Belief in another world, a joyful dimension that lies beyond death, cannot paper over the challenges and demands of this-world suffering.

As I have already said so many times already, Westerners, particularly Americans, have a hard time seeing shades of gray. We often see reality as a binary on-and-off button. In this case, ON is resilience; OFF is total failure and dysfunction. But that's not the nature of true resilience. Author Resmaa Menakem wrote, "In today's America, we tend to think of healing as something binary: either we're broken, or we're healed from that brokenness. But that's not how healing operates, and it's almost never how human growth works. More often, healing and growth take place on a continuum, with innumerable points between utter brokenness and total health."[354] Resilience, I would say, is the courage to commit to the long journey of healing, with all its ups and downs between brokenness and the abundant, full-bodied life God wants for us. Resilience is rooted in hope.

Hope and Resilience

When I looked up the etymology of both hope and resilience, I discovered that their oldest word roots are surprisingly similar. *Resilience* grew from a Latin word that meant "to jump, to leap"—and *hope* shares a common root with the word *hop*. The etymological foundations of both *resilience* and *hope* contain a sense of brisk, nearly airborne forward movement.

Our modern understanding of these words has, however, warped their original meanings until they are barely recognizable. Author Meg Llewellyn wrote, "We've lost sight of hope as something active and muscular—something practical and down-to-earth that gives meaning to our work. True hope isn't the same as either positive thinking or a goal-oriented perspective. . . . In Old English, *hopa* meant 'confidence in the future,' but it wasn't a cheery outlook that was immune to dark days. It wasn't even a glass-is-half-full mentality that hoped for the best. Instead, the ancient version of hope saw the empty half of the glass, and it knew that there was darkness all around—but it still believed there were possibilities, even in the darkness. There was action to take that would lead to something better."[355]

Hope, Lewellyn went on to say, is "less like the rungs of a ladder which must be climbed in an ascent to a heaven up there (or, indeed, out there) and rather more like the scaffolding being put in place which allows heaven to be built in the here and now of daily existence."[356] Hope and resilience are both practical and action-oriented.

This is what the Bible describes when it speaks of hope, not the wistful wishing we have in mind when we say things like, "I hope it doesn't rain tomorrow," "I hope you feel better soon," or "I hope I don't get COVID." Real hope and true resilience get busy; they're creative. They work with whatever is there to build something new, something fresh and unique that never existed before.

Resilience and Creativity

The hope and resilience of Black people created jazz music, Soul Food, and Black theology, to name just a very few examples. Neuroscientist and author Jonah Lehrer offers this paradox as a partial explanation: "The imagination is unleashed by constraints."[357] With constraints, psychological research suggests, we have the opportunity to use our mental energies more creatively. Challenge forces us to figure out new ways to cope; it gives us the impetus to leap forward. This impetus is resilience, and it is fueled by hope. Resilience builds on the strength of the past to create something new in the future.

Lehrer also wrote that creative insights come when "the rules of one place are shifted to a new domain."[358] This too describes the Black experience in the Americas, where enslaved groups of people confronted hardship and cruelty in colonized lands even as they remained rooted in the joys and beauties of Africa. Their hybrid experience, despite all its sorrow and oppression, produced something rich and unique that has nourished and enriched the entire world.

As a member of the Black community, I affirm with Isabel Wilkerson that "we must know our history to gain strength for the days ahead. We must love ourselves even if—and perhaps, especially if—others do not. We must keep our faith even as we work to make our country live up to its creed. And we must know deep in our bones and in our hearts that if the ancestors could survive the Middle Passage, we can survive anything."[359]

Whites are not excluded from this creative resilience, for, whether America acknowledges it or not, her society was birthed from the union of the Western world with Africa. You can't dismiss America's connection to Africa as a purely spiritual bond, felt only by Black folk, for the bond between Africa and America is tangible and visible. Imagine America without spirituals or jazz, rock'n'roll or hip-hop, gospel or the blues, without banjos and guitars, without tap or hip-hop dancing, and without watermelon or yams, barbecue or fried fish. Think how boring America would be without the rich visual, musical, gustatory, and spiritual flavors of Africa! Without Africa, America would not be who she is.

Without Black workers, America could not have grown into the industrial giant that allowed her to become a world power. In the years since Emancipation, Blacks continued to contribute their strength, courage, and creativity to America; they have fought for her in wars; cared for her young, her sick, and her elderly with tenderness and compassion; contributed new ideas to science, business, and government; and entertained us with their humor, athleticism, and artistic creativity. America also owes much of its current political freedom to her Black people; as journalist Nikole Hannah-Jones pointed out, "Our founding fathers may not have actually believed in the ideals they espoused, but black people did"[360]—and it was the resilience of Black people who were strong enough to stand up for justice that shaped the reality of our democracy today.

"Your country?" wrote DuBois. "How came it yours? Before the Pilgrims landed we were here. Here we have brought our gifts and mingled them with yours: a gift of story and song . . . , the gift of sweat and brawn to beat back the wilderness, conquer the soil, and lay the foundations of this vast economic empire. . . . Actively we have woven ourselves with the very warp and woof of this nation—we fought their battles, shared their sorrow, mingled our blood with theirs, and generation after generation have pleaded with a headstrong, careless people to despise not Justice, Mercy, and Truth. . . . Our song, our toil, our cheer, and warning have been given to this nation in blood-brotherhood. . . . Would America have been America without her Negro people?"

Too often, however, the Black community is described in terms of deficits and disease. We've told a single story about Blacks, and in doing so, we've failed to recognize the historical fact that as a population, Blacks have shown a sustained ability to not merely survive social, economic, and environmental adversities but to thrive. Oppression and prejudice have taken (and continue to take) a devastating toll, and yet Blacks, both as individuals and as a community, have endured with creativity and a tenacious pluck. They demonstrate what trauma experts E. K. Rynearson and Fanny Corea define as resilience: the ability to confront violence and death while still maintaining an interior sense of safety, separateness, and autonomy.[361] Forced again and again to bear death, Blacks have never stopped affirming life.

Bearing Death

The encounter with death, however, especially violent death, initially shatters any human being's sense of equilibrium. When that happens—when we find ourselves in a state of brokenness, our sense of security gone, our self-concepts fragmented— healthy storytelling can restore our resilience. Unfortunately, though, some of the stories we tell ourselves only thrust us deeper into despair, doubt, and fear—but other stories, Rynearson and Corea maintain, lift us and illumine us. When our understanding of life has been devastated, when we are lost, confused, despairing, and cynical, "restorative storytelling" allows us to "reconstruct a world of meaning."[362]

During the Zoom session I described earlier in this chapter, I explained the value of stories as a way to see the Divine Presence even in the terror and ugliness of violence and death. The story of the seventy-five Igbo is an example of using narrative to affirm meaning. My doubting-Thomas attendee took issue with that as well. "Stories," she said, "are fiction. They're not true. They're just a way to run away from reality."

She's not alone in her perception; the modern world often assumes that fiction is synonymous with falsehood, and that its purpose is purely as entertainment and escape. As a society, we've lost sight of the ancient world's understanding that narratives don't need to be factual to be true;[363] stories can be doorways into a deeper understanding of reality. Stories are one way we put our world back together, even when it keeps falling apart.

In these COVID years, we desperately need new stories that will help us make sense of our world. Even as Blacks have endured more than their share of COVID-caused suffering, the pandemic has forced the white community to also learn to bear death in new ways. As psychologist and grief researcher Robert Neimeyer explained, "The losses [dealt by COVID] include [the loss of] our sense of predictability, control, justice, and the belief that we can protect our children or elderly loved ones."[364] In the wake of the pandemic, we live in an uncertain and frightening world.

It's a world we Blacks have lived in for a very long time.

And like racism, COVID is ongoing. It keeps evolving, so that even as our sense of the initial crisis wanes, millions of people are still grieving the death of loved ones or enduring the debilitating aftereffects of long COVID (and meanwhile, people are still getting sick, still dying). Along with the sorrow of physical deaths, COVID has also devastated many individuals' sense of safety and independence. It has robbed millions of people of their employment and financial security, while the loss of physical strength because of long COVID has taken away their ability to work and participate in recreational activities.[365] In the future, while our world continues to seek scientific answers, individuals will experience still more COVID-related losses we can't yet predict. "We're talking about grieving a living loss—one that keeps going and going," says Dr. Neimeyer.[366] The same, of course, can be said of racism.

We can't overcome our world's ongoing powers of death and destruction with a single mighty act of healing. Instead, we must think of healing as a journey—a journey in which we bear death by affirming life.

Steps Toward Affirming Life

Restorative storytelling is one technique that grief experts offer for dealing with the ongoing trauma of both racism and COVID. Instead of trying to evade sorrow by putting it out of our minds, this technique encourages us to tell sorrow's story, in as many ways as we need to in order to find meaning in the midst of meaninglessness. This not only helps to reconstruct our sense of control and safety, psychologists say, but it also allows us to maintain a bond with the people death has taken away from us.[367] (See chapter 8 for other ways to maintain these connections beyond death.)

When we tell these narratives of hope and possibility to one another—as I do when I tell the story of the seventy-five Igbo—we give them even more power. We bring them out of the hazy realm of our personal and private beliefs, and we set them free in the larger world. They become a creative force.

Grief experts list additional ways to put our confidence in life even while we're carrying the crushing weight of death. These steps in the journey of bearing death by affirming life are techniques that encourage resilience. Too often, we think of resilience as an inner quality we either have or we don't, when in reality, there are specific things we can do to build resilience in both ourselves and others. These include:

Building and supporting kinship ties.[368] This applies both to the physically alive family members and to the kinship network that lives on in an invisible realm. "Only a living sense of the immortality of the personality," wrote cultural scholar Viacheslav Vsevolodovich Ivanov, "can make our society truly a society in the sense of the universal connection of all living people (after all, everyone is alive in God) and the voluntary acceptance of responsibility for all. . . . The true liberators . . . are filled with the understanding that is granted by love, love not only for their visible family but also for their unseen neighbors."[369] We gain strength from our family's life force, a force that stretches both backward and forward in linear time.

Creating and strengthening our connections to social networks beyond the family.[370] Trauma expert Bessel A. van der Kolk believes, "Social support is the most powerful protection against becoming overwhelmed by stress and trauma." He goes on to stress that "social support is not the same as merely being in the presence of others. The critical issue is reciprocity: being truly heard and seen by the people around us, feeling that we are held in someone else's mind and heart."[371] With active recognition of one another and a commitment to help, we tighten and strengthen the intimate connections between us.

Creating strong community networks where differences are encouraged and cherished. Physicist and ecologist Fritjof Capra, comparing human communities to ecosystems, wrote, "The more complex the network is, the more complex its pattern of interconnections, the more resilient it will be." He went on to explain, "Diversity means many different relationships, many different approaches to the same problem. A diverse community is a resilient community . . . sustained by a web of relationships."[372] In order to not only survive but also to thrive as communities, we need to recognize and value our differences, seeing them as strengths rather than barriers between us. As the Akan people say, "All fingers are not the same"; we need all five to function effectively. "Differences are not intended to separate, to alienate," wrote Desmond Tutu. "We are different precisely in order to realize our need of one another."[373]

In Kongo spirituality, community is not limited to Western definitions of commonality or geographical proximity. Instead, it is sacramental, a tangible embodiment of spiritual reality. According to Simon Bockie, a native of Zaire, the Kongo perspective perceives community as "a reality present everywhere, at all times. Each person realizes his or her nature through relationship with others in the community. . . . This community furthermore extends through all life to include not only the visible beings but also those who are unseen."[374]

Expanding and clinging to faith in a spiritual reality of love and purpose, which contains this world with all its sorrows.[375] When we believe in a larger unseen world, we are empowered to find meaning in the visible, everyday world. This, said theologian William Barber, "is how the slaves made it through slavery. Yes, they were called everything but children of God by the oppressive slave masters and system of slavery, but somehow deep in their spiritual DNA they were able to yet sing: *Before I be a slave, I'll be buried in my grave, and go home to my Lord and be free*. They knew they were not slaves."[376] When we are rooted in the vast perspective of a world outside linear time, a world of infinite wholeness and completion, we have the steadiness and flexibility we need to survive this world's tumult.

Imagining a society that's different from the one in which we live. This means we can no longer say, "But that's the way things have always been," as a justification for oppression and violence. Instead, we cast our mind's eye beyond the boxes of tradition and societal limitation. Theologian James Alison wrote that as human beings "our imaginations go round in death-bound cycles"; we need to open our minds to the "immense creative diversity" found in the Divine imagination.[377]

And, as with restorative storytelling, our imagination can become a catalyst for change when we put words to our ideas. According to African spirituality, "We have the power to build whatever we pronounce and make something tangible from nothing. We bring the tangible from the intangible, like God."[378]

Taking positive action in some way—whether through activism, advocacy, or some other form of active engagement—in order to go beyond imagination to build something tangible.[379] "Meaning is also 'made' through deliberate action—by performing intentional, meaningful acts."[380] As we act, seeking to build and heal rather than tear down and destroy, we not only change society; we also change ourselves. Our attention shifts away from the pain of the past, as we focus on the possibility of the present and the future.

Being willing to learn and adapt. We must, wrote Willie Jennings, "become radically adaptive learners always willing to expand our identities toward those to whom the Spirit is calling us to join."[381] To do this, we change our attitude toward people and events; instead of labeling circumstances as "terrible," "unbearable," or "impossible," we see them as opportunities for learning and growth. Instead of seeing other people as "dangerous," "strange," or "inferior," we regard them with a friendly curiosity that seeks to learn, that reaches out to others rather than pushes them away.

This doesn't mean we aren't heartsick when death and violence invade our lives; it doesn't mean we don't get angry with those who practice injustice and persecution. But we don't allow ourselves to be frozen by our emotions, unable to move forward. Instead, we explore stories that are yet untold, stories that leave room for innovative possibilities. We allow fresh identities and groundbreaking understandings to rise out of the dead ashes of our trauma. We know that hatred and prejudice, sorrow and death are all-too real—but we also know that one day we shall overcome them.

We Shall Overcome

In 1945, American Tobacco, a company in Charleston, South Carolina, had a long history of segregation and unequal payment practices. The Black women who worked there got together to ask for unpaid back wages and a raise of 25 cents an hour. When management refused to listen to them, the women walked out of the factory and began to picket.

As they marched, they sang an old song that had been around awhile, sung in various forms by both Blacks and whites.

We shall overcome, we shall overcome,
we shall overcome someday.
Oh, deep in my heart, I do believe,
we shall overcome someday.

The tobacco strike in Charleston was the first time this song was sung in a protest. The women made one alteration to the words: always before, it had been "I shall overcome," but they sang "we." In doing so, they changed the song from a simple tune of personal hope and faith into a powerful anthem of unity.

"We Shall Overcome" traveled from the Charleston strikers to the Highlander Folk School, where it was picked up by labor activists, including Pete Seeger. Pete then brought the song full circle back to the Black community, a beautiful example of racial cooperation and creativity.

This simple song, with its roots spread through both the Black and white experience, became the voice of the Civil Rights Movement. Protestors sang it as they marched for equality and an end to racial discrimination. They sang it as they were beaten by cops' batons and attacked by police dogs; they sang it while they struggled to breathe through tear gas; they sang it from jail cells.

New words were spontaneously added to the song, in response to the needs of the moment.

We are not afraid, we are not afraid,
we are not afraid today.
Oh, deep in my heart, I do believe,
we shall overcome someday.

We are not alone, we are not alone,
we are not alone today.
Oh, deep in my heart, I do believe,
we are not alone today.

John Lewis, the congressman from Georgia, described what the song meant to him during his time as a leader of the Civil Rights Movement. Lewis was jailed, he was beaten, and in Selma on Bloody Sunday, his skull was fractured. Through it all, he said, "We Shall Overcome" sustained him. "It gave you a sense of faith, a sense of strength, to continue to struggle, to continue to push on. And you would lose your sense of fear. You were prepared to march into hell's fire."[382]

"We Shall Overcome" has become a protest song among freedom movements around the world. The song's simple words and tune have united protestors in China, Northern Ireland, South Korea, Lebanon, Eastern Europe, and India.[383] It is a song for all human beings, a song of power and promise, an affirmation of unity, equality, and hope. It is the voice of resilience, teaching us to celebrate life even as we bear the reality of death. Victory will not come quickly or easily—but nevertheless, we *shall* overcome the forces of death.

Unfortunately, our modern-day myths have offered us unrealistic images of what victory looks like. In Tolkien's epic fantasy, every last evil orc flees Middle Earth once their master has been defeated; in the Star Wars world, the Death Stars are destroyed in dramatic explosions; and in the Star Trek universe, the entire Borg are soundly trumped when their queen is infected with a pathogen. We long for similar feats of glory in our own world, and we are bitterly disappointed when instead, we seem to be fighting a thousand-headed hydra that grows a new head as soon as we cut off one.

African author Simon Bockie wrote that for the Kongo people, the struggle between life and death is not seen in terms of epic battles, nor is it led by shining heroes who rise up to fight a single evil mastermind. Instead, this struggle is a constant daily effort, both individually and societally, to create a peace and equilibrium with a foundation beyond time. "Human life is not seen as rushing headlong through linear history toward death," Bockie wrote, "on a collision course with itself. . . . Evils endlessly arise and must be dealt with wisely, so that the prosperity and mutual goodwill of the community can continue always to thrive." Bockie also reminded that from the African perspective, "The social order has its roots in the invisible world. . . . God is the power of life."[384]

The message of "We Shall Overcome" is planted in this African insight. We are not bold knights wielding swords, seeking to kill before we can be killed, nor are we intrepid avengers retaliating against evil. We are simply ordinary people engaged in a struggle to slowly transform our world. We do not triumph as warriors using our enemies' methods of destruction, but rather we seek to be catalysts in a life-giving process that never ends. We use the forces of love—in whatever shape or form is most effective—to transform our enemies rather than annihilate them. We seek to bring them with us into eternity's new creation. As we participate daily in this ongoing struggle, we continue to affirm life even in the midst of death.

"Bearing death" does not mean vanquishing the traumas in our lives or forgetting them. It doesn't mean we will one day be able to live as if racism, COVID, and all the other life-robbing forces in our world had never happened. We're not going to "get better," and we will never go back to being who we were before our encounters with death and destruction. "The reality is that you will grieve forever," wrote Elisabeth Kübler-Ross. "You will not 'get over' the loss of a loved one; you will learn to live with it. You will heal and you will rebuild yourself around the loss you have suffered. You will be whole again but you will never be the same. Nor should you be the same nor would you want to."[385]

If we apply Kübler-Ross's words to the larger world beyond our personal sorrows, we do not learn to "live with" racism and violence. Instead, each time another innocent Black person is shot down or Tasered by police, we seek ways to rebuild and heal not only our own hearts but also the world that allows these things to happen. We look at the ongoing griefs born by people of color, and we work together to find paths of wholeness.

For that is the only way we shall overcome, and ultimately, that is the only we can all go home—together.

Home-Going

When we think of death as a home-going, we usually assume the "mansions" Jesus described[386] are our ultimate destinations, and we envision them as places of never-ending rest and peace, places where no more struggle is required. But I'm not sure where or when we came up with that story of static, changeless bliss.

And so, let me end our time together with another story, one that tells a different story about the afterlife. This story is entirely my own creation and yet, I believe, carries truth for us all.

Once more, you are one of those seventy-five Igbo, following your leader into the dark, deep water. Your heart is pounding; it's only natural to be afraid, for even as you sing your affirmation of hope, you know you are walking toward death. You watch as the person ahead of you sinks beneath the water, and you feel the cold current sucking at your legs, your belly, your arms, your chest . . .

And then, even as the darkness claims you and your breath leaves your body, something else happens. Your shoulder blades prickle, then burn, then seem to expand in an impossible way. Suddenly, wings unfurl from your body and catch the air, sweeping you into the sky. Joy explodes within your chest, for you know this is not the end after all. You are going home.

With your companions around you, your wings beat strong and steady as you cross the Atlantic. In what seems an impossibly short amount of time, you see through the clouds below you the coastline of your home. You recognize the familiar shapes of mountains and plains; you trace the river that brought life to your village; and then, as you draw still nearer, lower now, you see the familiar dwelling places of your community. With a last powerful flap of your wings, you land on the soil of your homeland, tears of joy rolling down your face.

The ancestors rush to greet you, surrounding you and your companions with loving hands and voices. You rejoice in their presence as you feel their love healing you and nourishing you. And then, you look past them—and now, there are no words for this part of the story, for you are face to face with the One who is both your Mother and your Father, the Giver of all life. You have come Home. . . .

You have come Home to joy unending, but this is not the end of the story. This is not a happily-ever-after story where there is no more action to come. A holy restlessness thrums through you; your wings lift and stretch; and you realize the Life-Giver is calling your name. You and your seventy-four companions step forward, your faces bright with joy, as you listen for the assignment that is yours.

But when you hear the Life-Giver say, "Go back," your heart drops. Go back to that world of suffering and oppression, far away from your kin, away from your Home? How can the Holy One ask this of you?

"You will bring this Home with you," the Life-Giver explains. "You will carry it on your wings and in your hearts, and you will share it with those who need it most. Be strong. Have courage. There is much work still to do."

And so the seventy-five of you lift into the air, and like a flock of immense geese, you fly across the ocean, back to that other world where your vocation lies. When you land, you realize you are invisible now, and yet you feel the Life-Giver's love and power coursing through you the way blood once flowed through your veins.

"What do we do now?" you ask—but before any of your companions can answer, you see a child sobbing as a white man drags her away from her mother. As one of your companions runs to the weeping mother and wraps her in his arms, you leap to the child's side. "I'm here, little one," you whisper into her heart. "You cannot be with your mother for a little while, but I will be here. I will not leave you."

And so you stay with this child as she is sold from enslaver to enslaver. Through all her suffering, you are there, lending her your strength, teaching her ways to endure, and opening her eyes to the presence of the Life-Giver in her life. As she grows older, she is forced to undergo terrible hardships— rape, grueling work, and the loss of her children—and you weep as you hold her in your arms, longing to free her from her pain. You cannot, though, and so, instead, you breathe love and power into her lungs, so that she grows strong and tall, filled with dignity and truth.

And when as an adult woman, freed from slavery at last, she wants a new name to call herself, you whisper in her mind, "Call yourself Sojourner—Sojourner Truth, for this world is not your home, and you carry with you your real Homeland's truth. It is your calling now to share that truth with others."

And so Sojourner spends her life working, with you invisible at her side, to build a world of justice and freedom. She is a powerful speaker who opens people's minds and stirs their hearts. With the force of her mighty voice, she fights tirelessly, not only for Black people's rights but also for all women's, as well as for prisoners'.

When at last, the time comes for her to leave this world of struggle, you are still beside her—and now, for the first time, she sees you. "Oh my!" she whispers as you spread your wings. You watch as plumes of flame sizzle and snap from her shoulders. "I'm not gonna die after all," she whispers. "I'm going Home like a shooting star."

And she does.

But of course Sojourner isn't one to sit on a cloud dangling her long, beautiful toes as she strums a harp. That same holy restlessness that drove her struggle for justice is still alive in her, and soon she too joins the network of truth-seekers and justice-builders that stretches around the Earth and out into the universe. Some of the activists in that network are visible, tangible to human senses, but many more—like you and Sojourner—are invisible, yet real and vigorous with the invincible force of love.

You are there when the mob slaughters seventeen-year-old Jesse Washington; you take his stripped and beaten body tenderly in your arms and you carry him Home. You are there, weeping uncontrollably, as Mary Turner is hung, burned, and stabbed. You welcome her bright spirit into the invisible world, where you reunite her with her baby and husband, and then you bring them all with you, back Home where they will be forever safe. You are there when white men kill sweet Emmett Till, and you are the one who stands beside his mother Mamie as she lifts her head and demands justice. And when George Floyd dies beneath the policeman's knee, you are there, waiting to wrap him in your arms. You walk among the protestors who shout for justice; you work side by side with every person who speaks out for freedom, who writes books and letters to newspapers and officials, who reaches out their hands to help.

The oppressed and suffering souls you bring Home are healed and renewed—and when they are ready, they too join the work of healing and renewal, building a new Earth, an Earth that overflows with abundance and beauty. And as you work together, you lift your voices in a song of resilience and hope.

We'll walk hand in hand, we'll walk hand in hand,
We'll walk hand in hand someday.
Oh, deep in my heart, I do believe,
We shall overcome someday.

We shall all be free, we shall all be free,
We shall all be free someday.
Oh, deep in my heart, I do believe,
We shall overcome someday.

God will see us through, God will see us through,
God will see us through each day.
Oh, deep in my heart, I do believe,
We shall overcome someday.

As I wrote this book, I found myself again and again seeking to see beyond the current chaos of racism and COVID, death and injustice. As a stranger in a strange land—or more precisely, as a Black Haitian in Nebraska—I often felt homesick. I wanted my friends, colleagues, students, and patients to see me as strong and resilient, but each time I heard another news story about racism or death, my sense of hope ebbed. Like a child who's frightened and exhausted, I longed for my old home with my grandmother. My childhood abode is no longer available to me, though, so I imagined a bright eternal Homeland, somewhere out past this world's confusion. I yearned to go there.

But now, as I have at last reached this book's end, I find myself seeing things more clearly, as I once saw them when I was living with my grandmother before her death. The sorrow of Tatie's death is not erased—its wound is now a permanent part of the makeup of my soul—but today, I see once again with my unclouded child's eyes.

Now, in the interior glow of my imagination, my grandmother comes to me and says, "You've been on a fool's errand, my beloved brat, trying to flatten out life's peaks and valleys, always looking for a smooth, straight road to take you home. But you'll never get there, not that way." She snaps her fingers under my nose. "Look at me now! Do you see?"

Tatie spreads out her arms—and I *see.* A glimmering web of life spreads out around us, connecting us to one another with luminous strands that cannot be broken. As I look more closely, I see my friends and my family woven into this tapestry of light. I see other faces I recognize and many more I do not. Small leafy things and towering trees, stars and shining angelic creatures, and furred, feathered, and scaled creatures of all sorts are also part of this endless, vibrant mesh. We are all here, I realize: Sojourner and Harriet and Frederick, Martin and Pete and Bobby, George and Breonna and Tamir, Daunte and Emmett and Mamie, and countless others—not one of us has been lost.

Now, for just a moment, stop reading and shut your eyes. Use your imagination and join me here. Look! Do you see this bright cloud of undying souls, each one itself and completely unique, each necessary to the living community? Watch! They're holding out their arms to you and me, inviting us to join them in their never-ending work of love and justice, the work that neither death nor racism can ever halt.

"Do you see now?" Tatie asks me. "Do you understand?"

Yes. I do. I understand now.

Hope and resilience are not something I must manufacture on my own, pulling these qualities out of myself by sheer determination and strength of character. No, I find these attributes simply by returning to my true Home. This Home is not somewhere far away, lost in the memories of childhood, nor does it lie ahead, beyond death's curtain. No, Home is *this*—this resilient network of constant, active love, an infinite filigree of

Divine life that holds us all, supports us, and helps us grow. It's right here, all around us.

And so, dear reader, now, before you turn another page, will you, in your mind's eye, reach out and take my hand?

Let's go Home together.

One thing alone I charge you.
As you live, believe in life!
Always human beings will live and progress
to greater, broader and fuller life.
The only possible death is to lose belief in this truth
simply because the great end comes slowly,
because time is long.

—W. E. B. DUBOIS[387]

MEDITATION PRACTICE

As we gain a new understanding of our relationships with each other and with the invisible world in which we live and move and have our being, sometimes guilt gets in the way of our experience. We have all let people down, and in the confrontation with death, we may be challenged to also confront these failures. This can be one more reason we avoid thinking about the many deaths that are interwoven through life.

In my practice, I often encounter this issue with my patients. I have found that guilt can be defined and intimate—the memory of hurtful words spoken, for example, or loving words unspoken—and it can also be so huge and embedded in the societal structure that it seems all-pervasive, impossible to address, and so we pretend it's not there.

In this meditation, I invite you to sit quietly for a moment, breathing in and out. Then gently shift your attention away from your breath and imagine yourself opening a door in your mind. The room on the other side of this door is dark, but where you are standing is a warm, bright space. In your imagination, stand in the doorway and say, "I know in the past I have hurt people who are no longer with me, who have already gone Home. I sorrow over my actions, and now I invite any guilt I have hidden in this room to come out into the light and talk with me."

Then simply wait and see what (or who) emerges from this dark room. It could be something that happened when you were a teenager and screamed words of hatred at a parent. It might be the lack of attention and understanding you gave a now-deceased friend. Or it could be the guilt you feel about the way people of color have been treated in our society. When your guilt emerges into the light, it may be something small and ugly—or something so massive that it seems to fill the entire space around you. Either way, welcome it. Invite it to engage with you in a conversation. Ask it to tell you more about itself. Without excuses—but also without anxiety or shame—listen to what it has to say to you. Ask it to reveal to you any ways in which you have hurt individuals who are now deceased.

Now imagine that those individuals have also entered the light where you are standing. I have found with my patients that saying these four things can be helpful at this point:

- *Please, forgive me.*

- *I forgive you.*

- *Thank you.*

- *I love you.*

These simple phrases connect us to those who are now in the invisible world. They can be the first steps toward healing a broken relationship that has branches outside of time.

I often hear people say, "But it's too late now!" If that sentence is hovering in your thoughts, let me assure you it is not too late to engage with the people who are no longer with us, not from a psychological perspective and not from a spiritual perspective. Through the powers of the imagination, we can connect at an emotional level, which I believe also has profound spiritual effects in our interior subjective worlds but also in the exterior "objective" world as well.

And if what came out of that dark room where you've hidden your guilt has to do with the racist society in which you are entangled, I suggest you imagine yourself speaking with one of the individuals whose stories I've told in this book. Whether it's one of the seventy-five Igbo, Mary Turner, Emmett Till, George Floyd, or someone else, I encourage you to have a conversation with this person. You may find it helpful to write this conversation as it emerges from your imagination.

Then, after you have spent some time on each of the four statements I listed above, ask a question: *What can I do now to help heal the hurt in which I participated?* Do not push or rush as you wait for an answer to surface.

If nothing specific or tangible comes to mind, carry this question with you. As you go through the next few days, weeks, or even months, hold the question at the back of your consciousness and return to it often. I believe that as you commit yourself to the intention of healing what has been damaged, new and transformative opportunities will reveal themselves to you. Trust that the web of life—the Homeland God invites us all to share—is supporting you. Have hope.

The Water Spirit brought you here—and the Water Spirit will bring you home.

Love is a form of sweet labor:
fierce, bloody, imperfect, and life-giving—
a choice we make over and over again. . . .
This labor engages all our emotions.
Joy is the gift of love.
Grief is the price of love.
Anger protects that which is loved.
And when we think we have reached our limit,
wonder is the act that returns us to love.

–VALARIE KAUR[388]

AFTERWORD

AS THIS BOOK WAS NEARLY READY to go to press, another Black man died at the hands of police officers. "I'm just trying to get home," twenty-nine-year-old Tyre Nichols told the officers as they punched and kicked him. When EMTs arrived on the scene, they stood chatting with the police, watching Tyre writhe in pain for another nineteen minutes. Finally, they took Tyre to the hospital, where he died from his injuries three days later.

At Tyre's funeral, the Reverend Al Sharpton said, "All he wanted to do was get home . . . home is not just a place, home is not just a physical location, home is where you are at peace, home is where you don't have to keep your dukes up, home is where you're not vulnerable, home is where everything is alright. He said all I want to do is get home." Rev. Sharpton went on to say, "The reason I keep going is all I'm trying to do is get home, I wanna get where they can't treat me with a double standard, I'm trying to get home, I want to get where they can't call me names no more, I want to get home, I want to get where they can't shoot now and ask questions later, I'm trying to get home, every Black in America stands up every day trying to get home."[389]

Dear readers, please—it's past time we all went home. Let's do whatever we can to show each other the way.

ENDNOTES

Introduction

1.   At the time of the slave trade, the Igbo were agricultural people
     with quite sophisticated iron tools. They lived in autonomous
     villages that were governed by their elders; their women and
     men had complementary rather than hierarchical roles. They
     also practiced slavery, and they actively participated in the trans-
     Atlantic slave trade. The quality of their lives cannot be reduced to
     these few sentences, though, for their lives were as rich with detail
     as ours are today.

2.   The forced voyage from Africa across the Atlantic was called the
     Middle Passage because it was the middle "leg" of the triangular
     trade route that first took goods (such as knives, guns, ammunition,
     cotton cloth, tools, and brass dishes) from Europe to Africa, then
     shipped Africans to work as slaves in the Americas and the West
     Indies, and finally, brought items, mostly raw materials, produced
     on the plantations (sugar, rice, tobacco, indigo, rum, and cotton)
     back to Europe.

3.   Frederick Douglass. *Narrative of the Life of Frederick Douglass*
     (Oxford, UK: Oxford University Press, 2009 [originally published in
     1881]).

4.   Malidoma Patrice Somé. *The Healing Wisdom of Africa: Finding
     Life Purpose Through Nature, Ritual, and Community* (New York:
     TarcherPerigee, 1999), pp. 167–168, 171–172.

5. Virginia Hamilton. *The People Could Fly* (New York: Alfred A. Knopf, 1985).

6. Georgia Writers' Project. *Drums and Shadows: Survival Studies among the Georgia Coastal Negroes* (Athens: University of Georgia Press, 1986), p. 108.

7. Fritjof Capra. *The Web of Life: A New Scientific Understanding of Living Systems* (New York: Doubleday, 1996).

8. The BaKongo are a group of Bantu-speaking people who today dwell mostly in Congo and Angola.

9. Gray Gundaker. "The Kongo Cosmogram in Historical Archeology and the Moral Compass of Dave the Potter," *Historical Archeology* 45(2: 2011), p. 159.

10. Robert Farris Thompson. *Flash of the Spirit: African & Afro-American Art & Philosophy* (New York: Vintage Books, 1984), p. 109.

11. Simon Bockie. *Death and the Invisible Powers: The World of Kongo Belief* (Indianapolis, IN: Indiana University Press, 1993), p. 137.

12. Thompson, p. 49; Wyatt MacGaffey. *Custom and Government in the Lower Congo* (Los Angeles: University of California Press, 1970), pp. 43–44.

13. Corey C. Stayton. "The Kongo Cosmogram: A Theory in African-American Literature" (Atlanta, GA: ETD Collection for AUC Robert W. Woodruff Library: 1997), paper 1972.

14. Robert Farris Thompson, pp. 108–111.

15. J. W. Joseph. ". . . All of Cross"—African Potters, Marks, and Meanings in the Folk Pottery of the Edgefield District, South Carolina," *Historical Archaeology* 45(2: 2011), pp. 147–148, https://www.jstor.org/stable/23070092. Also: Ferguson, "Magic Bowls," Park Ethnography Program—African American Heritage and Ethnography (Department of Interior—The National Park Service, 1999), https://www.nps.gov/ethnography/.

16. "YOWA—Continuity of Human Life," *African Burial Ground* (New York: The National Park Service, 2021), https://www.nps.gov/.

17. Robert Ellison. *Shadow and Act* (New York: Vintage, 1972), p. 253.

18. Fritjof Capra and Pier Luigi Luisi. *The Systems View of Life: A Unifying Vision* (Cambridge, MA: Cambridge University Press, 2014), p. 95.

19. Bockie, pp. 36–37.

20. 1 Corinthians 15:26: my translation is based on the literal Greek meanings.

21. Madeleine L'Engle. *A Wind in the Door* (New York: Farrar, Straus and Giroux, 1973), p. 111.

22. Romans 6:22, literal translation of the Greek.

23. Matthew 22:37, 39 TV.

24. Interview with James Ogude by Steve Paulson and Anne Strainchamps. "I Am Because You Are: An Interview with James Ogude," *CHCIdeas* (June 21, 2019), https://chcinetwork.org/ideas/.

25. According to Somé, water is also associated with focus and clarity; it permits us to slow down and notice what we have previously overlooked. Water helps us to perceive the world in terms of possibilities for community, relationship, love, and harmony. Our tears arise because of the gap between the possibilities and the reality of our current world, but those tears are the "cleansing taste of reconciliation." An elder told Somé, "My tears tell me my soul has heard something about the Other World" (Somé, p. 172.)

26. CDC. "Unfair and Unjust Practices and Conditions Harm Hispanic and Latino People and Drive Health Disparities" (June 27, 2022), https://www.cdc.gov/.

27. Miriam Makeba. *Makeba: My Story* (New York: Plume, 1989), p. 2.

28. Harold M. Schmeck Jr. "Modern Man's Origin Linked to a Single Female Ancestor, *New York Times* (March 26, 1986), https://www.nytimes.com/1986/03/26.

29. Kwame Gyeke. *An Essay on African Philosophical Thought: The Akan Conceptual Scheme* (Cambridge, MA: Cambridge University Press, 1987), pp. 85–128.

30. Carlyle Fielding Stewart. *Soul Survivors: An African American Spirituality* (Louisville, KY: Westminster John Knox Press, 1997), pp. 32, 37.

Chapter 1 – The Age of Pandemic:
Death and Racism

31. Kamala Harris. Milwaukee, WI: Democratic National Convention, August 2020.

32. James Baldwin. "Letter from a Region of My Mind," in *The 60s: The Story of a Decade,* Henry Finder, ed. (New York: Random House, 2016), p. 25.

33. John 11:35.

34. When I wrote this phrase (the waters of death), I became curious as to the original source of this metaphor. I assumed it was the Bible, but as it turns out, it comes from the Epic of Gilgamesh, which is, perhaps, the oldest written story on Earth. The story was written on clay tablets some five thousand years ago in Ancient Sumeria—but the hero of the story has a problem that is nearly identical to mine: confronted for the first time with the death of someone he loves, he tries to run away from the "waters of death." Our fear of death is truly ancient and universal.

35. World Health Organization. "The True Death Toll of COVID-19," https://www.who.int/data/stories/the-true-death-toll-of-covid-19-estimating-global-excess-mortality.

36. Johns Hopkins Center for Gun Violence Solutions. *A Year in Review: 2020 Gun Deaths in the U.S.* (Baltimore, MD: Johns Hopkins University, 2022), available online at https://publichealth.jhu.edu/gun-violence-solutions. On average, 124 people died from gun violence every day in 2020.

37. Shannon Sabo and Sandra Johnson. "Pandemic Disrupts Historical Mortality Patterns, Caused Largest Jump in Deaths in 100 Years," *United States Census Bureau,* March 24, 2022, https://www.census.gov/library/.

38. World Health Organization (WHO). This number includes anyone who may have technically died from some other health condition when they would have been unlikely to die if they had not also had COVID. The WHO states as well that it believes there is an "excess mortality" (unreported deaths) of more than a million.

39. William Barber, co-written with Liz Theoharis on behalf of Poor People's Campaign: A National Call for a Moral Revival. "Poverty Amidst Pandemic: A Moral Response to COVID-19" (letter to President Donald Trump, Vice President Mike Pence and Members of the 116th Congress, March 19, 2020).

40. Rob Stein. "Doctors and Grief Experts on the Milestone of 1 Million COVID Deaths," *All Things Considered* (NPR, May 12, 2022), https://www.npr.org.`

41. Sarah Elizabeth Petry, Dalton Hughes, and Anthony Galanos. "Grief: The Epidemic Within the Epidemic," *American Journal of Hospice and Palliative Medicine 38*(4: 2020), pp. 419-422

42. Quoted in "COVID Has Put the World at Risk of Prolonged Grief Disorder" by Katherine Harmon Courage, *Scientific American,* May 19, 2021, https://www.scientificamerican.com/.

43. Susan D. Hillis, Alexandra Blenkinsop, Andrés Villaveces, et al. "COVID-19–Associated Orphanhood and Caregiver Death in the United States," *Pediatrics 148*(6: 2021), https://doi.org/10.1542/peds.2021-053760.

44. Amy Goldstein and Emily Guskin. "Almost One-Third of Black Americans Know Someone Who Died of COVID-19, Survey Shows," *Washington Post,* June 26, 2020, https://www.washingtonpost.com/health/.

45. Elise Gould and Melat Kassa. "Low-Wage, Low-Hours Workers Were Hit Hardest in the COVID-19 Recession," Economic Policy Institute, May 20, 2021, https://www.epi.org/.

46. Mary-Frances O'Connor. "Grief: A Brief History of Research on How Body, Mind, and Brain Adapt," *Psychosomatic Medicine 81*(8: 2019), pp. 731–738.

47. Christian R. Schultze-Florey, Otoniel Martínez-Maza, Mary-Frances O'Connor, et al. "Bereavement Induced Systemic Inflammation Is a Question of Genotype," *Brain, Behavior, and Immunity 26*(7: 2012), pp. 1066–1071, https://www.sciencedirect.com/.

48. Da'Mere T. Wilson and Mary-Frances O'Connor. "From Grief to Grievance: Combined Axes of Personal and Collective Grief Among Black Americans," *Frontiers in Psychiatry 13,* 2022, 10.3389/fpsyt.2022.850994. Wilson and O'Connor also report that a review of research between 1998 and 2014 found that of the approximately four thousand articles published on grief and bereavement, only about a hundred of these studies included Blacks in their samples.

49. ACLU. *The Other Epidemic: Fatal Police Shootings in the Time of COVID-19* (New York: ACLU, 2020).

50. Ibid. The ACLU also points out that police have historically always played a primary role in anti-Black violence, citing a 1933 study that found that "white police officers had participated in at least half of all lynchings, and that in 90 percent of others, law enforcement stood by, complicit in their inaction, as mobs murdered Black people." These statements from the ACLU are based on statistics from the Bureau of Justice and studies performed by the National Academy of Sciences.

51. *Mapping Police Violence,* https://mappingpoliceviolence.org (updated March 3, 2022).

52. "Fatal Force," *Washington Post* (updated January 19, 2023), https://www.washingtonpost.com/graphics/investigations/police-shootings-database/.

53. Naomi Washington-Leapheart. "Do Black Lives Matter Only After Someone's Death?" *City of Philadelphia* (November 25, 2020), https://www.phila.gov.

54. John Shelby Spong. *Eternal Life: A New Vision* (New York: HarperOne, 2010), p. 8.

55. Garrett Hardin. "The Tragedy of the Commons," *Science 162*(3859: 1968), pp. 1243-1248, 10.1126/science.162.3859.12.

56. Harlan Krumholz. "Racism as a Leading Cause of Death," *MedPageToday* (April 13, 2022), https://www.medpagetoday.com/publichealthpolicy/ethics/.

57. Anne Cheng. *The Melancholy of Race: Psychoanalysis, Assimilation, and Hidden Grief* (New York: Oxford University Press, 2001), pp. x, 7.

58. Eric Weiner. "Preparing Your Mind for Uncertain Times," *The Atlantic* (August 25, 2020), https://www.theatlantic.com/.

59. Meera Jagannathan. "Social Justice Donations Soared in the Months After George Floyd's Murder, but Then Fell—What Happened?" *MarketWatch* (May 25, 2021), https://www.marketwatch.com/.

60. Martin Luther King Jr. "Letter from a Birmingham Jail" (1963), available online at https://www.africa.upenn.edu/Articles_Gen/Letter_Birmingham.html.

61. Note that Kübler-Ross never perceived her stages as consecutive steps within a linear model but rather as stepping stones that we may need to land on again and again before we can begin to heal.

62. Frantz Fanon. *Black Skin, White Masks* (New York: Grove, 1967), p. 194.

63. Elisabeth Kübler-Ross and David Kessler. *On Grief and Grieving: Finding the Meaning of Grief Through the Five Stages of Loss* (New York: Simon and Schuster, 2014), pp. 20, 21.

64. Ibid., pp. 24, 25.

65. Audre Lorde. *Sister Outsider: Essays and Speeches* (Berkeley, CA: Crossing Press, 1984), p. 110.

66. Jeremy Lent. "A House on Shaky Ground: Eight Structural Flaws of the Western Worldview," *Resilience* (May 22, 2017), https://www.resilience.org/.

67. Working Effectively with Indigenous Peoples.® "Indigenous Peoples Worldviews vs Western Worldviews," *Indigenous Corporate Training* (January 26, 2016), https://www.ictinc.ca/blog/.

68. Lesiba Baloyi. "The African Conception of Death: A Cultural Implication," in *Toward Sustainable Development Through Nurturing*

Diversity: Proceedings from the 21st International Congress of the International Association for Cross-Cultural Psychology, https://scholarworks.gvsu.edu/.

69. Desmond Tutu. Nobel Peace Prize acceptance speech, 1984.

70. Howard Thurman. *Jesus and the Disinherited* (Boston: Beacon Press, 1996), p. 78.

71. Jennifer Green, Jennifer Huberty, Megan Puzia, and Chad Stecher. "The Effect of Meditation and Physical Activity on the Mental Health Impact of COVID-19–Related Stress and Attention to News," *JMIR Mental Health 8* (4: 2021), https://mental.jmir.org/2021/4/e28479/.

72. Ibid.

73. Howard Thurman. *The Inward Journey* (New York: Harper, 1961).

Chapter 2 – The Work of Mourning:
Death as an Opportunity to Learn

74. Sarah H. Seeley and Mary-Frances O'Connor. "Seeing Grieving as Learning," *Psyche* (May 25, 2022), https://psyche.co/ideas/.

75. Quoted in *Radical Equations: Civil Rights from Mississippi to the Algebra Equation* by Robert Moses and Charles Cobb (Boston: Beacon Press, 2001), p. 3

76. Sigmund Freud. "Mourning and Melancholy," *Collected Papers Vol. IV* (London, UK: Hogarth Press, 1950), pp. 152–170.

77. Ibid.

78. Ibid, p. 154.

79. Quoted in "Mourning in America: Racial Trauma and the Democratic Work of Mourning," by David McIvor, Duke University Dissertation (2010), p. 62, https://www.academia.edu/.

80. In Freud's words: "Mourning, as we know, however painful it may be, comes to a spontaneous end. When it has renounced everything

that has been lost . . . our libido is once more free . . . to replace the lost objects by fresh ones equally or still more precious." From "On Transience," *The Standard Edition of the Complete Psychological Works of Sigmund Freud. Volume XIV,* James Strachey, trans. (London, UK: Hogarth Press, 1964), p. 307.

81. Kimbwandènde Kia Bunseki Fu-Kiau. *Kongo Cosmology* (Kinshasa, Zaire: ONRD, 1969).

82. Ibid.

83. Gray Gundaker. "The Kongo Cosmogram in Historical Archaeology and the Moral Compass of Dave the Potter," *Historical Archaeology* 45(2: 2011), p. 176.

84. Fu-Kiau. *African Cosmology of the Bântu-Kôngo: Tying the Spiritual Knot* (Brooklyn, NY: Athelia Henrietta Press, 2001), pp. 127–150.

85. Herbert Kohl. "The Discipline of Hope: Lessons from a Lifetime of Teaching and Learning," *rethinking schools 12*(3:1998), https://rethinkingschools.org/articles/.

86. Mary-Frances O'Connor in an interview with Kim Mills, "Speaking of Psychology: How Grieving Changes the Brain," episode 184, American Psychological Association (March 2022), https://www.apa.org/news/podcasts/.

87. Ibid.

88. Fanny Brewster. *Archetypal Grief: Slavery's Legacy of Intergenerational Child Loss* (New York: Routledge, 2019), p. 29.

89. Critical race theory was developed in the 1980s, based on the ideas of attorney Derrick Bell.

90. Jelani Cobb. "The Man Behind Critical Race Theory," *New Yorker* (September 13, 2021), https://www.newyorker.com/magazine/2021/.

91. Julia Zenkevich. "Mars Area School Board Bans Teaching Critical Race Theory, Passes 'Patriotism Amendment,'" *WESA* (August 17, 2021), https://www.wesa.fm/.

92. Quoted in Bess Levin's "Trump Tells Supporters They Must Fight to the Death to Stop Schools from Teaching Kids About Systemic

Racism," *Vanity Fair* (March 14, 2022), https://www.vanityfair.com/news/2022/.

93. Kevin M. Spivak. "Patriotism Starts in the Classroom," *National Review* (July 3, 2022), https://www.nationalreview.com/2022/07/.

94. Martin Luther King Jr. "The Role of the Behavioral Scientist in the Civil Rights Movement. *American Psychologist 23* (1968), p. 156, https://doi.org/10.1037/h0025715.

95. Saidiya Hartman. "The Time of Slavery," *South Atlantic Quarterly 101*(4: Fall 2002), pp. 757–777, 10.1215/00382876-101-4-757.

96. Ediho Lokango. "The Concept of Space and Time: An African Perspective," *International Journal of Recent Advances in Physics 10*(1/2/3: August 2021), p. 7, https://doi.org/10.14810/ijrap.2021.10301.

97. Simon Stow. "Agnostic Homegoing: Frederick Douglass, Joseph Lowry, and the Democratic Value of African American Public Mourning," *American Political Science Review 104*(4: 2010), p. 686.

98. Drew Gilpin Faust. *This Republic of Suffering: Death and the American Civil War* (New York: Knopf, 2008), p. xv.

99. Bill Farrell. "All in the Family: Ken Burns's *The Civil War* and Black America," *Transition: An International Review 58* (1993), p. 170.

100. Quoted in Da'Mere T. Wilson and Mary-Frances O'Connor's "From Grief to Grievance: Combined Axes of Personal and Collective Grief Among Black Americans," *Frontiers of Psychology 13*(2002), 10.3389/fpsyt.2022.850994.

Chapter 3 – Clad in Mourning:
Death as a Never-Ending Reality

101. Quoted in D. R. Roediger. "And Die in Dixie: Funerals, Death & Heaven in the Slave Community 1700–1865," *The Massachusetts Review 22*(1: 1981), pp. 163–183.

102. Karla Holloway. *Passed On: African American Mourning Stories* (Durham, NC: Duke University Press, 2002).

103. PBS. "White Louisiana Man Charged with Murder in Separate Killings of Black Men in Baton Rouge" (September 19, 2017), https://www.pbs.org/newshour/nation/.

104. BBC. "Tamir Rice Killing" (December 30, 2020), https://www.bbc.com/news/world-us-canada-55481339. Tamir Rice was a twelve-year-old with a toy gun when he was shot by police officers in 2014; no charges were brought against officers.

105. BBC. "Timeline of Black Deaths and Protests" (April 22, 2021), https://www.bbc.com/news/world-us-canada-52905408. Walter Scott was shot in the back five times after being pulled over for having a defective light on his car by a white police officer, who was later fired and eventually sentenced to 20 years in prison.

106. Ibid. Philando Castile was pulled over by the police during a routine check. He was shot as he was reaching for his license, according to his girlfriend, who live-streamed the encounter on Facebook. The officer involved was cleared of murder charges.

107. Ibid. Stephon Clark died after being shot at least seven times in his grandmother's backyard in Sacramento, California, by police who were investigating a nearby break-in. The two officers involved did not face criminal prosecution.

108. CBS News. "Fired Atlanta Officer Charged with Murder in Rayshard Brooks Shooting" (June 18, 2020), https://www.cbsnews.com/news/.

109. NPR. "The Buffalo Supermarket Shooter Pleads Not Guilty to Federal Charges" (June 18, 2022), https://www.npr.org/.

110. NPR. "5 Years After Charleston Church Massacre, What Have We Learned?" (June 17, 2020), https://www.npr.org/.

111. Jonathan Franklin. "Watering Flowers While Black: A Pastor Shares His Story of Wrongful Arrest," *NPR* (September 1, 2022), https://www.npr.org/.

112. Samantha Michaels. "Breonna Taylor Is One of a Shocking Number of Black People to See Armed Police Barge into Their Homes,"

Mother Jones (May 20, 2020), https://www.motherjones.com/crime-justice.

113. BBC. "Woman Shot Dead By Texas Police Through Bedroom Window" (October 13, 2019) https://www.bbc.com/news/.

114. Josh Campbell, Michelle Watson, and Emma Tucker. "Texas District Attorney Names San Antonio Officer Who Shot 17-Year-Old in a McDonald's Parking Lot," *CNN* (October 10, 2022), https://www.cnn.com.

115. Madison J. Gray. "Besides the Horror in Buffalo, Here Are 5 Other Recent Mass Shootings Spurred by Racial Hate" (May 19, 2022), https://www.bet.com/.

116. J. Bittel. "People Called Police on This Black Birdwatcher So Many Times That He Posted Custom Signs to Explain His Hobby" *Washington Post* (June 5, 2020), https://www.washingtonpost.com/science/; E. Hannon. "A Black Man Bird-Watching in Central Park Asked a White Woman to Leash Her Dog. She Called the Cops," *Slate* (May 2020), https://slate.com/news-and-politics/.

117. Claudia Rankine. "The Condition of Black Life is One of Mourning," in *Rebellious Mourning: The Collective Work of Grief*, Cindy Milstein, ed. (Oakland, CA: AK Press, 2017).

118. John Gramlich. "Safety Concerns Were Top of Mind for Many Black Americans Before Buffalo Shooting," *Pew Research* (May 20, 2022), https://www.pewresearch.org/fact-tank/.

119. Rankine.

120. Ibid.

121. Frantz Fanon. *Black Skin, White Masks* (London, UK: Pluto Press, 1967), p. 112.

122. United Nations, https://www.un.org/en/observances/decade-people-african-descent/slave-trade.

123. "Death Toll from the Slave Trade: The African Holocaust," World Future Fund, http://www.worldfuturefund.org/Reports/.

124. In *American Holocaust* (Oxford University Press, 1993), David

Stannard estimates that some 30 to 60 million Africans died because of being enslaved. (This is roughly equivalent to the twentieth century's Holocaust (6 million Jews and millions of others were killed; see "Holocaust Misconceptions," Illinois Holocaust Museum, https://www.ilholocaustmuseum.org/), as well as the number of Indigenous people in the Americas who died because of Europeans' arrival on their land (see Alexander Koch, et al., "Earth system Impacts of the European Arrival and Great Dying in the Americas After 1492," *Quaternary Science Reviews* *207*(March 1, 2019), pp. 13–36).

Stannard claims a 50 percent mortality rate among new slaves while being gathered and stored in Africa, a 10 percent mortality among the survivors while crossing the ocean, and another 50 percent mortality rate in the first phase of being enslaved.

125. Common nutrition-related diseases among enslaved populations included beriberi, caused by a thiamine deficiency; pellagra, caused by niacin deficiency; tetany, caused by deficiencies of calcium, magnesium, and Vitamin D; rickets, caused by a deficiency of Vitamin D; and kwashiorkor, caused by severe protein deficiency. See "Historical Context: Facts About the Slave Trade and Slavery" by Steven Mintz, *History Resources* (Gilder Lehrman Institute of American History), https://www.gilderlehrman.org/history-resources/.

126. Mintz.

127. J. Mellon. *Bullwhip Days: The Slaves Remember* (New York: Grove, 1988), p. 239.

128. Tom Costa. "Runaway Slaves and Servants in Colonial Virginia," *Encyclopedia Virginia,* https://encyclopediavirginia.org/.

129. E. B. O'Callaghan, ed. *Documents Relative to the Colonial History of the State of New York, vol. 5* (Albany, NY: Weed, Parsons, 1858), p. 341.

130. According to Herbert Aptheker in *American Negro Slave Revolts* (International Publishers, 1983), during the years of slavery, there were at least 250 revolts that involved at least ten enslaved persons.

Aptheker's research indicates that "rebelliousness" was exceedingly common and an aspect of the African psyche.

131. Olaudah Equiano. *The Interesting Narrative of the Life of Olaudah Equiano, or Gustavus Vassa, the African. Written by Himself* (London, UK: self-published, 1789), available online from Project Gutenberg, https://www.gutenberg.org/.

132. Quoted in George Francis Dow's *Slave Ships and Slaving* (Salem, MA: Marine Research Society, 1927), V.

133. For more on slavery and suicide, see *The Power to Die* by Terri L. Snyder (University of Chicago Press, 2015). To read primary-source, first-person accounts of enslaved people's experiences with suicide, see "Suicide Among Slaves" in *The Making of African American Identity: Vol. I, 1500–1865*, available from the National Humanities Center, https://nationalhumanitiescenter.org/.

134. A paragraph similar to this one appears in my book, *The Crucible of Racism: Ignatian Spirituality and the Power of Hope* (Orbis, 2022). Most of this information comes from the NAACP's *Thirty Years of Lynching in the United States, 1889–1919* (New York: NAACP, 1919), which recorded year, state, color, sex, and alleged offense.

135. Patricia Bernstein. "The Lynching of Jesse Washington," in *Lynching in Texas* (Huntsville, TX: Sam Houston State University, 2022).

136. Isabel Wilkerson. "Where Do We Go from Here?" *Essence* (October 27, 2020), https://essence.com.

137. Quoted in Derrick Jensen's *The Culture of Make Believe* (White River Junction, VT: Chelsea Green, 2004), p. ix.

138. Deneen L. Brown. "'It Was a Modern-Day Lynching': Violent Deaths Reflect a Brutal American Legacy," *National Geographic* (June 3, 2020), https://www.nationalgeographic.com/history/.

139. Quoted in "Hundreds of Black Americans Were Killed During 'Red Summer.' A Century Later, Still Ignored," Associate Press in *USA Today* (July 23, 2019), https://www.usatoday.com/story/news/nation/. Tuttle is the author of *Race Riot: Chicago in the Red Summer of 1919* (University of Illinois Press, 2019).

140. Ibid.

141. David Nakamura and Margaret Coker. "Three White Men Guilty of Hate Crimes Charges in Connection with Ahmaud Arbery Murder," *Washington Post* (November 22, 2022).

(February 22, 2022).

142. Quoted in Eric McDaniel, "Lynching Is Now a Federal Hate Crime After a Century of Blocked Efforts," *NPR* (March 29, 2022), https://www.npr.org/.

143. Discussed in Thomas Hübl's *Healing Collective Trauma: A Process for Integrating Our Intergenerational and Cultural Wounds* (Boulder, CO: Sounds True, 2020), p. 6.

144. Like the lynchings of the Jim Crow era, these deaths aren't furtive crimes done in the dark; they take place in public places, in the broad daylight, out in the open where everyone can see. Officers of the law are doing the killing; and the police were also often involved in the Jim Crow era lynchings. Historically, the Southern police forces evolved from the government-sponsored slave patrols who were charged with three tasks: catching escaped Blacks; using terrorist tactics to deter potential revolts; and disciplining enslaved Blacks for breaking plantation rules. This racist legacy is still clear in many Southern police officers. (See Connie Hassett-Walker's "How You Start Is How You Finish? The Slave Patrol and Jim Crow Origins of Policing," *American Bar Association Human Rights Magazine* 46(2: January 11, 2021), https://www.americanbar.org/groups/crsj/publications/human_rights_magazine_home/.

145. Khiara M. Bridges. "The Many Ways Institutional Racism Kills Black People," *Time* (June 22, 2020), https://time.com/5851864/institutional-racism-america/.

146. Elizabeth Hinton. "An Unjust Burden: The Disparate Treatment of Black Americans in the Criminal Justice System" (New York: Vera Institute of Justice, 2018), https://www.vera.org/.

147. Rachel Nania. "The Surprising Impact of Racism on the Brain," *AARP* (August 2, 2022), https://aarp.org/health.

148. Bridges.

149. Debra Umberson, Julie Skalamera Olson, Robert Crosnoe, et al. "Death of Family Members as an Overlooked Source of Racial Disadvantage in the United States," *PNAS 114* (5: 2017), pp. 915–920, https://doi.org/10.1073/pnas.1605599114.

150. A. Rochaun Meadows-Fernandez. "The Unbearable Grief of Black Mothers," *Vox* (May 28, 2020), https://www.vox.com/first-person/.

151. Frantz Fanon. *Black Skin, White Masks* (London, UK: Pluto Press, 1967), p. 53.

152. Saidiya Hartman. *Lose Your Mother: A Journey Along the Atlantic Slave Route* (New York: Farrar, Straus & Giroux, 2007), p. 6.

153. Vinson Cunningham. "The Argument of 'Afropessimism,'" *New Yorker Magazine* (July 20, 2020).

154. Jared Sexton. "Ante-Anti-Blackness: Afterthoughts," *Lateral: Journal of the Cultural Studies Association 1* (2012), https://csalateral.org/.

155. Fanon, p. 60.

156. Quoted in "Finding Inner Harmony: The Underappreciated Legacy of Karen Horney" by Scott Barry Kaufman, *Scientific American* (May 11, 2020), https://blogs.scientificamerican.com/.

157. W. E. B. DuBois. *The Souls of Black Folk* (Chicago: A. C. McClurg, 1903), preface, available online at https://etc.usf.edu/lit2go/203/the-souls-of-black-folk/.

158. Rhonda V. Magee. *The Inner Work of Racial Justice: Healing Ourselves and Transforming Our Communities Through Mindfulness* (New York: Penguin, 2021), p. 33.

159. Resmaa Menakem. *My Grandmother's Hands: Racialized Trauma and the Pathway to Mending Our Hearts and Bodies* (Central Recovery Press, 2017), chapter 2.

160. Bessel A. Van der Kolk. *The Body Keeps the Score: Brain, Mind, and Body in the Healing of Trauma* (New York: Penguin, 2014), p. 273.

161. Thomas Hübl. *Healing Collective Trauma: A Process for Integrating*

Our Intergenerational and Cultural Wounds (Boulder, CO: Sounds True, 2020), pp. xvi–xvii, 11.

Chapter 4 – Racism and Trauma:
Death's Lasting Imprint

162. Resmaa Menakem. *My Grandmother's Hands: Racialized Trauma and the Pathway to Mending Our Hearts and Bodies* (Las Vegas, NV: Central Recovery Press, 2017), p. 10.

163. American Psychological Association. "Trauma" (Washington, DC: APA, 2022), https://www.apa.org/.

164. Bessel A. Van der Kolk. *The Body Keeps the Score: Brain, Mind, and Body in the Healing of Trauma* (New York: Penguin, 2015), pp. 21, 53.

165. Vivian M. Rakoff. "A Long-Term Effect of the Concentration-Camp Experience," *Viewpoints* (1: 1966), pp. 17–22.

166. H. A. Barocas and C. B. Barocas. "Wounds of the Fathers: The Next Generation of Holocaust Victims," *International Review of Psycho Analysis* (6: 1979), pp. 331–340; J. T. Freyberg JT. "Difficulties in Separation – Individuation as Experienced by Offspring of Nazi Holocaust Survivors. *American Journal of Orthopsychiatry* (50: 1980, pp. 87–95; Y. Danieli. "Differing Adaptational Styles in Families of Survivors of the Nazi Holocaust: Some Implications for Treatment," *Child Today* 10(6–10: 1981), pp. 34–35.

167. Luciana Lorens Braga, Marcelo Feijó, and José Paulo Fiks. "Transgenerational Transmission of Trauma and Resilience: A Qualitative Study with Brazilian Offspring to Holocaust Survivors," *BMC Psychiatry* (12: 2012), p. 134, https://www.ncbi.nlm.nih.gov/pmc/articles/.

168. Maria Yellow Horse Brave Heart. "*Oyate Ptayela*: Rebuilding the Lakota Nation Through Addressing Historical Trauma Among Lakota Parents," *Journal of Human Behavior in the Social Environment* 2(1–2: 1999), pp. 109–126, https://doi.org/10.1300/J137v02n01_08.

169. Benedict Carey. "Can We Really Inherit Trauma," *New York Times* (December 10, 2018), https://www.nytimes.com/.

170. Rachel Yehuda and Amy Lehrner. "Intergenerational Transmission of Trauma Effects: Putative Role of Epigenetic Mechanisms," *World Psychiatry 17*(3: 2018), pp. 243–257.

171. Joy DeGruy. *Post Traumatic Slave Syndrome: America's Legacy of Enduring Injury and Healing* (New York: Amistad, 2017), p. 57.

172. Harriet Jacobs. *Incidents in the Life of a Slave Girl* (Boston: Thayer & Eldridge, 1861), p. 55.

173. Marimba Ani. *Let the Circle Be Unbroken: The Implications of African Spirituality in the Diaspora* (New York: Nkonimfo, 1980), p. 13.

174. Solomon Northup. *Twelve Years A Slave* (Auburn, NY: Derby and Miller, 1853), pp. 78–82.

175. Kelly L. Schmidt. "Augustine Queen and His Family" (Slavery, History, Memory, and Reconciliation Project: 2021), https://www.jesuits.org/.

176. Kenneth B. Clark and Mamie P. Clark. "Racial Identification and Preference in Negro Children," available online at https://i2.cdn.turner.com.

177. Ijemoa J. Madubata, Mary O. Odafe, David C. Talavera, et al. "Helplessness Mediates Racial Discrimination and Depression for African American Young Adults," *Journal of Black Psychology 44*(7: 2018), p. 626, https://doi.org/10.1177/0095798418811476.

178. DeGruy, p. 110.

179. Arline T. Geronimus, Margaret T. Hicken, Jay A. Pearson, et al. "Do US Black Women Experience Stress-Related Biological Aging?" *Human Nature 21*(1: 2010), pp. 19–38, https://www.ncbi.nlm.nih.gov/pmc/articles/.

180. Joanne Lewsley. "What Are the Effects of Racism on Health and Mental Health?" *Medical News Today* (July 28, 2020), https://www.medicalnewstoday.com/.

181. Eric Suni. "What's the Connection Between Race and Sleep Disorders?" *Sleep Foundation* (April 21, 2022), https://www.sleepfoundation.org/.

182. Jeanne L. Alhusen, Kelly M. Bower, Elizabeth Epstein, and Phyllis Sharps. "Racial Discrimination and Adverse Birth Outcomes: An Integrative Review," *Journal of Midwifery & Women's Health 61*(6: 2016), pp. 707–720, https://doi.org/10.1111/jmwh.12490.

183. American Academy of Pediatrics. "Policy Statement: The Impact of Racism on Child and Adolescent Health," *Pediatrics 144*(2: 2019), https://doi.org/10.1542/peds.2019-1765.

184. Kelly M. Hoffman, Sophie Trawalter, Jordan R. Axt, et al. "Racial Bias in Pain Assessment and Treatment Recommendations, and False Beliefs About Biological Differences Between Blacks and Whites," *PNAS 113*(16: 2016), pp. 4296–4301, https://doi.org/10.1073/pnas.1516047113; Monika K. Goyal, Nathan Kupperman, Sean D. Cleary, et al. "Racial Disparities in Pain Management with Children with Appendicitis in Emergency Departments," *JAMA Pediatrics 169*(11: 2015), pp. 996–1002, https://jamanetwork.com/journals/jamapediatrics/.

185. Ejim Sule, Ryan M. Sutton, Debbie Jones, et al. "The Past Does Matter: A Nursing Perspective on Post Traumatic Slave Syndrome," *Journal of Racial and Ethnic Health Disparities 4*(2017), pp. 779–783.

186. F. C. Harris. "The Rise of Respectability Politics," *Dissent 61*(1: 2014), pp. 33–37.

187. Ibram X. Kendi. "Post-Traumatic Slave Syndrome Is a Racist Idea," *Black Perspectives* (African American Intellectual History Society, June 21, 2016), https://www.aaihs.org/.

188. Menakem.

189. Jacobs, p. 46.

190. Lawrence G. Calhoun and Richard G. Tedeschi. *Handbook of Posttraumatic Growth: Research and Practice* (New York: Psychology Press, 2006), pp. 4–6.

191. Hübl, p. 233.

192. Pim van Lommel. *The Science of the Near-Death Experience* (New York: Harper Collins, 2010).

193. For more on this, see "The Nonlocal Universe" by Andrew Lohrey and Bruce Boreham, *Communicative and Integrative Biology 13*(1: 2020), pp. 147–159. The authors note that "along with the absolute dualism of local realism comes a series of binary values and preferences, such as quantity in preference to quality; the physical in preference to the mental; objectivity in preference to subjectivity; explicit details in preference to hidden implicit contexts; controlled variables in preference to hidden and uncontrolled variables; the local in preference to the nonlocal."

194. Gabor Maté, in Hübl, p. 70.

195. van Lommel. "Getting Comfortable with Near-Death Experiences: Dutch Prospective Research on Near-Death Experiences During Cardiac Arrest," *Missouri Medicine 111*(2: 2014), pp. 126–131.

196. Hübl, p. 7.

197. "Dr Peter Evans—Retro-Causality: Unravelling the Mysteries of Quantum Cosmology," *Scientia* (August 14, 2019), https://www. scientia.global/.

198. John Mbiti. *New Testament Eschatology in an African Background* (London, UK: SPCK, 1978), p. 24.

199. William James. "A Pluralistic Universe" in *The Works of William James,* Frederick Burkhardt and Fredson Bowers, eds. (Cambridge, MA: Harvard University Press, 1977), p. 139.

200. Donald Kalsched. *Trauma and the Soul* (New York: Routledge, 2013), p. 25.

201. Malidoma Patrice Somé. *The Healing Wisdom of Africa: Finding Life Purpose Through Nature, Ritual, and Community* (New York: Putnam, 1999), p. 97.

202. Fanny Brewster. *Archetypal Grief: Slavery's Legacy of Intergenerational Child Loss* (New York: Routledge, 2019), p. 53.

203. Menakem.

204. Jenny Escobar. "The Role of Memory Practices in Building Spiritual Solidarity for Survivors of State Violence," *American Journal of*

Community Psychology 69 (2022), p. 412.

205. Brewster, p. xxii.

206. Menakem.

207. B. A. van der Kolk. "Clinical Implications of Neuroscience Research in PTSD," *Annals of the New York Academy of Sciences 1071* (1: 2006), pp. 277–293, doi:10.1196/annals.1364.022; B. A. van der Kolk, L. Stone, J. West, et al. "Yoga as an Adjunctive Treatment for Posttraumatic Stress Disorder," *The Journal of Clinical Psychiatry 75* (6: 2014), doi:10.4088/jcp.13m08561.

208. Bessel van der Kolk. *The Body Keeps the Score: Brain, Mind, and Body in the Healing of Trauma* (New York: Penguin, 2014), p. 103.

Chapter 5 – Grief and Rage:
Death as a Shout for Justice

209. James Baldwin. *Nobody Knows My Name: More Notes of a Native Son* (New York: Dial, 1961), p. 205.

210. Stokely Carmichael (Kwame Ture) in Paula Span's "The Undying Revolutionary," *Washington Post* (April 8, 1988), https://www.washingtonpost.com/archive/lifestyle/.

211. I have paraphrased most of this story from the account in Mamie Till-Mobley and Christopher Benson's *Death of Innocence: The Story of the Hate Crime That Changed America* (New York: Random House, 2003).

212. As quoted in Ruth Feldstein's *Motherhood in Black and White: Race and Sex in American Liberalism, 1930–1965* (New York: Cornell University Press, 2000), p. 107.

213. Simon Stow. *American Mourning: Tragedy, Democracy, Resilience* (Cambridge, MA: Cambridge University Press, 2017), p. 685.

214. Martin Luther King Jr. *The Papers of Martin Luther King, Jr., Volume VII: To Save the Soul of America, January 1961 August 1962*, Vol. 7 (Los Angeles, CA: University of California Press, 2014).

215. Larry Buchanan, Quoctrung Bui, and Jugal K. Patel. "Black Lives Matter May Be the Largest Movement in U.S. History," *New York Times* (July 3, 2020), https://www.nytimes.com/.

216. Judith Butler. *Frames of War: When Is Life Grievable?* (New York: Verso Books, 2016), p. 39.

217. Sigmund Freud. *Beyond the Pleasure Principle* (London, UK: International Psycho-Analytical Press, 1922).

218. Jacques Lacan. *The Ethics of Psychoanalysis 1959–1960* (London, UK: Routledge, 1992), p. 246.

219. Unfortunately, Black creativity is often treated as a commodity that can be bought and sold—and it allows white society to appreciate (and even imitate) Black culture without having to actually respect and value Black human beings.

220. L. Z. Tiedens. "Anger and Advancement versus Sadness and Subjugation: The Effect of Negative Emotion Expressions on Social Status Conferral," *Journal of Personality and Social Psychology 80* (2001), pp. 86–94. Also: Jessica M. Salerno, Liana C. Peter-Hagene, and Alexander C. V. Jay. "Women and African Americans Are Less Influential When They Express Anger During Group Decision Making." *Group Processes & Intergroup Relations 22* (1: 2019), pp. 57–79, doi:10.1177/1368430217702967.

221. Seneca. "On Anger," *Sophia Project Philosophy Archives,* pp. 1, 2, http://www.sophia-project.org/.

222. Karl A.E. Enenkel and Anita Traninger. *Discourses of Anger in the Early Modern Period* (Leiden, NL: Brill, 2015), pp. 3, 144, 327.

223. Ibid., p. 389.

224. Harriet Lerner. *The Dance of Anger* (New York: HarperCollins, 2009), p. 1

225. Quoted in "A Philosopher's Defense of Anger" by Helen Rosner, *New Yorker Magazine* (October 14, 2021), https://www.newyorker.com/culture/.

226. Lacan, p. 103.

227. Myisha Cherry in an interview with Helen Rosner, "A Philosopher's Defense of Anger."

228. Frederick Douglass. *The Portable Frederick Douglass,* Henry Louis Gates and John Stauffer, eds. (New York: Penguin, 2016), p. 288.

229. D. W. Winnicott. *Collected Papers: Through Paediatrics to Psychoanalysis* (Levittown, PA: Brunner-Mazel, 1992), p. 188.

230. Ibid.

231. bell hooks. *Killing Rage: Ending Racism* (New York: Holt, 1996), p. 14.

232. Howard C. Stevenson, Jr. "Wrestling with Destiny: The Cultural Socialization of Anger and Healing in African American Males," *Journal of Psychology and Christianity 21*(3; 2002), pp. 357–364

233. K. Davidson K, M. W. MacGregor, J. Stuhr, et al. "Constructive Anger Verbal Behavior Predicts Blood Pressure in a Population-Based Sample," *Health Psychology 19*(1: 2000), pp. 55–64, doi: 10.1037/0278-6133.19.1.55. S. Also, J. Kitayama, J. M. Park, J. M. Boylan, et al. "Expression of Anger and Ill Health in Two Cultures: An Examination of Inflammation and Cardiovascular Risk," *Psychological Science 26*(2: 2015), pp. 211–220, doi: 10.1177/0956797614561268; and Jiyoung Park, Abdiel J. Flores, Kirstin Aschbacher, and Wendy Berry Mendes. "When Anger Expression Might be Beneficial for African Americans: The Moderating Role of Chronic Discrimination," *Cultural Diversity & Ethnic Minority Psychology 3* (2018), pp. 303–318, doi: 10.1037/cdp0000185.

234. E. H. Johnson and A. Greene. "The Relationship Between Suppressed Anger and Psychosocial Distress in African American Male Adolescents," *Journal of Black Psychology 18* (1991), pp. 47–65. J. R. Gibbs. "Anger in Young Black Males: Victims or Victimizers?" In R. G. Majors and J. U. Gordon, eds., *The American Black Male: His Present Status and His Future* (Chicago: Nelson-Hall, 1993), pp. 127–144. H. C. Stevenson. Managing Anger: Protective, Proactive, or Adaptive Racial Socialization Identity Profiles and Manhood Development, *Journal of Prevention and Intervention in the Community 16* (1997), pp. 35–61.

235. Audre Lorde. "The Uses Of Anger," keynote presentation given at the National Women's Studies Association Conference (Storrs, Connecticut: 1981), available online at https://www.blackpast.org/.

236. Cherry. *The Moral Psychology of Anger* (Lanham, Md: Rowman & Littlefield, 2017), p. 113.

237. Quoted in an interview with Gaamangwe Mogami, "Rage Is the Softness I'm Learning to Own: A Dialogue with Vuyelwa Maluleke," *Africa In Dialogue* (October 26, 2017), https://africaindialogue.com/.

238. This story is told in all four of the Gospels, though the timing of the incident differs. See Matthew 21:12–17, Mark 11:15–19, Luke 19:45–48, and John 2:13–17. I have, admittedly, inserted my own interpretation into my retelling.

239. Cole Arthur Riley. *This Here Flesh: Spirituality, Liberation, and the Stories That Make Us.* (New York: Convergent, 2022), chap. 9.

240. Riley, chapter 10.

241. Ibid., chapter 11.

242. John 17:21 TV.

243. James Alison. *Raising Able* (London, UK: SPCK, 2010), pp. 115–116.

244. Rienzo Colpo. "Is South Africa 'Really an Angry Nation'?" *News24* (March 26, 2013), //www.news24.com/.

245. Desmond Tutu in *The Book of Joy: Lasting Happiness in a Changing World* by Desmond Tutu and the Dalai Lama (New York: Penguin, 2016).

246. Fred Moten. "Blackness and Nothingness: Mysticism in the Flesh," *The South Atlantic Quarterly 112*(4: 2013), doi 10.1215/00382876-2345261.

Chapter 6 – Crossing the Waters:
Death as an Affirmation of Identity

247. Quoted in "And Die in Dixie: Funerals, Death, & Heaven in the Slave

Community 1700–1865" by David R. Roediger, *The Massachusetts Review 22*(1: 1981), p. 177.

248. Danielle Broadway. "The Unbreakable Spirits of Black Gospel During Funerals," *The Order of the Good Death* (September 18, 2020), https://www.orderofthegooddeath.com/. There is some question as to whether "It takes a village. . . ." is actually a proverb from Africa. Although the proverb has become so much a cliché that it has nearly lost its true meaning, I personally believe it to be a translation of a proverb from the Swahili people of East Africa.

249. Christiane Owusu-Sarpong. *La mort Akan. Etude des formes d'énonciation propres aux rites funéraires Akan,* PhD thesis, Université de Franche-Cornpté (Besancon, FR: 1992). Owusu-Sarpong is referring to Akan funerals in Africa, but the same can be said for almost any funeral in the Black diaspora.

250. James Alison. *Raising Abel: the Recovery of the Eschatological Imagination* (New York, Crossroad, 1996), p. 116.

251. Kimbwandende Kia Bunseki Fu-Kiau. "Ntangu-Tandu-Kolo: The Bantu-Kongo Concept of Time," in *Time and the Black Experience,* Joseph K. Adjaye, ed. (Westport, CN: Greenwood, 1994), pp. 27, 41.

252. Alison, p. 59.

253. Quoted in "The 'Grief Pandemic' Will Torment Americans for Years" by Liz Szabo, *NPR* (June 2, 2021), https://www.pbs.org/newshour/health/.

254. Robert Farris Thompson. *Flash of the Spirit: African & Afro-American Art and Philosophy* (New York: Vintage, 1983), p. 42.

255. Melville J. Herskovits. *The Myth of the Negro Past* (Boston, MA: Beacon, 1958), p. 63.

256. Souleymane Bachir Diagne (2000), p. 2.

257. Roediger, p. 178.

258. Lawrence Levine. *Black Culture and Black Consciousness: Afro-American Folk Thought from Slavery to Freedom* (New York: Oxford University Press, 1977), pp. 32–33.

259. Jason R. Young. "All God's Children Had Wings: The Flying African in History, Literature, and Lore," *Journal of Africana Religions* 5(1: 2017), p. 62.

260. Timothy Powell. "Summoning the Ancestors: The Flying Africans' Story and Its Enduring Legacy," in *African American Life in the Georgia Lowcountry: The Atlantic World and the Gullah Geechee*, Philip Morgan, ed. (Athens, GA: University of Georgia Press, 2011), p. 254.

261. Y. Okeyinka and B. Amole. "The Meaning of Home in Yoruba Culture," *Ethiopian Journal of Environmental Studies and Management* 5(4:2012), p. 493, http://dx.doi.org/10.4314/ejesm. v5i4.S8.

262. Gaston Bachelard. *The Poetics of Space*, Maria Jolas, trans. (Boston: Beacon. 1964), pp. xxxvi, 4, 5.

263. Brian Collinson. "Symbolism of the Home #3," *Journeying Toward Wholeness* (September 18, 2017), https://www.briancollinson.ca/.

264. James Baldwin. *Giovanni's Room* (London, UK: Penguin, 1991), p. 88.

265. Baldwin. *The Price of the Ticket: Collected Nonfiction, 1948–1985* (New York: St. Martin's Press/Marek, 1985), p. xix.

266. Toni Morrison. *Song of Solomon* (New York: Vintage, 2004), p. 67.

267. Based on Luke 12:13,15–24.

268. Moten.

269. *Maranasati* is the Buddhist term for meditating on death. If you'd like to find out more about it, a good starting place is this article by Jo Nash, PhD: "Maranasati Meditation: How to Practice Mindfulness of Death," *Positive Psychology* (November 20, 2022), https:// positivepsychology.com/.

270. Ralph Ellison. *Invisible Man* (New York: Knopf Doubleday, 1991), p. 243.

Chapter 7 – The Fear of Hell, the Hope of Heaven: Death and the Call to Community

271. Simon Bockie. *Death and the Invisible Powers: The World of Kongo Belief* (Bloomington: Indiana University Press, 1993).

272. See M. Cickara, E. Bruneau, J. J. VanBavel, and R. Saxe, "Their Pain Gives Us Pleasure: How Intergroup Dynamics Shape Empathic Failures and Counter-Empathic Responses," *Journal of Experimental Social Psychology* 55 (2014), pp. 110–125. This research study demonstrated that when sports fans viewed members of their own team being harmed, they felt empathy—but when they viewed fans of a rival team being harmed in the same way, they felt little or no empathy—and they even felt pleasure.

273. Augustine of Hippo. *The Works of Saint Augustine: A Translation for the 21st Century,* Maria Boulding, trans. (Hyde Park, NY: New City Press, 2008), p. 63.

274. Augustine, in *Isaiah: Interpreted by Early Christian Medieval Commentaries,* Robert L. Wilkin, ed. (Grand Rapids, MI: Eerdmans, 2007), pp. 535, 536.

275. Steven Lawson, interview with Nathan W. Bingham at Ligonier's 2021 National Conference, https://ask.ligonier.org/.

276. Friedrich Nietzsche. *On the Genealogy of Morals and Ecce Homo* (New York: Knopf Doubleday, 2010), p. 49.

277. David R. Roediger. "And Die in Dixie: Funerals, Death, and Heaven in the Slave Community, 1700–1865," *The Massachusetts Review* (Spring, 1993), p. 179.

278. Ibid., p. 180.

279. Quoting David Hamstra in "Will We All Be White in Heaven? Dissecting a Strange Statement from Ellen White," *Compass Magazine* (August 23, 2019), https://thecompassmagazine.com/blog/.

280. Nathan Placencia. "Will There Be Races in Heaven" in *Death, Immortality, and Eternal Life,* T. Ryan Byerly, ed. (Abingdon, UK: Routledge, 2021), pp. 192–206.

281. Sandra Bland was a twenty-eight-year-old Black activist who was found hanged in a Texas police cell in July 2015 after she was arrested during a traffic stop.

282. Stephen S. Bush. "Is There Racism in Heaven," *Marginalia* (August 2, 2017), https://themarginaliareview.com/.

283. Jacque Lacan, "The Mirror Stage," in *Écrits: The First Complete Edition in English,* Bruce Fink, trans. (New York, NY: Norton, 2007).

284. Ilia Delio. "Beatrice Bruteau, Pope Francis and Global Community," *Global Sisters Report* (September 27, 2015), https://www.globalsistersreport.org/column/speaking-god/.

285. Daniel Cho. "Thanatos and Civilization: Lacan, Marcuse, and the Death Drive," *Policy Futures in Education* 4(1: 2006), p. 28.

286. Beatrice Bruteau. *The Holy Thursday Revolution* (Maryknoll, NY: Orbis, 2005), p. 6.

287. Alma Gottlieb. *The Afterlife Is Where We Come From: The Culture of Infancy in West Africa* (Chicago: University of Chicago Press, 2004), p. 82.

288. Quoted in Linda O. McMurry's *George Washington Carver: Scientist and Symbol* (New York: Oxford University Press, 1982), p. 107.

Chapter 8 – Death's Love Story:
Kinship Beyond Death

289. Malidoma Patrice Somé. *The Healing Wisdom of Africa: Finding Life's Purpose Through Nature, Ritual, and Communion* (New York: Putnam, 1999), p. 53.

290. Gabriele Lübbers. *Mitteilungen zur Kulturkunde*, Volumes 52–53 (Stuttgart: Franz Steiner, 2006), p. 323.

291. May Joseph and Jennifer Fink, eds. *Performing Hybridity* (Minneapolis, MN: University of Minnesota Press, 1999), p. 119.

292. Oprah. "Death Shows Up to Remind Us to Live More Fully," https://www.oprah.com/spirit/.

293. José Esteban Muñoz. *Cruising Utopia* (New York: New York University Press, 2011), p. 95.

294. Haoua Diatta. *Fighting and Beating COVID-19: Sharing an African Perspective* (San Francisco: Alpha, 2021), p. 13.

295. Hans L. Loewald. "On the Therapeutic Action of Psychoanalysis," in *Papers on Psychoanalysis* (New Haven, CT: Yale University Press, 1980), pp. 221–256.

296. W. Dewi Rees. "The Hallucinations of Widowhood," *British Medical Journal 4* (1974), pp. 37–41. Anna Castelnovo, Simone Cavallotti, Orsola Gambini, and Armando D'Agos. "Post-Bereavement Hallucinatory Experiences: A Critical Overview of Population and Clinical Studies," *Journal of Affective Disorders 186* (1: 2015), pp. 266–274. Vaughan Bell. "Ghost Stories: Visits from the Deceased," *Scientific American* (December 2, 2008), https://www.scientificamerican.com/. Karina Stengaard Kamp, Edith Maria Steffen, Ben Alderson-Day, et al. "Sensory and Quasi-Sensory Experiences of the Deceased in Bereavement: An Interdisciplinary and Integrative Review," *Schizophrenia Bulletin 46* (6: 2020), pp. 1367–1381, https://doi.org/10.1093/schbul/sbaa113. The *Scientific American* article concedes "that in cultures of non-European origin the distinction between 'in here' and 'out there' experiences is less strictly defined" and suggests that Latinos, the Hopi Indians, and the Mu Ghayeb people from Oman all take these experiences as aspects of reality. The article does not mention either Africans or Black Americans.

297. The Institute of Noetic Sciences (founded by Apollo 14 astronaut Dr. Edgar Mitchell) studies the issue of life and after death, and the University of Arizona has a "Laboratory for Advances in Consciousness & Health," which studies phenomena related to a larger, invisible world. A good review of the evidence is in the American Psychological Association's *Death as an Altered State of Consciousness: A Scientific Approach* (2023) by Imants Baruss.

298. My study would have been more accurate had I repeated it multiple times over the course of a year. However, I was concerned I might get arrested for being a lurker!

299. Michael Lesy. *The Forbidden Zone* (New York: Farrar Straus & Giroux, 1987), introduction.

300. Technically, Baron Samedi is the first male buried in a cemetery, while the first female becomes his wife, Maman Brigitte (the Haitian manifestation of the Celtic St. Brigid). However, I choose to affirm that the advent of nongendered roles applies also to the dead.

301. Mary and Frederic Brussat. "Rituals," *Spirituality & Practice*, https://www.spiritualityandpractice.com/books/.

302. Birago Diop. "Breath" in *Poems of Black Africa*, Wole Soyinka, ed. (London: Heinemann, 1975), pp. 45–46.

303. Daniel Foor. "Animism and Earth Reverence," *Ancestral Medicine*, https://ancestralmedicine.org/ancestors-animism-ritual/.

304. John Paul II. *The Threshold of Hope* (New York: Knopf, 1994), p. 82.

305. Krystin E. Stiefel. "Burning Stars in *The Lion King*," *Science On* (June 7, 2018), https://scienceonblog.wordpress.com/.

306. John 3:8, my paraphrase of the Greek.

307. Ethan Siegel. "Observing The Universe Really Does Change the Outcome," *Forbes* (May 26, 2020), https://www.forbes.com/sites/startswithabang/.

308. Ruha Benjamin. "Black Afterlives Matter," *Boston Review* (July 16, 2018).

309. This translation is based on meanings given for the individual words in *Strong's Concordance* and in *Thayer's Greek Lexicon*.

310. The literal meaning is actually "penis"; make what you will of that!

311. Jean-Paul Sartre. *Being and Nothingness* (New York: Atria, 2021), p. 142.

312. Carlo Rovelli. *The Order of Time* (New York: Riverhead, 2019).

313. Immanuel Kant. *Critique of Pure Reason*, Norman Kemp Smith, trans. (London: Palgrave Macmillan, 2003), p. 77.

314. Jenny Escobar. "The Role of Memory Practices in Building Spiritual Solidarity for Survivors of State Violence," *American Journal of Community Psychology 69* (2022), p. 409.

315. Quoted in "How Memorial Tattoos Can Help With The Grieving Process," by Caroline Bologna, *HuffPost* (January 5, 2021), https://www.huffpost.com/.

316. Viacheslav Vsevolodovich Ivanov. *Selected Essays*, Robert Bird, trans. (Evanston, IL: Northwestern University Press, 2001), p. 146.

317. Gabriele Lübbers. "The Graffiti of Grief," *Paideuma: Mitteilungen zur Kulturkunde 53* (2007), pp. 149–150.

318. Benjamin.

319. Ivanov, p. 146.

320. Luke 22:19 TV.

321. James Cone. *The Cross and the Lynching Tree* (Maryknoll, NY: Orbis, 2011), pp. 2, 22.

322. Malidoma Patrice Somé. *The Healing Wisdom of Africa: Finding Life Purpose Through Nature, Ritual, and Community* (New York: TarcherPerigee, 1999), p. 54.

323. Elizabeth Jelin. *State Repression and the Labors of Memory* (Minneapolis, MN: University of Minnesota Press, 2003), p. 5.

324. Quoted in Anthony Shafton's *Dream Singers: The African American Way with Dreams* (New York: Wiley, 2010), p. 18.

325. See Joshua D. M. Black's "Dreams of the Deceased: Who Has Them and Why?" (St. Catherines, ON: Brock University, 2018) for a listing of this research.

326. See, for example, Genesis 28, 37, 40, 41; Numbers 12:6; Judges 7:13–14; Job 33:14; Daniel 2, 4; Matthew 1:20, 2:12–13, 27:19; Acts 2:17.

327. Quoted in "Dream Divination and the Neoplatonic Search for Salvation" by Sebastian Gertz in *On Prophecy, Dreams and Human Imagination: Synesius, De insomniis*, Heinz-Ginther Nesselrath and Donald Russell, eds. (Tübingen, DE: Mohr Siebeck, 2014), pp. 111, 119, 123.

328. Anton Adamut. "Oneiric Foundations of Philosophy: Saint Augustine," *Meta: Research In Hermeneutics, Phenomenology, and Practical Philosophy X* (1: 2018), pp. 188–195.

329. Montague Ullman and Nan Zimmerman. *Working with Dreams* (Detroit, MI: Aquarian Press, 1987).

330. M. Stroebe, M. M. Gergen, K. J, Gergen, and W. Stroebe. "Broken Hearts or Broken Bonds: Love and Death in Historical Perspective," *American Psychologist 47* (1: 1992), pp. 205–212.

331. Donna Klass, Phyllis R Silverman, and Steven L. Nickman. *Continuing Bonds: New Understandings of Grief* (Washington, DC: Taylor & Francis, 1996).

332. John Mbiti. "Dreams as a Point of Theological Dialogue Between Christianity and African Religion," *Missionalia 25* (4: 1997), pp. 511–522.

333. Anthony Shafton. *Dream-Singers: The African Way with Dreams* (Hoboken, NJ: Wiley, 2002).

334. Joseph C. Miller. *The Way of Death: Merchant Capitalism and the Angolan Slave Trade, 1730–1830* (Madison: University of Wisconsin Press, 1996), pp. 269, 403, 404.

335. Gregory the Theologian, Oration 19, available online at https://www.newadvent.org/fathers/310218.htm.

336. Jerome. "Against Vigilantius," W.H. Fremantle, trans., in *Nicene and Post-Nicene Fathers, vol. 6* (New York: T & T Clark, 1893), pp. 346-415.

337. Gertz, p. 112.

338. For more on the philosophy of Jacques Derrida, see Tom Cohen's *Jacques Derrida and the Humanities: A Critical Reader* (Cambridge, MA: Cambridge University Press, 2001).

339. Hebrews 12:1 TV.

340. Valarie Kaur. *See No Stranger: A Memoir and Manifesto of Revolutionary Love* (New York: Random House, 2021), p. 11.

341. This practice is adapted from the New Afrikan Spirituality website.

Chapter 9 – Bearing Death, Affirming Life: Death and Resilience

342. Michele Prettyman Beverly. "No Medicine for Melancholy: Cinema of Loss and Mourning in the Era of #BlackLivesMatter," *Black Camera 8* (2: 2017), p. 100.

343. Matt Strassler. "Virtual Particles: What Are They?" *Of Particular Significance* (October 10, 2011), https://profmattstrassler.com/.

344. Chad Orzel. "Six Things Everyone Should Know About Quantum Physics," *Forbes* (July 8, 2015), https://www.forbes.com/.

345. Ibid.

346. Elizabeth Landau. "How Dark Matter Could Be Measured in the Solar System," *NASA* (February 1, 2022), https://www.nasa.gov/.

347. Tom Siegfried. "Hidden Space Dimensions May Permit Parallel Universes, Explain Cosmic Mysteries," *Dallas Morning News,* https://aloper.physics.ucdavis.edu/siegfr.txt.

348. James Baldwin. *The Fire Next Time* (New York: Vintage, 1992), pp. 105–106.

349. Chimamanda Adichie. "The Danger of a Single Story," TED (2009), https://www.ted.com/talks/chimamanda_ngozi_adichie_the_danger_of_a_single_story.

350. James W. Coleman. *Faithful Vision: Treatments of the Sacred, Spiritual, and Supernatural in Twentieth-Century African American Fiction* (Baton Rouge: Louisiana State University Press, 2009), Introduction.

351. Toni Morrison. "Unspeakable Things Unspoken: The Afro-American Presence in American Literature," *Michigan Quarterly Review 28* (1: 1989), http://hdl.handle.net/2027/spo.act2080.0028.001:01.

352. Coleman.

353. Michael Orsini. "Stop Asking Us to Be Resilient," *Policy Options* (October 19, 2020), https://policyoptions.irpp.org/magazines/.

354. Resmaa Menakem. *My Grandmother's Hands: Racialized Trauma and the Pathway to Mending Our Hearts* (Las Vega, NV: Central Recovery Press, 2017), p 12.

355. Meg Llewellyn. "The Power of Hope" in *Persistent Resistance: Calls for Justice from the Celtic Traditions* (Vestal, NY: Anamchara Books, 2019), pp. 153, 154.

356. Ibid.

357. Jonah Lehrer. *Proust Was a Neuroscientist* (Mariner Books, 2008), p. 23.

358. Lehrer. *Imagine: How Creativity Works* (New York: Houghton Mifflin, 2012), p. 11.

359. Isabel Wilkerson. "Where Do We Go From Here?" *Essence* (October 27, 2020), https://www.essence.com/news/.

360. Nikole Hannah-Jones. "Our democracy's founding ideals were false when they were written. Black Americans have fought to make them true," *New York Times Magazine* (August 14, 2019), https://www.nytimes.com/interactive/.

361. E. K. Rynearson and Fanny Correa. *Accommodation to Violent Dying: A Guide to Restorative Retelling and Support* (Seattle, WA: Violent Death Bereavement Society, July 2008), http://www.vdbs.org/docs/ATVDENGLISH_JUN2013.pdf.

362. Robert A. Neimeyer, Dennis Klass, and Michael Robert Dennis. "A Social Constructionist Account of Grief: Loss and the Narration of Meaning," *Death Studies 38* (8: 2014), p. 485.

363. This confusion is also the source of some of the arguments between fundamentalists, other people of faith, and atheists. As Joseph Campbell wrote in *Thou Art That* (New World, 1971), "Half the people in the world think that the [stories] of their religious traditions, for example, are facts. And the other half contends that they are not facts at all. As a result we have people who consider themselves believers because they accept [stories] as facts, and we have others who classify themselves as atheists because they think religious [stories] are lies." Campbell refers to these stories as "metaphors."

ENDNOTES

364. Quoted in "Grieving Life and Loss" by Kirsten Weir, *Monitor on Psychology 51* (4: 2020), https://www.apa.org/monitor/2020/06/ covid-grieving-life.

365. According to the US Bureau of Labor Statistics, nearly 10 million people are out of jobs because their employers closed or lost a business during the pandemic (https://www.bls.gov/cps/effects-of-the-coronavirus-covid-19-pandemic.htm). A 2022 Brookings report found that as many as 4 million people are unable to work because of long COVID (https://www.forbes.com/sites/ williamhaseltine/2022/09/02/long-covid-is-keeping-millions-of-people-out-of-work/?sh=45be825652cc).

366. Neimeyer quoted in Weir.

367. Ibid.

368. Alison Salloum and Edward K. Rynearson. "Family Resilience After Violent Death," *Accommodation to Violent Dying: A Guide to Restorative Retelling and Support* (Seattle, WA: Violent Death Bereavement Society, July 2008), http://www.vdbs.org/docs/ ATVDENGLISH_JUN2013.pdf.

369. Viacheslav Vsevolodovich Ivanov. *Selected Essays,* Robert Bird, trans. (Evanston, IL: Northwestern University Press, 2001), p. 146.

370. The America Psychological Association (APA) includes these items on its list of ways to build resilience: "prioritizing meaningful personal relationships; joining groups that provide social support and foster hope" (https://www.apa.org/topics/resilience).

371. Bessel A. van der Kolk. *The Body Keeps the Score: Brain, Mind, and Body in the Healing of Trauma* (New York: Penguin, 2015), p. 81.

372. Fritjof Capra. *The Web of Life: A New Scientific Understanding of Living Systems* (New York: Knopf Doubleday, 1997), p. 303.

373. Desmond Tutu. *10 Pieces of Wisdom from Desmond Tutu on His Birthday* (Desmond Tutu Foundation, 2015).

374. Simon Bockie. *Death and the Invisible Powers: The World of Kongo Belief* (Bloomington: Indiana University Press, 1993), p. 1.

375. Janice Harris Lord. "Spiritual Essentials" in *Accommodation to Violent Dying: A Guide to Restorative Retelling and Support.*

376. William J. Barber II. *Forward Together: A Moral Message for the Nation* (Saint Louis, MO: Chalice Press, 2014), p. 9.

377. James Alison. *Raising Abel* (Freiberg, DEU: Herder & Herder, 1996), p. 69.

378. Anthony Ephirim-Donkor. *African Spirituality: On Becoming Ancestors* (Washington, DC: Rowman & Littlefield, 2021), p. 65.

379. The APA's recommendations for building resilience include finding purpose by helping others, constructive problem-solving, and setting and moving toward realistic goals.

380. Marilyn Peterson Armour. "Meaning Making for Survivors of Violent Death" in *Accommodation to Violent Dying: A Guide to Restorative Retelling and Support.*

381. Willie James Jennings. "Overcoming Racial Faith," *Divinity* (Spring: 2015), p. 9.

382. Quoted in Mary Lynne Gasaway Hill's *The Language of Protest: Acts of Performance, Identity, and Legitimacy* (New York: Springer, 2018), p. 140.

383. "We Shall Overcome: The Story Behind the Song," *The Kennedy Center,* https://www.kennedy-center.org/education/resources-for-educators/classroom-resources/media-and-interactives/media/music/story-behind-the-song/the-story-behind-the-song/we-shall-overcome/. To hear "We Shall Overcome" sung in seven of India's languages, go to https://www.youtube.com/watch?v=qkGUOs-O7GM.

384. Bockie, p. 140.

385. Elisabeth Kübler-Ross. *On Grief and Grieving: Finding the Meaning of Grief Through the Five Stages of Loss* (New York: Scribner, 2005), p. 230.

386. See John 14:1–3.

387. This is part of a letter that DuBois wrote on June 26, 1957, with instructions that it be opened after his death (which occurred August 27, 1963). The whole letter can be read in his obituary published in the *Harvard Crimson* on November 19, 1963, https://www.thecrimson.com/article/.

388. Valarie Kaur. *See No Stranger: A Memoir and Manifesto of Revolutionary Love* (New York: Random House, 2021), p. xv.

Afterword

389. Al Sharpton. "Eulogy for Tyre Nichols" (Memphis, TN: February 1, 2023), https://www.youtube.com/watch?v=u4VCLQ7-gvg.

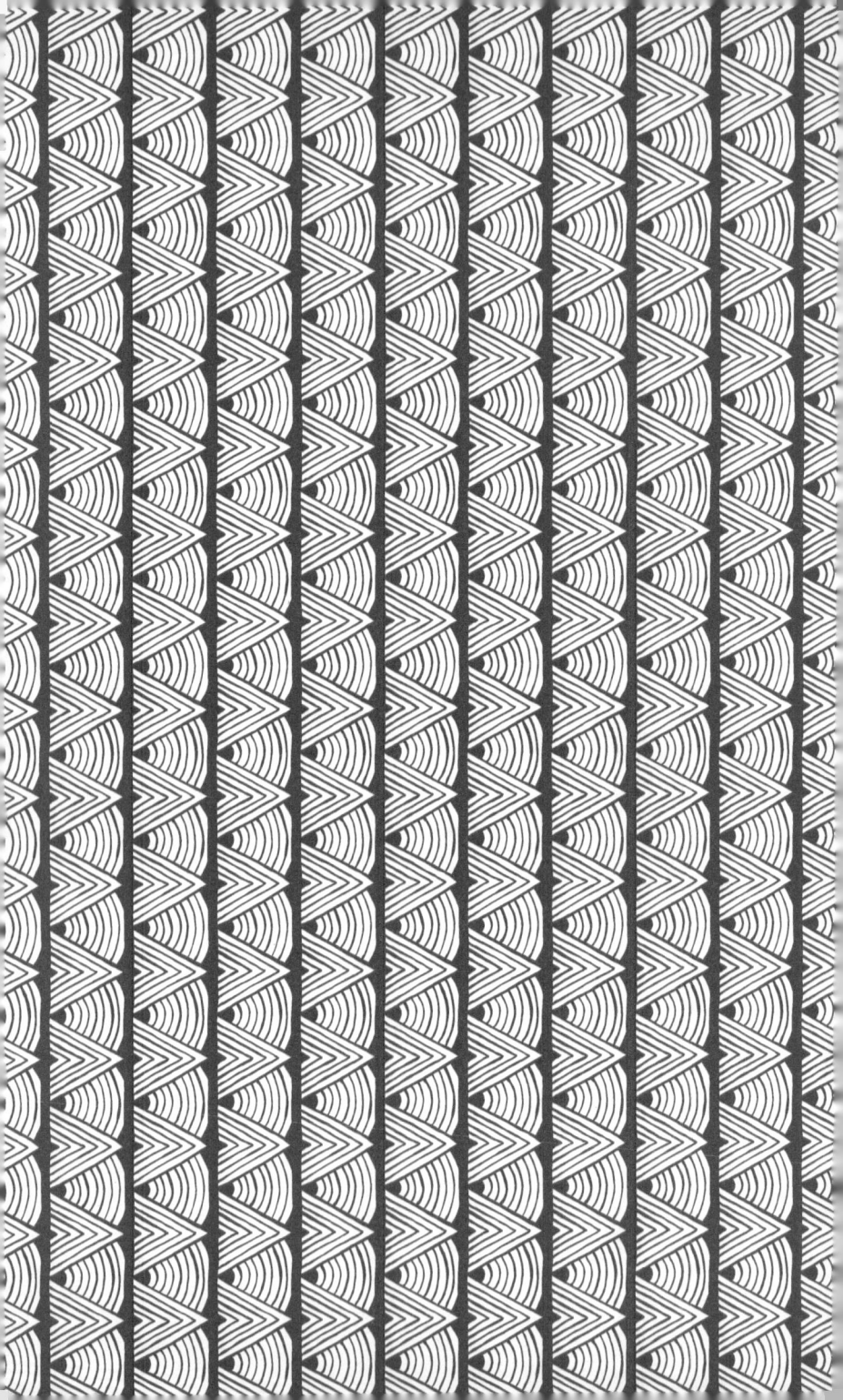

READING LIST

James Alison. *Raising Abel: the Recovery of the Eschatological Imagination* (New York: Crossroad, 1996).

Marimba Ani. *Let the Circle Be Unbroken: The Implications of African Spirituality in the Diaspora* (New York: Nkonimfo, 1980).

James Baldwin. *Nobody Knows My Name: More Notes of a Native Son* (New York: Dial, 1961).

———. *The Price of the Ticket: Collected Nonfiction, 1948–1985* (New York: St. Martin's Press/Marek, 1985).

Edward E. Baptist. *The Half Has Never Been Told: Slavery and the Makings of American Capitalism* (New York: Basic Books, 2016).

William J. Barber II. *Forward Together: A Moral Message for the Nation* (Saint Louis, MO: Chalice Press, 2014).

Simon Bockie. *Death and the Invisible Powers: The World of Kongo Belief* (Bloomington: Indiana University Press, 1993).

Fanny Brewster. *Archetypal Grief: Slavery's Legacy of Intergenerational Child Loss* (New York: Routledge, 2019).

Beatrice Bruteau. *The Holy Thursday Revolution* (Maryknoll, NY: Orbis, 2005).

Fritjof Capra. *The Web of Life: A New Scientific Understanding of Living Systems* (New York: Doubleday, 1996).

Fritjof Capra and Pier Luigi Luisi. *The Systems View of Life: A Unifying Vision* (Cambridge, MA: Cambridge University Press, 2014).

Anne Cheng. *The Melancholy of Race: Psychoanalysis, Assimilation, and Hidden Grief* (New York: Oxford University Press, 2001).

Myisha Cherry. *The Case for Rage: Why Anger Is Essential to Anti-Racist Struggle* (New York: Oxford University Press, 2021).

James W. Coleman. *Faithful Vision: Treatments of the Sacred, Spiritual, and Supernatural in Twentieth-Century African American Fiction* (Baton Rouge: Louisiana State University Press, 2009),

Joy DeGruy. *Post Traumatic Slave Syndrome: America's Legacy of Enduring Injury and Healing* (New York: Amistad, 2017).

Haoua Diatta. *Fighting and Beating COVID-19: Sharing an African Perspective* (San Francisco: Alpha, 2021).

Frederick Douglass. *The Portable Frederick Douglass,* Henry Louis Gates and John Stauffer, eds. (New York: Penguin, 2016).

George Francis Dow. *Slave Ships and Slaving* (Salem, MA: Marine Research Society, 1927).

W. E. B. DuBois. *The Souls of Black Folk* (Chicago: A. C. McClurg, 1903).

Robert Ellison. *Shadow and Act* (New York: Vintage, 1972).

———. *Invisible Man* (New York: Knopf Doubleday, 1991).

Frantz Fanon. *Black Skin, White Masks* (London, UK: Pluto Press, 1967).

Kimbwandènde Kia Bunseki Fu-Kiau. *Kongo Cosmology* (Kinshasa, Zaire: ONRD, 1969).

———. *African Cosmology of the Bântu-Kôngo: Tying the Spiritual Knot* (Brooklyn, NY: Athelia Henrietta Press, 2001).

Alma Gottlieb. *The Afterlife Is Where We Come From: The Culture of Infancy in West Africa* (Chicago: University of Chicago Press, 2004).

Kwame Gyeke. *An Essay on African Philosophical Thought: The Akan Conceptual Scheme* (Cambridge, MA: Cambridge University Press, 1987).

Saidiya Hartman. *Lose Your Mother: A Journey Along the Atlantic Slave Route* (New York: Farrar, Straus & Giroux, 2007).

Mary Lynne Gasaway Hill. *The Language of Protest: Acts of Performance, Identity, and Legitimacy* (New York: Springer, 2018).

Karla Holloway. *Passed On: African American Mourning Stories* (Durham, NC: Duke University Press, 2002).

bell hooks. *Killing Rage: Ending Racism* (New York: Holt, 1996).

Thomas Hübl. *Healing Collective Trauma: A Process for Integrating Our Intergenerational and Cultural Wounds* (Boulder, CO: Sounds True, 2020).

Viacheslav Vsevolodovich Ivanov. *Selected Essays,* Robert Bird, trans. (Evanston, IL: Northwestern University Press, 2001).

Harriet Jacobs. *Incidents in the Life of a Slave Girl* (Boston: Thayer & Eldridge, 1861).

Elizabeth Jelin. *State Repression and the Labors of Memory* (Minneapolis, MN: University of Minnesota Press, 2003).

Donald Kalsched. *Trauma and the Soul* (New York: Routledge, 2013).

Valarie Kaur. *See No Stranger: A Memoir and Manifesto of Revolutionary Love* (New York: Random House, 2021).

Donna Klass, Phyllis R Silverman, and Steven L. Nickman. *Continuing Bonds: New Understandings of Grief* (Washington, DC: Taylor & Francis, 1996).

Elisabeth Kübler-Ross and David Kessler. *On Grief and Grieving: Finding the Meaning of Grief Through the Five Stages of Loss* (New York: Simon and Schuster, 2014).

Jacques Lacan. *The Ethics of Psychoanalysis 1959–1960* (London, UK: Routledge, 1992).

Lawrence Levine. *Black Culture and Black Consciousness: Afro-American Folk Thought from Slavery to Freedom* (New York: Oxford University Press, 1977).

Audre Lorde. *Sister Outsider: Essays and Speeches* (Berkeley, CA: Crossing Press, 1984).

Rhonda V. Magee. *The Inner Work of Racial Justice: Healing Ourselves and Transforming Our Communities Through Mindfulness* (New York: Penguin, 2021).

John Mbiti. *New Testament Eschatology in an African Background* (London, UK: SPCK, 1978).

J. Mellon. *Bullwhip Days: The Slaves Remember* (New York: Grove, 1988).

Resmaa Menakem. *My Grandmother's Hands: Racialized Trauma and the Pathway to Mending Our Hearts and Bodies* (Las Vegas, NV: Central Recovery Press, 2017).

Joseph C. Miller. *The Way of Death: Merchant Capitalism and the Angolan Slave Trade, 1730–1830* (Madison: University of Wisconsin Press, 1996).

Cindy Milstein, ed. *Rebellious Mourning: The Collective Work of Grief* (Oakland, CA: AK Press, 2017).

Philip Morgan, ed. *African American Life in the Georgia Lowcountry: The Atlantic World and the Gullah Geechee* (Athens, GA: University of Georgia Press, 2011)

Toni Morrison. *Song of Solomon* (New York: Vintage, 2004).

NAACP. *Thirty Years of Lynching in the United States, 1889–1919* (New York: NAACP, 1919).

Solomon Northup. *Twelve Years A Slave* (Auburn, NY: Derby and Miller, 1853).

Cole Arthur Riley. *This Here Flesh: Spirituality, Liberation, and the Stories That Make Us.* (New York: Convergent, 2022).

Ellyn Sanna, ed. *Persistent Resistance: Calls for Justice from the Celtic Traditions* (Vestal, NY: Anamchara Books, 2019).

Anthony Shafton. *Dream Singers: The African American Way with Dreams* (New York: Wiley, 2010).

Pamela Felder Small, Marco J. Barker, and Marybeth Gasman, eds. *Sankofa: African American Perspectives on Race and Culture* (Albany, NY: SUNY Press, 2020).

Terri L. Snyder. *The Power to Die* (Chicago: University of Chicago Press, 2015).

Malidoma Patrice Somé. *The Healing Wisdom of Africa: Finding Life Purpose Through Nature, Ritual, and Community* (New York: Putnam, 1999).

David Stannard. *American Holocaust* (Oxford University Press, 1993).

Carlyle Fielding Stewart. *Soul Survivors: An African American Spirituality* (Louisville, KY: Westminster John Knox Press, 1997).

Simon Stow. *American Mourning: Tragedy, Democracy, Resilience* (Cambridge, MA: Cambridge University Press, 2017).

Robert Farris Thompson. *Flash of the Spirit: African & Afro-American Art & Philosophy* (New York: Vintage Books, 1984).

Howard Thurman. *The Inward Journey* (New York: Harper, 1961).

———. *Jesus and the Disinherited* (Boston: Beacon Press, 1996).

Mamie Till-Mobley and Christopher Benson. *Death of Innocence: The Story of the Hate Crime That Changed America* (New York: Random House, 2003).

Bessel A. Van der Kolk. *The Body Keeps the Score: Brain, Mind, and Body in the Healing of Trauma* (New York: Penguin, 2015).

Violent Death Bereavement Society. *Accommodation to Violent Dying: A Guide to Restorative Retelling and Support* (Seattle, WA: Violent Death Bereavement Society, July 2008).

INDEX

INDEX

faith 111–112, 164, 168, 195, 225, 252, 262–263, 268, 274, 278
Fanner, Robert and Peter 81–82
Fanon, Frantz 50, 80, 96, 98
Farrell, Bill 72
Faust, Drew Gilpin 71
Floyd, George 39, 48, 89, 142, 285, 291
flying Africans 16, 19–20, 171–172, 178, 256, 258–261, 270, 281–282
food (see also, diet) 48, 180, 214, 219, 263
Fort Lauderdale, Florida 43
Freedom Riders 92
Freud, Sigmund 58–61, 93, 142, 143, 205, 241, 302
Fuhr, Shaun 42
Fu-Kiau, Kimbwandende Kia Bunseki 166
funerals
    African 19, 214, 239
    Black 140–141, 164–170

Galatians, Epistle to 193
Gedeus, Barry 43
Genesis, Book of 154
Georgetown University 234
Georgia
    Atlanta 40
    Brunswick 93
    St. Simons Island 15
    Savannah 13
    Smyrna 41
    Sylvania 42
Ghana 62, 164
Gordon, Maurice Jr. 42
ghosts 217

Gospels (see also, individual books) 54, 204, 206, 236
graffiti 234
Graham, North Carolina 43
grandmother (author's) 33, 53, 58, 60–61, 68, 70, 104–106, 132, 190, 215, 244, 248, 286–287
graves (see, cemeteries)
Green, William Howard 43
Gregory of Nyssa 246
Gregory the Theologian 247
grief 34, 35, 38–39, 47, 48, 53, 59–60, 64, 69, 72, 79, 108, 112, 115, 137–139, 144, 158, 218
    stages 4751, 138–139
    theorists 242, 272
guns 34, 40, 42, 43, 134, 135

Haiti 119, 165, 221, 286
Hannah-Jones, Nikole 268
Hardin, Garrett 46
Harris, Kamala 31, 37
Hartman, Sadiya 68, 96
health 36, 96, 150, 265
    care 35, 38, 65, 95, 115
    effects of racism on 21, 95, 97, 114–115, 264
    insurance 95
    intergenerational 96
heart disease (see cardiovascular disease)
heaven 62, 111, 189–197, 199–201, 221, 245, 247
    realm of 203–205, 208–211, 235, 266
Hebrew
    scriptures 145, 176, 230, 240

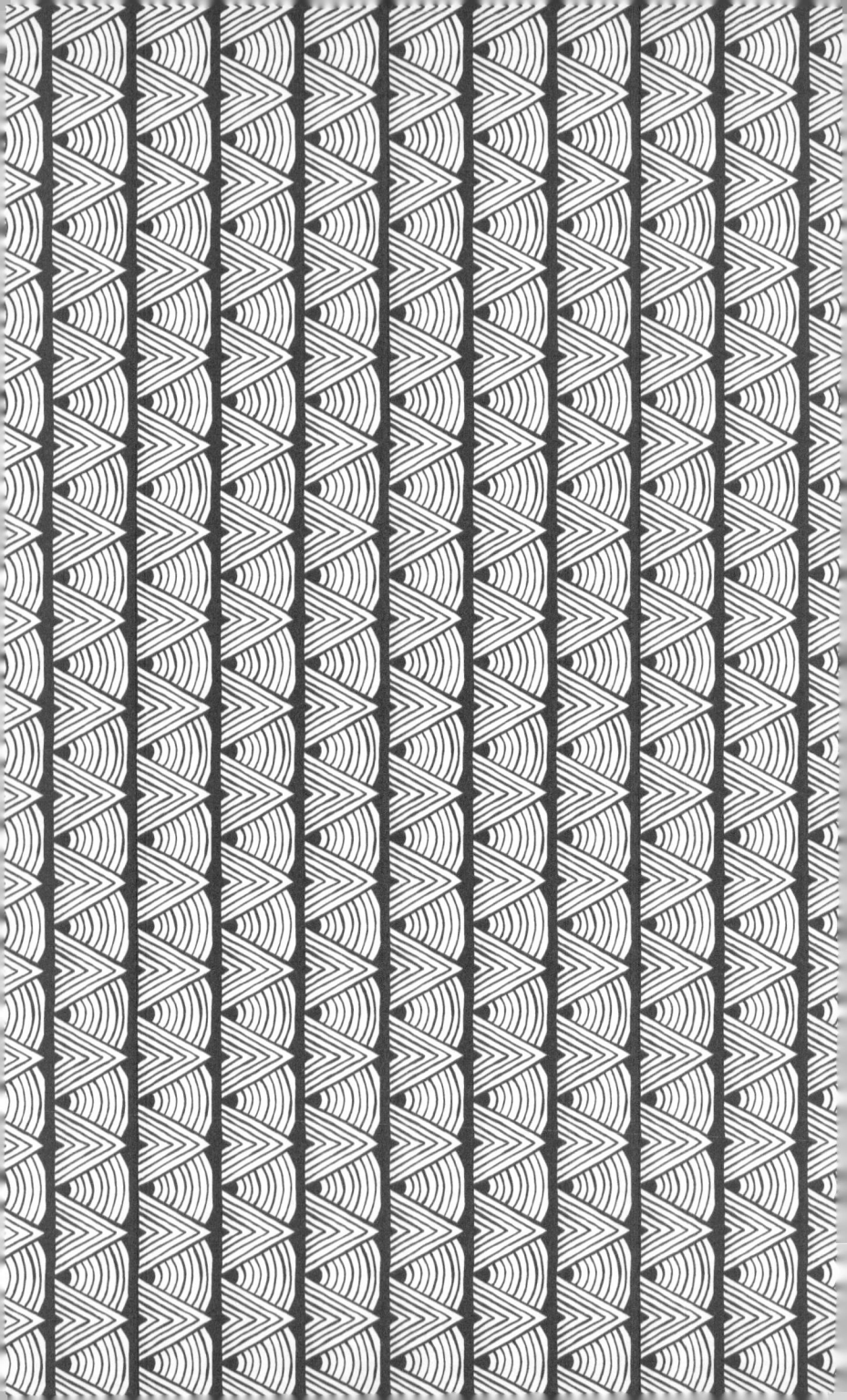

ACKNOWLEDGMENTS

WHEN MY DEAR BEST FRIEND ELLYN SANNA
approached me about this project, I was initially reluctant; I
wanted to postpone tackling such a difficult topic until I felt
readier—but she convinced me now was the best time to write
this book, and so I embarked on her boat of ideas. I let my fears
drop, and I trusted Ellyn's guidance.

During the process of this book's creation, like the seventy-
five Igbo people whose story I've told, I found myself again
and again entering the Kalunga, the waters of death and life.
Ellyn was right. This point in time, when we are beset with the
ongoing onslaught of both racist violence and COVID, is the
right moment for this book to be born. If not for Ellyn, however,
you would not be able to hold this monumental project in your
hands. I am forever in her debt for convincing me of this book's
right to be told. Thank you, my beloved Mother of Mercy, for yet
again helping me to send the stories and wisdom of my people
out into the world.

In the early spring of 2022, Ellyn's advice was affirmed on a trip to New York City when I had dinner with a dear friend, Fr. Bryan Massingale. As soon as I described this project, he said, "Patrick, I see what you are getting at. This is a good idea! It is deeply needed at this time." Ironically, the very next day, however, I stopped in Philadelphia to visit another friend, and when I again described the project, his response was: "Why would you want to publish a book like that, especially right now? You need to be careful to not keep shaming white people. It will damage your academic reputation. They will see you as a weak intellectual."

I sighed, and for a moment I struggled to come up with an answer for him. Was he really correct that my options were to either write my truth and face harsh criticism and even violent push-back (it's happened before, after my last book was published), or else tiptoe around the realities of death and racism in order to advance my professional career? At that moment, though, as though coming from a long way away, I thought I heard my brother Bob singing, *Get up, stand up, . . . don't give up the fight.* Brother Abraham's voice gently inserted, *You can please some of the people some of the time, all of the people some of the time, some of the people all of the time, but you can never please all of the people all of the time.* So I simply smiled at my friend, thinking, *Oh well. C'est la vie!*

To be clear, though, my intention in this book is not to shame white people (or anyone else). Instead, I hope to empower us all—no matter our skin color—to face the past, confront the present, and together build a stronger, healthier future. Racism is a cancer that threatens the well-being and happiness of all of us who share Planet Earth. And so, let me say to all the members of the white, brown, Indigenous, and Asian communities: *This book is for you as much as it is for the Black community.* We all face death; we are all called to challenge racism wherever we encounter it; and only together can we find our places in the eternal, Love-begotten community that includes us all. We each have so much to contribute to the network of life; may this book inspire us to work with one another instead of against each other.

If you have read the book already, you will know that key experiences and individuals in my life have shaped my stories and insights. I would like to express my gratitude to everyone who has helped me understand the meaning of death more deeply. At the top of that list is my grandmother, Tatie, both her life and her death. My experiences living and working in Congo are also on this list, as well as my years of research, clinical practice, and many conversations with friends, family, acquaintances, and strangers. Spiritual direction, my graduate studies, and countless hours of continuing education and recertifications have contributed to this text as well. In addition, many individuals in particular helped me to grasp this topic better. These include my discussion partners, Jill Brown, PhD, and Maya Khanna, PhD. I will also always be grateful to Dr. Maryellen Vonlanthen; Georgia Gutierrez; Dr. Jessica Mora; Elizabeth Volmar; Josianne Joseph; Emily Eckwahl-Sanna; Fr. Antonio Mondesir; Gina Sidor and family; Amos Perde and family; Nathaneal Sidor and family; all my other cousins, aunties, and uncles; and finally, Dr. Kimberly O'Connor, a great friend who always challenges me to think better. I owe a deep debt of gratitude to the Society of Jesus—my religious family—especially Fr. Karl Kiser, SJ, Fr. Charlie Rodriguez, SJ, Fr. Nicolas Santos, SJ, Fr. Daniel Hendrickson, SJ, Br. Mark Mackey, SJ, Br. Ralph Cordero, SJ, and many more who share this Society with me. Last but certainly not least, I want to say thank you to the Creighton Community in Omaha, Nebraska, including Dr. Jennifer Petter and everyone at the counseling center, as well as my chair Dr. Corey Guenther and the rest of the staff in the psychology department. Their support, prayers, and friendship make me a better person, and their patience with me throughout this project means that their love is interwoven through my words. Thank you very much.

—*Patrick Saint-Jean, SJ*

ABOUT THE AUTHOR

BORN IN HAITI, PATRICK SAINT-JEAN, SJ, IS
now a member of the USA Midwest Jesuits; he is also a practicing psychotherapist and a psychology professor. He did his
undergraduate education at the Université Victor Segalen de
Bordeaux in France and received his graduate degree in psychoanalysis from the Parisian Ecole Lacanienne de Psychanalyse in
Paris and his PsyD from the Universidad Nacional Autonoma
de Mexico. He did additional theology studies at the Catholic
Theological Union in Chicago. Before joining the Jesuits, he
studied, conducted research, and worked in various countries
throughout Europe, Africa, the Caribbean, and South America.
He is fluent in several languages, enjoys jazz music, and is a
frequent speaker and writer on the topic of antiracism. He is
also engaged in ongoing research into the effects of intergenerational trauma on the descendants of enslaved Blacks.

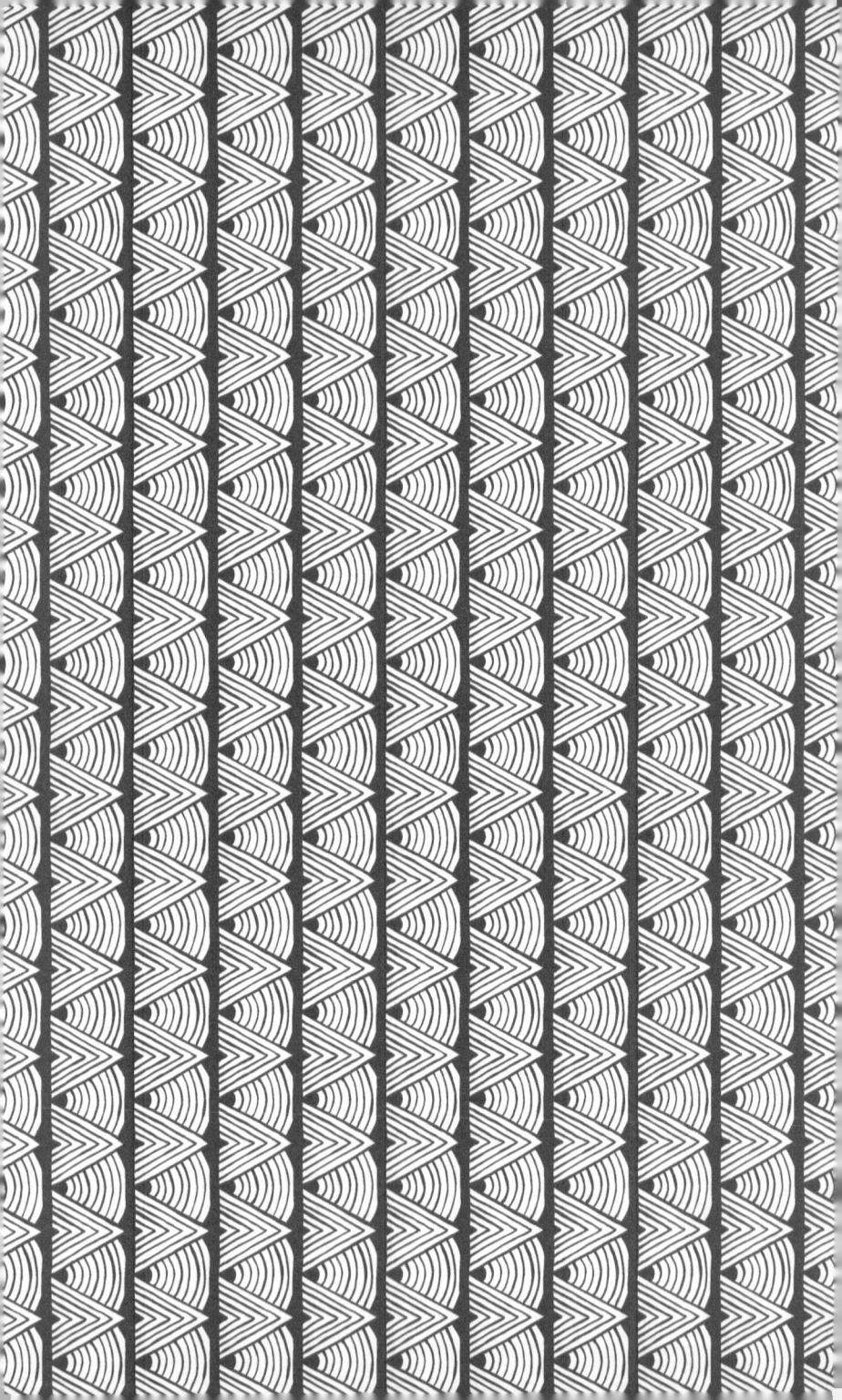

More from
Anamchara Books...

The Spiritual Work of Racial Justice
A Month of Meditations with Ignatius of Loyola

"The Spiritual Work of Racial Justice is a meaningful and practical resource for our times. Through Ignatian Spiritual Exercises, Patrick Saint-Jean, S.J. offers an opportunity to continue the pursuit of racial justice as a necessary component of faith. Each meditation includes relevant history and grounded spiritual practices. The book is refreshing and accessible to all."

— Barbara Holmes, author of *Joy Unspeakable: Contemplative Practices of the Black Church* and *Liberation and the Cosmos*

"Saint-Jean's book beautifully weaves together several threads: the author's personal experience as a Jesuit in formation who is both an immigrant and a Black man; poignant reminders of the long history of race-based violence; calls for racial justice; and the perennial wisdom of the Spiritual Exercises of St. Ignatius of Loyola, with their focus on examining our sin so that we are free to love God and neighbor. The end result is an invitation to the interior work necessary to deepen our commitment to racial justice."

— Very Rev. Brian G. Paulson, S.J., Provincial Superior, USA Midwest Province of the Society of Jesus

Persistent Resistance
Calls for Justice from the Celtic Traditions
A Collection of Essays

The Celts were activists for justice. They persuaded kings to change their policies; they stood up for women and others who were endangered by prejudice; and they worked with tireless love on behalf of all Earth's creatures. They resisted the injustice of their day—and they persisted throughout their entire lifetimes, until their deaths. (And some would say that they are still hard at work fighting injustice from the Otherworld.) Following in their footsteps requires a mystical experience of the Divine that expresses itself in acts of tangible justice and compassion

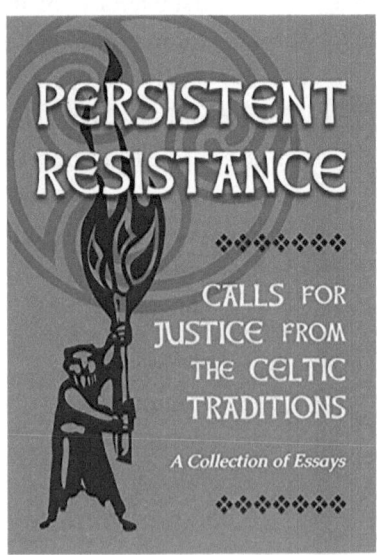

These essays build on Celtic stories, myths, and tradition to inspire and challenge us. They remind us that we cannot consider ourselves faithful to God if we are not faithful to our entire community (a community that not only includes humans, but also animals, plants, and the entire Earth).

Paths of Justice

Celtic Prayers for a World of Equity, Unity, and Healing

Energize us with Your compassion, Giver of Life,
to help the dispossessed, to listen to those without voices,
and to reach out in friendship to all.
Empower us with Your love; encourage us with Your Spirit;
make us strong to bring Your justice
to individuals, communities, nations, and the entire globe.

Our society often assumes that "justice" has to do with punishment. We think it means we make criminals pay for their crimes. The biblical meaning of the word "justice," however, means "to make right." This concept of justice has to do with healthy

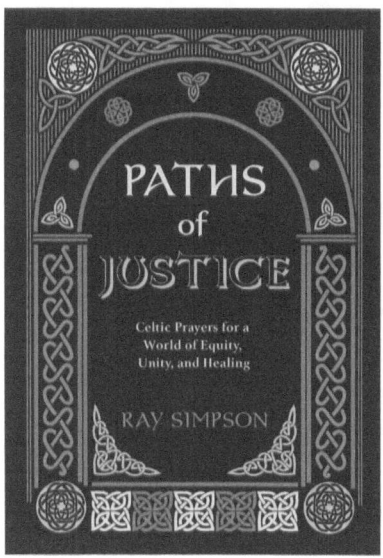

relationships based on equity and kindness; it refers to a society based on life-giving relationships between God, human beings, and the natural world. This is the world Ray Simpson seeks to build, and he offers these prayers as openings into the Divine power that constantly seeks to heal and restore.

ANAMCHARA
BOOKS

AnamcharaBooks.com

www.ingramcontent.com/pod-product-compliance
Lightning Source LLC
Chambersburg PA
CBHW030747060526
44539CB00043B/827